DIVIDED THEY STAND

DIVIDED THEY STAND

A Background Book on the Two Germanies
by JOHN SCOTT
with a Preface by ROBERT D. MURPHY

Parents' Magazine Press

NEW YORK

Each Background Book is concerned with the broad spectrum of people, places, and events affecting the national and international scene. Written simply and clearly, the books in this series will engage the minds and interest of people living in a world of great change.

Copyright © 1973 by John Scott
All rights reserved
Printed in the United States of America

Library of Congress Cataloging in Publication Data

Scott, John, 1912-
  Divided they stand.

  (A Background book)
  SUMMARY: A personal narrative of German history which stresses the political and economic development since World War II.
  Bibliography: p.
  1. Germany (Federal Republic, 1949-   )—Description and travel.
  2. Germany (Democratic Republic, 1949-   )—Description and travel.
  [1. Germany—History] I. Title.
  DD43.S365   914.3'03'87   72-12817
  ISBN 0-8193-0680-0
  ISBN 0-8193-0681-0 (lib. bdg.)

CONTENTS

	Preface	VII
1	Introduction	1
2	Germany Defeated	24
3	Germany Divided	48
4	The Soviet Zone Bids for Nationhood	70
5	The Federal Republic of Germany	91
6	The Economic Miracle	111
7	The DDR's Coercive Economy	131
8	Brandt Assumes Power in a Troubled Federal Republic	147
9	Soviet Policy on Germany	169
10	The New German Democratic Republic	194
11	The Federal Republic Moves Toward Leadership of Europe	218
12	The Future of the Two Germanies	242
	Notes	260
	Selected Reading List	268
	Index	271

ACKNOWLEDGMENTS

My thanks to Ruth Knutson and Paula Pembrook for their help in preparing this manuscript.

My thanks also to TIME in whose employ I spent many years studying and writing about Germany and traveling around the country.

My thanks, finally, to Holt, Rinehart and Winston, Inc. for permission to quote from *A Peace Policy for Europe* by Willy Brandt, translated by Joel Carmichael. Quotations appear on pages 149 through 153.

PREFACE

It is not an everyday occurrence to enjoy the rich experience and knowledge of an author writing on a subject which has attracted his intensive interest and with which he has been associated for many years at an extraordinary historical period.

As a young man, John Scott went to the Soviet Union in the early stages of that exciting social experiment. He saw much of its development and was employed there as an industrial worker for five years. During much of that period he lived almost as a Russian, speaking the language, and marrying a Russian girl. His father was an early American radical.

John Scott also had German friends and took an active interest in the German scene. Actually, as I have observed through the years, Scott indulges a rather global sweep of curiosity and interest in people, their psychology, their welfare and aspirations, the various social and political systems under which they live, their deeds and misdeeds. In the case of Germany he found an entrancing subject and has written an impressive account of his findings.

I became acquainted with the author during the immediate postwar years in Berlin where he was then stationed representing Time Inc. Here was a gifted American journalist equipped, among other things, with an intimate knowledge of the Russian and German people at a moment when their relationship was a major historical element.

Scott's book is instructive in its dynamic recording of wartime drama in the savage conflict of World War II and its aftermath. He is able to interpret mistakes of judgment as well as successful achievements and relate them to personalities. The Soviet and German political structures and policies are subjected to accurate illumination. The contrasts between German and Russian thinking, action, and tradition are vividly portrayed. Scott brings to the German problem and future a solid assessment. His comments on American policy *vis à vis* both defeated Germany and Japan as well as our Allies are persuasive. Certainly the facts would seem to justify his opinion that the German people will remain divided into two nations for the indefinite future. My own opinion differs but I would have difficulty proving it.

Scott's final conclusion, after examining the American postwar record, is that American realism in maintaining a sound relationship between our ambitions and our resources has been wanting. He suggests that in this area the United States may have something useful to learn from the two Germanies. One can only agree.

—*Robert D. Murphy*

Honorary Chairman of the Board of Corning Glass International; former U.S. Ambassador to the Federal Republic of Germany; former Under Secretary of State for Political Affairs.

1

Introduction

I first saw Germany one June afternoon in 1927. A German friend and I rode our bicycles down the ordered Alpine slopes, across a bridge, and into the somewhat less ordered Bavarian countryside. I was fifteen at the time; for a year I had been in school in the French part of Switzerland, during which time I had bicycled extensively around Switzerland itself, and made several trips down the Rhone to Provence, and over the passes into northern Italy. Now I had cajoled and persuaded my parents to let me make a trip in the other direction — down the Rhine through Germany to Holland. My friend and companion, Ernst, was then a university student, and for the next several months served as my guide and teacher, as we wound our way northward through the picturesque Schwarzwald, or Black Forest, and on past the castles and vineyards of the Rhineland, through the smoky industrial region along the lower Rhine and the Ruhr. We spent most nights in our sleeping bags in fields, or, when the weather was bad, in youth hostels; we cooked some of our meals, bought others in country inns, and sometimes stopped to visit Ernst's friends along the way. We met my mother according to plan in Amsterdam; then Ernst and I took the boat back up the Rhine to his home in Koblenz. By then my German was considerably better than his English, and during the next few weeks, which I spent in his home, we made occasional trips to local points of interest. His guidance was invaluable, and he helped select books for me to read which would give some depth and substance to my scattered visual impression of Germany.

At that time, the last of the American occupation forces had just departed from Koblenz, leaving behind some unpleasant memories which were beginning to merge in local minds with even more unpleasant memories of the spiral inflation, and the war, even though little fighting had taken place on German territory in World War I. The local economy was now reasonably prosperous. The war had been a great misfortune, everyone agreed, but now at last things were straightened out again, one could get a fair day's pay for a good day's work, and life could and should be enjoyed.

In this idyllic setting, with Ernst's help, I began reading about Germany. We visited the nearby valley where early German tribesmen had defeated Roman legionnaires garrisoned in a small town at the confluence of the Rhine and the Mosel, which later became known as Koblenz. Looking down on the busy Rhine from a terrace, I began to get a feeling for the ancient myths of the Volsungs and Niebelungen; groping through ruined castles high up on cliffs overlooking the river gave reality to the tales of knights and heroes who had lived and fought on this land for centuries before there was a Germany.

At the risk of oversimplifying a subject on which hundreds of weighty volumes of typically thorough German scholarship have been written, let me sketch out in broad outline the historic events that shaped Germany.

The country was inhabited, of course, very early. The Neanderthal valley a few miles north of Koblenz was the home of early primates some 300,000 years ago, whose remains were found in 1856 and today bear the name of the valley. Early Germanic tribesmen suffered periodic invasions by Celts from the north and west, by Slavs and Goths from the north and east, by the Etruscans and, later, the Romans from the south, and occasionally from Asia, as when Attila made his devastating advances in the seventh century.

The Romans had never really established themselves and enforced their way of life on most of Germany as they did in Gaul and in England, so when an illiterate Frankish king from Aachen (now on the frontier between France and Germany) was crowned Charlemagne, Emperor of the Holy Roman Empire, in Rome in 800 A.D., for the first time some degree of centralized authority and unity was imposed on what later became western and southern Germany. But conflict between local pagan princes and the church, and the local wars among these early princes prevented any effective unification, although repeated attempts were made, as under the rule of Frederick Barbarossa, who reigned briefly as emperor until his death by drowning in 1190 while on his way to fight the infidels in the Holy Land with the Third Crusade. For the most part, however, the country remained fragmented, gradually developing small cities with artisans and local burghers, who exchanged goods and services with peasants in the countryside under the general surveillance of princes and princelets in their castles high up in the hills. During the generations of the Crusades, bards and lyric poets emerged to create such works as Wolfram von Eschenbach's *Parzival* and Gottfried von Strassburg's *Tristan;* growing trading centers began to draw together into what later became known as the Hanseatic League, which gradually attracted merchant trade from the Baltic Sea and Scandinavia; and at the same time the power of the church increased and in the larger cities magnificent cathedrals were built to replace the primitive early churches.

During the fourteenth and fifteenth centuries, while feudal princes and dukes in France and England began to draw together into larger units leading toward national unification, Germany muddled on under a multiplicity of princes, each seeking to protect or extend his own principality, but none strong enough to enforce his will on the others. And this may have been fortunate for the people and for culture, because it was during this period—the fourteenth century—that the universities of Prague and Cologne, Vienna, Erfurt, and Heidelberg were organized under the loose leadership of Emperor Charles IV. After his death, the local princes took to fighting among themselves more than ever, the Hanseatic League began to lose ground to the prosperous Dutch,

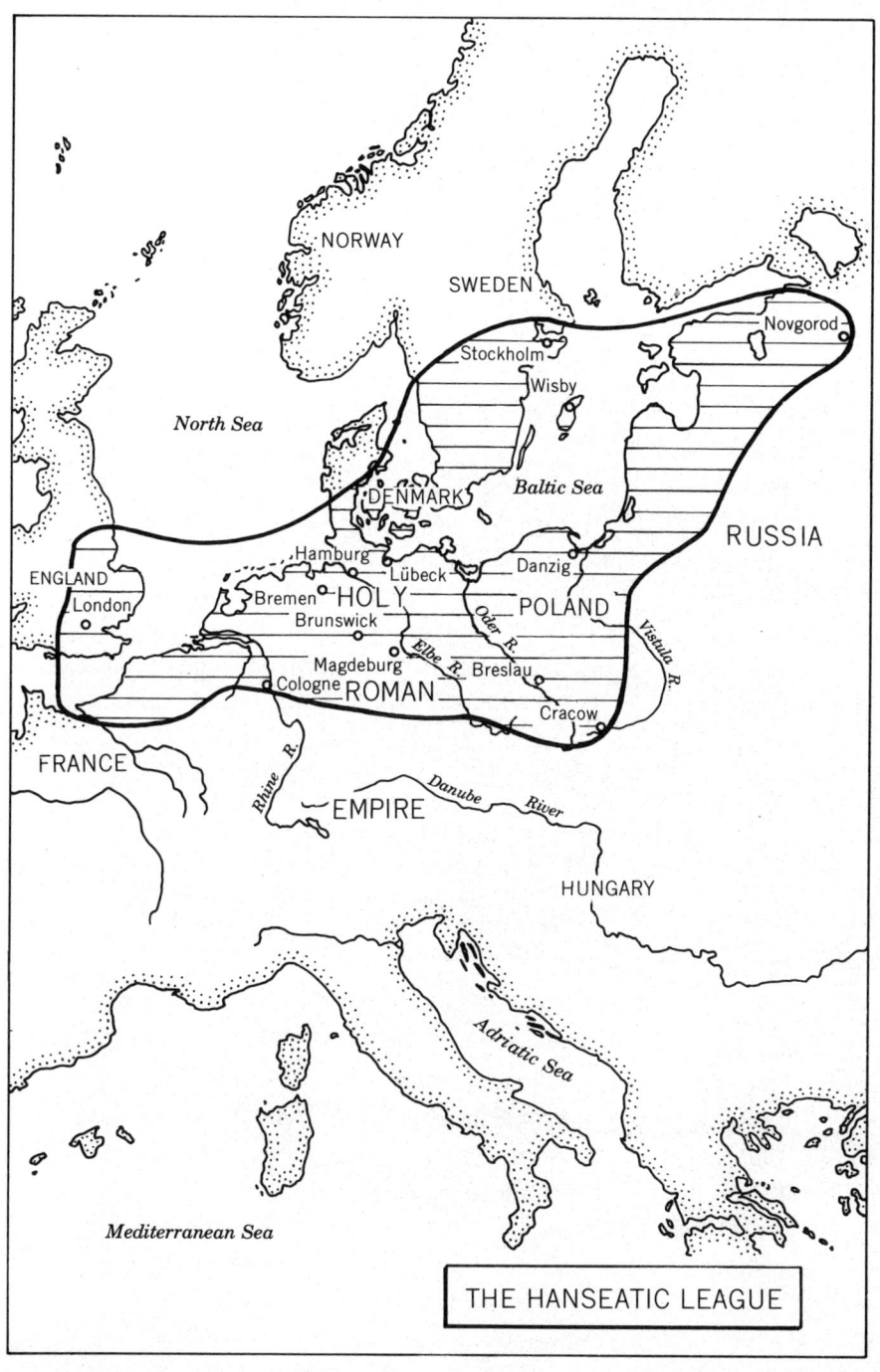

the Alpine peasant communities associated themselves into the Swiss League. Life in most of what now is Germany was insecure and poor. Most Germans were ignorant of the momentous events taking place beyond the Alps in Italy, where thinkers, poets, and painters such as Thomas Aquinas, Dante, and Giotto were leading the world in a spiritual and artistic renaissance.

Knowledge of these happenings began to penetrate into Germany under Maximilian I, who reigned from 1493 to 1519. His patronage of the arts encouraged men like Hans Holbein, Albrecht Dürer, and Tilman Riemenschneider to create their great works, although this artistic and intellectual creativity was largely limited to several cities and universities. The Hapsburg princes Charles IV and Charles V were successful in establishing their authority in their own principality and even in acquiring some overseas territories, but they were not strong enough, or perhaps did not have sufficient vision, to attempt to unify any substantial part of Germany, whose local princes continued to squabble and fight.

These local conflicts assumed a more general character early in the sixteenth century when Martin Luther, after visiting Rome in 1511, became convinced that the Roman Catholic church was corrupt and wicked, and launched his demands for reformation. After the Edict of Worms (1521) declared Luther and his associates heretics, the Protestant movement gradually assumed political overtones. The Peace of Augsburg declared that each German prince was free to determine which religion was to be practiced in his domain, and this was followed by vigorous reforms within the Catholic church in an attempt to counteract the Protestant heresy.

Martin Luther meanwhile settled down to work on his monumental translation of the Bible into German, thereby in effect creating the modern German language. From that time on, although people in Hamburg continued to speak a patois not understandable to their cousins in Freiburg or Munich, all Germans had one common language, now known as *Hochdeutsch*, or classical German, which is shared today by some 80 million Germans, as well as several million citizens in parts of Switzerland, France, Austria, Italy, Yugoslavia, Rumania, and the Soviet Union, in addition to being often a sort of *lingua franca* for millions of Slavs of Eastern Europe.

During the latter half of the sixteenth century, the reforms which had taken place within the Catholic Church, and the pressures which the Church applied succeeded in bringing many Protestants back into the fold, which in turn antagonized and terrorized a number of Protestant princes, who feared the loss of their independence and authority. Thus German society became polarized and the stage was set for catastrophe.

The Thirty Years War began in 1618, and by 1648, when the Peace of Westphalia finally put an end to the mayhem, Germany was decimated. Not only had Germans killed each other for a generation, but Swedish and French armies had also become involved in the bloody religious struggle. It is estimated that the population of Germany fell from 16 million to 6 million during the course of the conflict,[1] and unification, or even cooperation among the dissident German princes seemed even further away than it had before the hostilities began. Several free cities survived the war reasonably intact, but only gradually did the larger and more populous principalities begin to reestablish themselves. Within a century Prussia became the most powerful of them, thanks in part to the Junkers — East German landholders with strong traditions of discipline and authority.

Prussia became a world power under Frederick II in the eighteenth century, but it was to be another one hundred years before Germany was united under Prussian leadership. In the intervening century, Germany produced a brilliant harvest of creative artists. Beginning with Telemann, Bach, and Handel in the early 1700s, the highest standards of musical composition were set, then further developed and refined by Mozart and Haydn. During and after the intellectual and political ferment caused by the French Revolution and Napoleon, came Beethoven, Schubert, and Schumann, followed by the later nineteenth-century Romantics — Wagner, Liszt, Brahms, and Richard Strauss. Thus, in five generations, during most of which Germany did not exist as a nation, the Germans gave the world a galaxy of musical creativity unmatched by any other country. Some of these composers were patronized by members of the surviving aristocracy, such as Haydn, who spent most of his creative life in the court of the powerful Hungarian Prince Esterhazy; some, like Bach, served as organists and Kapellmeisters in German churches; others traveled farther afield — Mozart to Paris and Italy, Handel and Haydn to London. Many migrated unhappily between Prague, Vienna, Salzburg, and small German courts, sporadically supported by the commissions of assorted princes, kings, and wealthy merchants, or by mysterious unidentified music lovers — such as the man who appeared in Mozart's impoverished household in Vienna in 1791 as the young composer, beset with family problems, was dying of tuberculosis, commissioned the great Requiem Mass, paid for it, and was never heard of again. The contribution of these German masters of music to Western civilization more than matches that of the Italians from Monteverdi and Vivaldi through Verdi and Puccini, and far outshines the more episodic efforts of the French, Czechs, English, Poles, and Spaniards at musical creativity.

In literature and science the Germans also produced a bounty of creative genius. Goethe, Schiller, and Lessing gave wings to Martin Luther's religious German, while Nietzsche, Schopenhauer, Kant, and Hegel used it to write some of the most profound and provocative philosophy of all time. In science one of the most important developments began when Isaac Newton, René Descartes, and Gottfried Wilhelm Leibnitz concurrently and independently developed the calculus, each unaware of what the others were doing. This essential tool of mathematical analysis created the theoretical basis for the burst of technical creativity which came during the eighteenth and nineteenth centuries in England, France, and Germany, and to which the Germans contributed bountifully, particularly with Heisenberg, Planck, and Einstein in the early twentieth century.

It was only at the end of the 1800s that Germany finally became a nation, thanks largely to the efforts of a unique Junker aristocrat named Prince Otto von Bismarck, who became prime minister of Prussia in 1862. Basing his operations on the ideals of hard work and frugality, religious puritanism and respect for authority, coupled with relative cultural insensibility and a dedication to austerity and duty, Bismarck set the tone for his efforts to unify Germany in an early speech: "Germany does not look to Prussia for liberalism, but for power. . . . the great issues of the day will not be settled by speeches and majority resolutions, but by blood and iron."[2]

And so it was. The victory over France in 1871 unified Germany and made it the most powerful nation on the European continent. Bismarck—the "Iron Chancellor"—controlled the new Germany almost single-handedly for a generation, until Wilhelm II acceded to the Prussian throne in 1890 and decided to run things his own way. Bismarck resigned in a fit of pique, hoping that the inexperienced and politically unskilled kaiser would shortly founder in a morass of problems and be forced to beg the crafty prime minister to return. But Kaiser Wilhelm had no intention of allowing his newfound power to slip from his hands back into Bismarck's. He appointed his own advisors, and for twenty years the German economy did very well. The country built a heavy industrial base, more formidable than that of either Britain or France, and managed to acquire some left-over colonies in Africa and the Pacific. At the same time, innumerable diplomatic blunders were made and the blustering and overbearing kaiser managed to antagonize nearly every other government in Europe.

In Germany itself developments were characterized by relative enlightenment. Though Karl Marx had been forced into exile in London, the German "Establishment"—both employers and government—had sense enough to act on his warning: "A spectre is haunting

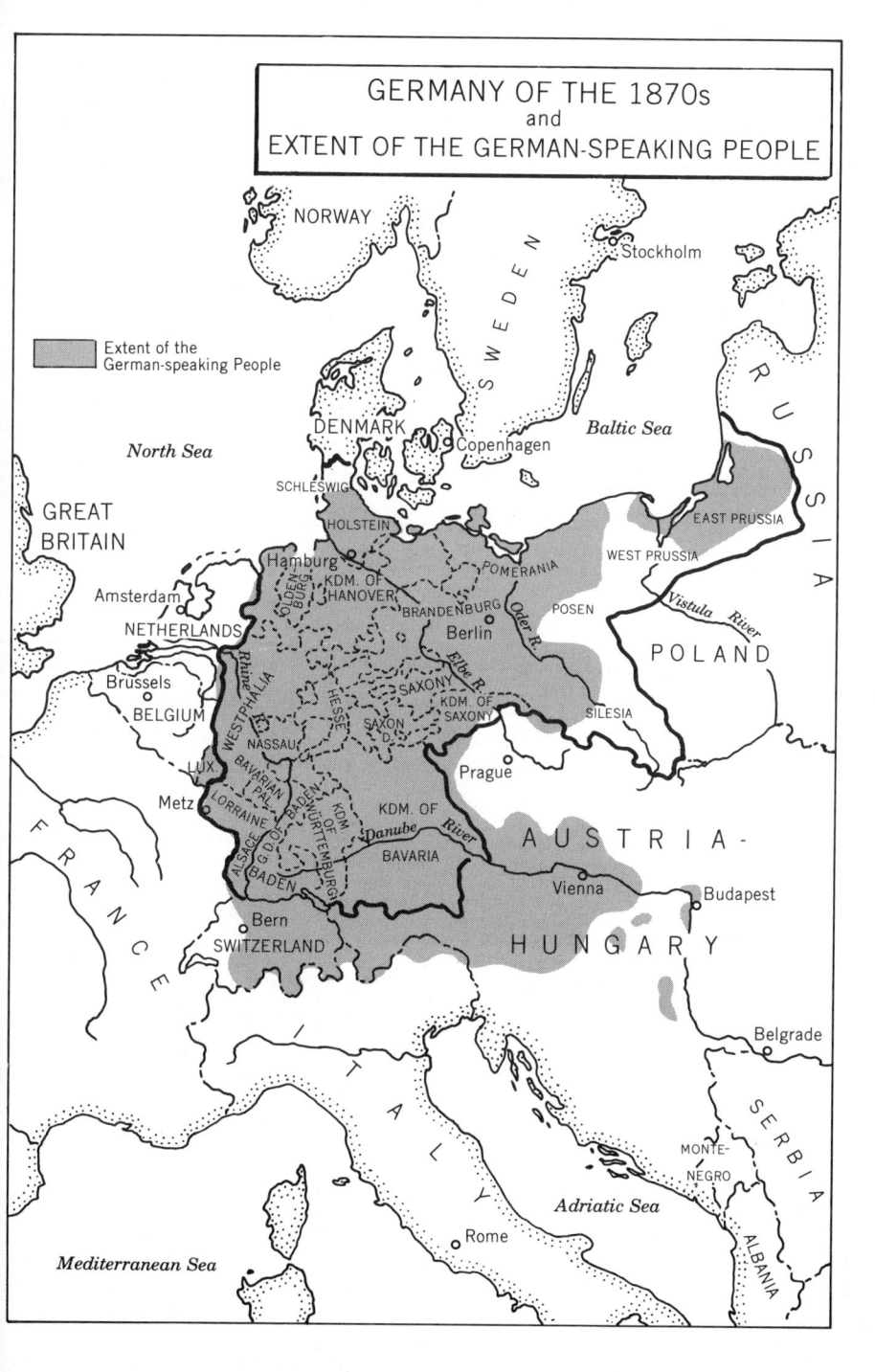

Europe—the spectre of Communism."³ Wage levels rose, workers' jobs and managers' careers opened up to talent from below. The first full-fledged social security system in the world was in operation by the turn of the century, as the German economy boomed, building new factories and seaports, universities and research institutions, and a powerful navy. It was this navy, and the implicit threat it posed to Britain's control of the seas, which made World War I inevitable.

Scores of excellent books have been written about the Balkan Wars of 1912 and 1913, the growing tension between the kaiser and his cousin Czar Nicholas II of Russia, the mobilization on both sides, and then the crisis triggered by the assassination of Archduke Ferdinand and his wife in Sarajevo, followed by war. Well-trained and nationalistically motivated German divisions swept across neutral Belgium into France according to plans worked out with meticulous skill by the matchless German general staff. At the same time, less well-armed but more numerous and equally patriotic Russians invaded East Prussia. Throughout Europe, and particularly in Germany, nationalism dominated the scene. Germany's Socialist deputies voted for the appropriations to finance the war. Bach and Mozart were forgotten both in Germany and elsewhere. In America, still far away, bigotry and jingoism took hold. The citizens of my birthplace, a suburb of Philadelphia, decided to change its name from Germantown to Mount Airy. The teaching of the German language was discontinued in many American schools and colleges.

For four bloody years the modern tribal war swept back and forth across Europe, causing the death of some

26 million people and reducing hundreds of cities and towns in France and Belgium, Poland and Russia to smoking ruins. The German generals had calculated well, and German soldiers fought with stoic heroism. But the entry of the United States in 1917, fresh and rich, and the gradual collapse of Bulgaria and Turkey, turned the tide. Revolution in Russia seemed briefly to have constituted a countervailing factor in early 1918 as German troops swept into the Ukraine, but the food and resources they had hoped to find were already exhausted, and so were the Germans. During the summer German troops began to mutiny, and the kaiser fled into exile in Holland, leaving Germany defeated and without a government, but largely undamaged by the war which the Germans had inflicted on millions of others. And this created the insidious myth later embraced by the Nazis—German armies had not been defeated, but betrayed.

The Weimar Republic, set up in 1919 under a constitution which combined the principle of federalism with coordination under a central government, had only limited powers. Allied troops were occupying the Rhineland; the border provinces of Alsace and Lorraine were rejoined to France, though their populations were largely German-speaking. The Czechs took over the Sudeten German region, and Poland occupied a large "corridor" of land between East Prussia and Germany proper. Germany was bound by Versailles to pay an unprecedented war reparation of approximately 150 billion gold marks. German colonies such as the Cameroons and Tanganyika in Africa and the Marshall Islands in the Pacific were divided up among the victorious allies.

Most of Germany's foreign assets were confiscated as were most vessels of the merchant marine and navy still afloat. Demoralized, racked by unemployment and inflation, the Germans did not know where to turn, and their economy, like a dead whale on the beach, threatened to pollute Europe.

As early as 1923 various groups within Germany had started organizing themselves with the aim of putting Germany back on its feet. One such group was headed by an Austrian named Schickelgruber, who had served as a corporal in the German army during the war. With a poorly organized band of cronies he tried to overthrow the government of Bavaria in a Munich-based *Bierhallputsch* which failed and landed its organizers in jail, where Schickelgruber, under the adopted name of Adolph Hitler, utilized his time by spelling out his racist and mendacious philosophy in his book, *Mein Kampf*.

Another group, far different in every respect, was composed of the remnants of the German General Staff. Its members had decided that the best way for a nucleus of German military power to survive and prepare to serve the German nation in some future conflict was to make common cause with Europe's other pariah, the young and struggling Soviet Union. This group succeeded first in making a commercial agreement with the Soviet Union as early as May 1921, then the broader Treaty of Rapallo in 1922, and finally a Soviet-German Treaty of Neutrality and Nonaggression, which was signed in Berlin in 1926. These agreements were implemented with specific arrangements under the terms of which the German military establishment, prohibited under the Treaty of Versailles to maintain or train large regular army units, or to develop or manufacture new weapons, was able to develop and test new weapons, and to train German units in the Soviet Union. Under these arrangements, as the world was later to learn, by 1923 Germany was spending more on its armed forces than Great Britain, and the German army was more than double its proscribed size.[4]

The third group of Germans who had specific plans and programs for Germany was the Communist Party. They had organized a structure of party cells or units both within the remains of the German armed forces, particularly in the navy, and also among workers in Germany's industries. With covert support from the Soviet Union through the Communist International, or Comintern, the Communists advocated a German Soviet Republic to be associated with the Soviet Union. But several attempts at local armed insurrection during the early 1920s were defeated, and the KPD, or German Communist Party, was forced to follow a legalistic program, running candidates for elections in competition with the usually more powerful and numerous Social Democrats and other German political parties.

And so, harassed by unemployment, disillusionment, and bitterness, plagued by an inflation which reduced the value of the German mark from twenty-five cents in 1921 to half a cent by January 1922, to the point where one dollar was worth more than a trillion marks by November 1923, the Germans lost their assets and savings and any sense of personal security. Beset by dissident opponents from three sides, and unsure in any case of its own objectives, the Weimar Republic struggled for survival. Gustav Stresemann became chancellor and foreign minister in August 1923, and managed initially to achieve a certain stability under which emerged that level of superficial well-being I found in Koblenz in 1927.

German genius in technology and the arts reappeared and thrived in such institutions as the Bauhaus for architecture and design, in the German film industry which proved innovative and creative as expressed by such early films as *The Cabinet of Dr. Caligary*. Bremen and Hamburg again became active ports, and German vessels plied the North Atlantic. In Britain, North America, Scandinavia, and elsewhere millions of people realized that World War I had accomplished nothing, that its jingoistic nationalism had served no useful purpose. In a wave of local sheepish contrition Mount Airy again became Germantown, German classical music became popular again, and young people such as those organized in England's Oxford Movement, vowed never again to allow themselves to be persuaded and cajoled into nationalistic wars.

During my stay in Koblenz I was too young to appreciate many of these contemporary developments, and in any case my German stay was cut off when I returned to the United States to finish my schooling. But the financial crisis of 1929, and the subsequent economic depression in the United States and elsewhere combined to influence my own life in such a way as to give me another vivid glimpse of Germany during its rapid transformation from the peaceful and permissive Weimar Republic into the strident and aggressive Third Reich.

In 1931 I dropped out of the University of Wisconsin to find job opportunities extremely limited; there was a

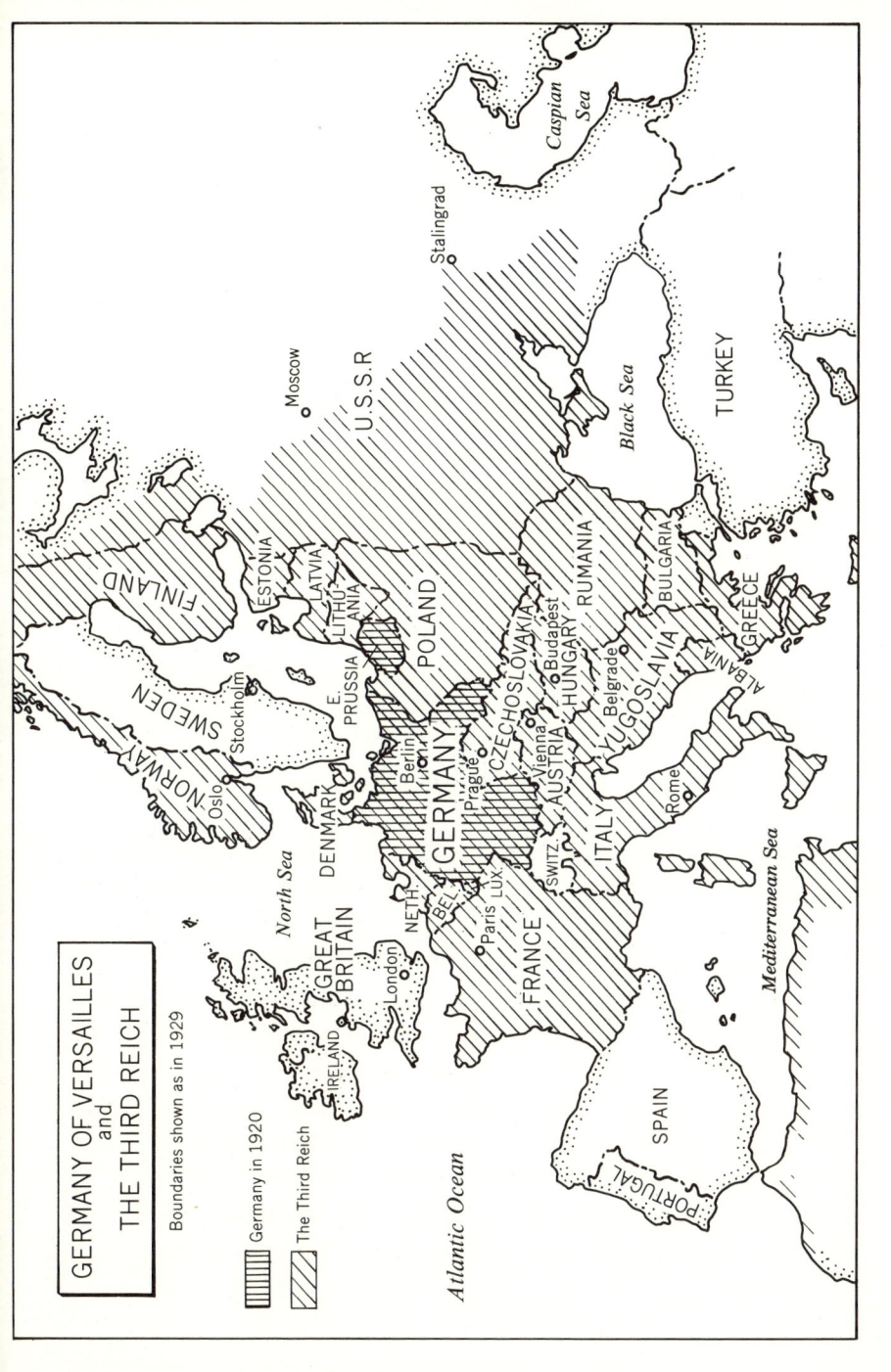

widespread conviction among my contemporaries and nearly everyone else that the capitalist system as practiced in the United States and western Europe was imperfect, and that alternatives should be examined. Encouraged by my parents, I went to a welding course offered by the General Electric Company, and then made arrangements to go to the Soviet Union to work in industry and get a look at the operation of a planned economy. There were no diplomatic relations between the United States and the USSR at that time; therefore I went to Germany to apply for a Soviet visa. While waiting for it to be granted, I spent some time in Berlin and Amsterdam, visiting friends and attending several international conferences.

The Germany I saw in the summer of 1932 was in vivid contrast to what I remembered from the 1920s. I re-visited my friend Ernst in Koblenz; he was now deeply involved in work among the country's millions of unemployed. I wandered for two days around the Ruhr; the grass was growing hip-high between the railroad ties in what had been some of Europe's most vigorous and productive industrial enterprises. In the Ruhr and in Berlin I saw mammoth demonstrations in which the National Socialists, now emerging as Germany's most vigorous and violent political force, fought the Social Democrats and Communists for popular support. Wise friends, both Socialists and Communists, told me unhappily that if these two groups would only work together, they could easily prevent the Nazis from making further political gains. But local Social Democratic Party (SPD) leadership was unwilling to work with the Communists, while the Communist international leadership in Moscow still did not take the Nazis seriously, and insisted that the "Social Fascists" of the SPD were the principal enemies.

At the Anti-War Congress in Amsterdam I witnessed one of the most impressive gatherings I was ever to see. Some ten thousand delegates from a score of countries met under Communist leadership (the Communist control was often indirect). The chairman of the meeting was Willy Muenzenberg, nominally a leader of the SAP or Socialist Workers Party, a splinter group lying somewhere between the KPD and the SPD, but used by the former to try to infiltrate the latter. Among the speakers I remember most vividly the French writer Henri Barbusse, already then in poor health and frustrated by the inability of anti-Nazi forces to get together to stop Hitler's relentless march toward power.

Then my Soviet visa came through, and I went off to Moscow, then Magnitogorsk, where I spent the next five years working in a steel mill, and learning about communism in operation. In 1937 I returned to the United States for a brief vacation, and on this trip had another glimpse of a much-changed Germany.

I arrived in Berlin early in the morning on April 20, Hitler's birthday. At the suggestion of one of my few remaining friends in Berlin I went down to Hitler's residence on Friedrichstrasse, where a huge crowd was gathering. When, as scheduled, Hitler appeared on the balcony to say a few words to his birthday well-wishers, a roar of enthusiasm burst from thousands of German throats. Then Hitler spoke in his staccato crescendo. A woman near me fainted and was promptly carried off by smartly dressed Storm Troopers stationed there for that purpose. The Nazis now controlled Germany completely. The Communists were in jail, had fled, or were deep underground. The Social Democrats were impotent. Some joined the Nazis reluctantly, as did my friend Ernst in Koblenz, in order to keep their jobs, and to bide their time. Others gave way to the pervasive hysteria of the times; convinced that the Nazi slogan "Today Germany—Tomorrow the World" would be realized to the general benefit of all concerned (although some would doubtless suffer), they became enthusiastic *Parteigenosse* (party members) in Hitler's NSDAP—the National Socialist German Workers' Party.

I did not return to Germany again until the end of the war, although I did see something of German operations during that time. Like millions of others, I cowered under German bombs in London and elsewhere, and as a journalist studied German military and politico-diplomatic organs at work in Scandinavia and in Japan during the war. With the rest of the world, I followed carefully the ebb and flow of World War II, the initial military successes, then Stalingrad, the long German retreat from Russia, Africa, and then Italy, concurrent with the systematic destruction of Germany by air attack—first night bombing, then precision daylight attacks on Schweinfurt, Hamburg, Dresden, and so many others. In Sweden I watched the crippled flak-rent Allied bombers nurse their way into Malmö and talked with a few—a very few—German defectors. I also maintained contact with several highly placed German dissidents such as Adam von Trott zu Solz, as they tried to persuade the British and Americans to modify their objective from unconditional surrender and negotiate with the German anti-Hitler opposition, which was virtually unknown in the world until its heroic but unsuccessful attempt to assassinate Hitler on July 20, 1944.

Then, at war's end, I went back to Germany, courtesy of the U.S. Seventh Armored Division. I flew into Berlin in July 1945, just before the Potsdam conference, to set up *Time*'s Central European bureau, and to report on the state of Germany as the smoke cleared above the devastated cities, as the hungry, hopeless refugees returned to their cindered homes to live under four occupying armies, their young and middle-aged men dead or in prison camps from Siberia to Texas.

For this time Germany had been truly defeated, and every German knew it. In spite of three years of progressively intensive air attacks, the German armies had kept on fighting, and the civilian economy had somehow continued to produce the bare essentials for survival and for carrying on the war effort until Russian and Allied divisions invaded from both sides and met in the middle on the Elbe. Mercifully, German plans to continue the war with guerrilla operations based on the *Werwolf** collapsed; the Germans are excellent soldiers, but they do not make good guerrillas. In any case, the country was completely exhausted, reserves were gone, the organs of government—the police and fire departments, the courts, schools, hospitals, trade unions, banks, stores, communication, and transportation facilities— had all but disappeared along with their Nazi leaders.

I remember flying into Berlin in a stripped-down DC 3, and peering through the tiny windows at mile after

---

*Werwolf: Units of young Germans who were intended to continue resistance to the occupying forces.

mile of hollow shells of buildings — roofs collapsed or burnt out, streets strewn shoulder-deep with charred vehicles, rubble, and debris. On the ground — quiet. Where were the Germans? One had to look for them — furtive figures emerging from their cellars and shelters, beating narrow paths over the heaps of rubble as they went to look for water, food, then some way to make a living.

I was billeted in a battered house in the western suburb of Zehlendorf, within walking distance from a makeshift press center which included an officers' mess and some improvised communications facilities. On my way to lunch on the first day I had my first talk with a post-war German. Dietrich was about twelve, although he looked small, gaunt, and shriveled. He was hovering near the mess with several comrades, waiting for the Americans to flick their cigarette butts into the gutter before entering the building. They would pounce on each butt, and, squabbling among themselves, make off with it. I grabbed his arm as he passed. Fearful, suspicious, but resigned, he whined:

"Wat willst Du, Onkel?" ("What do you want, Uncle?")

"Show me that," I said, pointing to something he had tightly gripped in his hand. Reluctantly he showed me the small battered metal box, in which were half a dozen cigarette butts.

"What do you do with them?" I asked.

"What do you mean?" he said in astonishment. "For a big one like that I can get a potato. The small ones my mother smokes."

"What do you do between mess hours?" I asked.

"I look in the Grunewald where there are many fallen Germans still unburied. My father fell somewhere there. I know his dog-tag number."

"Don't you go to school?" I asked.

"Ach, nein," he muttered. "Six months ago our school was requisitioned as a hospital. And anyhow, what good would it do? Before, we were told in school that the Germans were right and the Russians and the others were wrong. Now we are told that the others were right and we Germans were wrong. I don't believe anything any more. War is wrong. People are all the same."

2

Germany Defeated

Germany had not merely been defeated, it had been atomized.

Eighty-odd million Germans who had been conditioned and disciplined during their entire lives by their country's institutions and restraints were now just so many individuals. The social cement, which had tied them to their families and jobs and structured their duties and actions, had been dissolved.

Moreover, the functioning mechanism of their lives was gone. While some still had ration cards, there were no rations. In Berlin more than two hundred bridges had been destroyed and since the subway system wasn't working, it was possible to get from one part of town to another only by swimming the canals and the river Spree, or with boats, which were hard to find. Many streets were impassable even by foot; only a few had been cleared enough so that vehicular traffic was possible, and the only vehicles were those of the occupation forces, all of which converged in Berlin. In the rest of the country, each of the occupying powers was taking over every aspect of administration.

For Germany had already been divided.

The details for the division of Germany had been worked out in London by the European Advisory Commission during 1944 and early 1945. This group consisted of United States, British, and Soviet representatives on an ambassadorial level, aided by a fairly large administrative and military staff. It was the function of this body to lay out the zones of occupation of Germany, so that when the victorious armies entered the country, each might take over its designated area in an orderly fashion, without risk of conflict among themselves by accident or exuberance.

Much criticism was later levied at this body for the many imperfections in its work, and it is well known that its meetings were often acrimonious. Each of the three main Allies had its own ideas as to what post-war Germany should be. The Russians wanted a Soviet German Republic, as large as possible. The British wanted an orderly and well-behaved Germany able to maintain European balances in cooperation with Whitehall. The Americans were divided among themselves. The Morgenthau Plan group favored an agrarian Germany, greatly reduced in size, its industries removed, and its small population making a modest living from the land. Other Americans agreed with the British. The French would have been happiest if there were no Germany.[1]

These wide differences in the objectives among the Allies were wisely kept off the agendas of the meetings of all kinds of wartime inter-allied bodies in order to facilitate getting on with the job of winning the war. But it was the duty of the European Advisory Commission to lay out the blueprints for post-war Germany, and the disagreements had to be faced and dealt with. Unfortunately for historians, Ambassador Winant, the U.S. representative to the Commission, committed suicide shortly after the end of the war and his principal deputy, Professor Philip Mosley, died of cancer in 1972. In the interim, neither he nor any of the British or Russian members of the group evidenced any willingness to write substantive memoirs on the subject.

Having tried, late in 1944 in London, to write a story on the subject, I know that the British had insisted that the heavy industry region around the Ruhr be included in the British zone of occupation, while the Russians wanted the East and as much of central Germany as possible, leaving the "scenery" to the United States. The Americans insisted on, and got, the port of Bremen as an enclave. Everyone, of course, wanted Berlin, as the symbol of control of the country. British and American insistence had gone far toward forcing the Russians into accepting three-power occupation of Berlin, when the Ardennes offensive in December 1944 administered a heavy setback to the Western Allies while the Russians were sweeping across Poland and the eastern Balkans. Many military men thought the war would end with the Russians on the Rhine. It was in this climate that the body agreed to Soviet occupation of a large part of Germany. The border ran just east of Lübeck, then in a

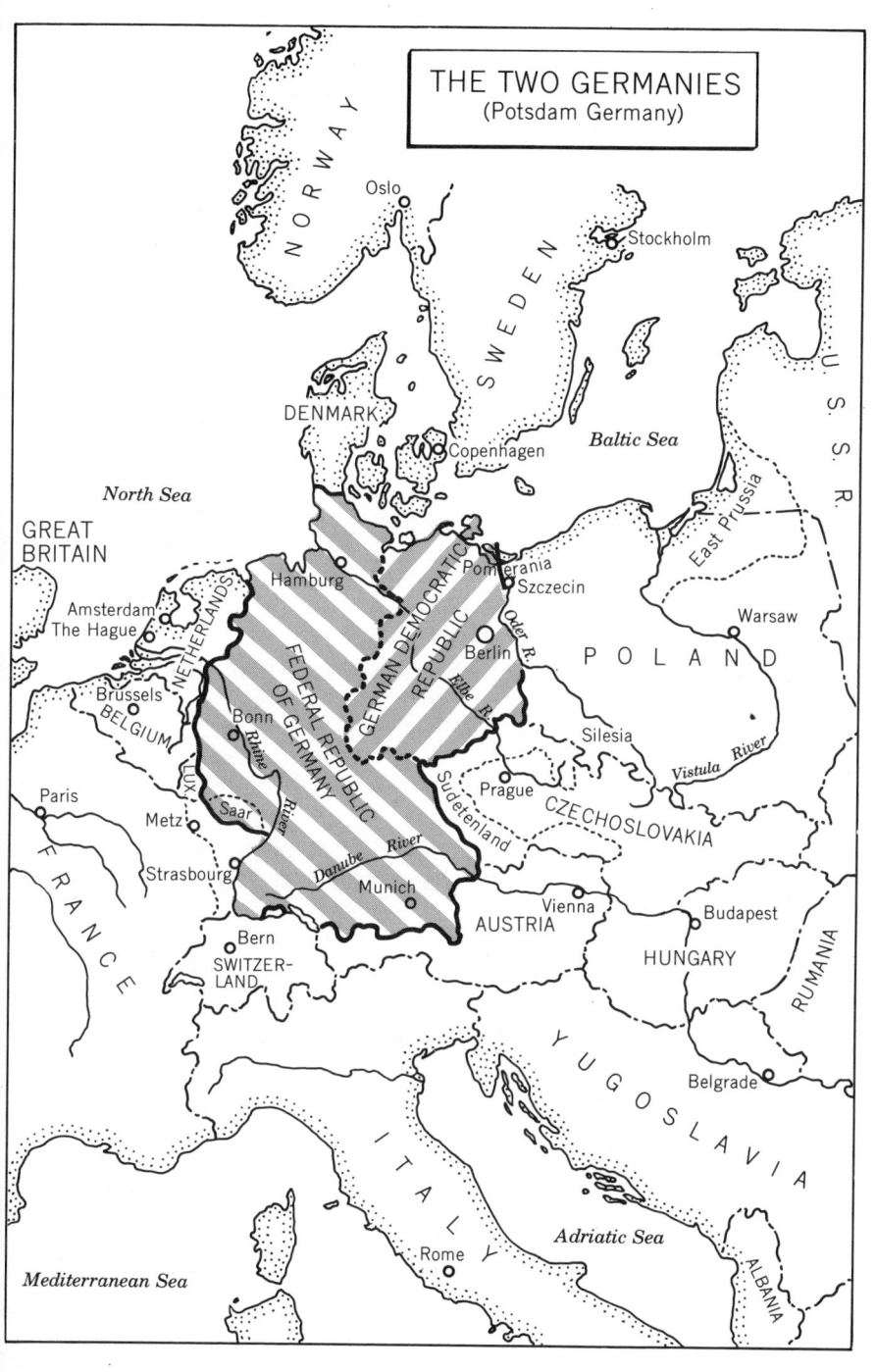

wavering line southward, turning sharply to the east at Fulda to join the Czech border near Hof (see map).

Berlin was to be a separate enclave within the Soviet zone; the city was to be divided into sectors, each administered by a commandant of its occupation power. Unfortunately, nothing was put in writing about access to Berlin from the west, probably because the Russians would not agree to a corridor, while the Western Allies would not accept a statement to the effect that their access was to be at the discretion of and by courtesy of the Russians. This ambivalence later caused endless trouble, and could have caused World War III during any one of the several Berlin crises during the 1950s and 1960s.

Another shortcoming of the work of the European Advisory Commission was the fact that while agreeing at the outset that Germany would be administered as a unit, it did not spell out what kind of German civilian authorities would be established, nor what their jurisdiction would be. This was almost certainly the result of the hope, fairly widespread in Allied governmental circles in 1944, that after the war Britain, the United States, and the USSR would cooperate in all areas of endeavor and reach compromise agreements on issues in dispute. This confidence was rapidly dispelled in the late spring of 1945, as the Soviet Union proceeded to install Communist governments in Poland, Bulgaria, and Rumania in flagrant violation of its agreement at Yalta to allow "free and unfettered" elections to determine the governments of liberated areas.

In February 1946, at Charles deGaulle's insistence, the British and American governments agreed that France should join the Big Three as one of the occupying powers of Germany. The Soviet attitude was, in effect, to shrug and say to London and Washington: "It's O.K. with us. If you want to carve out a French zone from your zones, go ahead." This was done, and a smaller French zone was created along the southern and western frontiers of Germany, encompassing the cities of Baden-Baden, Landau, Offenburg, Zweibrücken, and the highly prized Saar area.

These were the preliminary arrangements made for governing post-war Germany, agreed to at the Potsdam conference which was convened on July 17, 1945 with Churchill, Stalin, and Truman in attendance. But the facts had far outrun the plans. The actual behavior of the four armies of occupation and the day-to-day policies they followed were already very different. Nor could it have been otherwise, given the conditions in the countries involved.

The Soviet Union had suffered losses during the war comparable to those suffered by the Germans. Millions in the Soviet Union were starving. I knew Soviet officers who got bread crusts from Allied mess halls in Berlin, wrapped them in packages, and sent them home to their families in Russia. Soviet industry was short of everything, reflected in the much-publicized Soviet demand for $10 billion in reparations from Germany, and even before Potsdam, Soviet military authorities were taking machinery, equipment, motor vehicles, railroad rolling stock, even railroad rails and telephone poles from German areas under their control. The Soviet troops in Germany had survived a bitter campaign, and had been promised "the victor's right" by their commanders after the end of the war. And they were taking it. All over eastern Germany, Soviet soldiers, alone and in groups, often completely out of contact with their units and commanders, were knocking down the doors of the houses still standing, taking anything they could find, including women and girls, and shooting any German who tried to resist. I saw many incidents in Berlin during the weeks I was there before the Potsdam conference began, in which Russian soldiers, often staggering drunk on looted liquor, struggled toward their quarters with radio sets, sewing machines, kitchenware, furniture, and other goods. I saw Russian soldiers with a dozen wristwatches on each arm grinning with satisfaction as they rode eastward on "liberated" bicycles. I saw one Soviet officer interfere with a Soviet soldier who was seizing a bicycle from a German woman with a red cross on her sleeve. The soldier argued: "I walked and crawled from Kiev to Berlin fighting these Fascists. And now that we have won, should I walk while these pigs ride? NO!"

Not that British and American and French soldiers did not "liberate" jewelry and motor vehicles. But they had chocolate bars with which to pay for these things, and for the favors of German girls. The Russians had only their guns.

After the beginning of the Potsdam conference, the Soviet commanders took vigorous measures to restore discipline among their troops. Some Soviet soldiers were shot for looting and rape, and battle-weary combat troops were sent eastward to be demoblized as soon as transport facilities permitted. But disorders continued for months, and millions of Germans were permanently embittered toward the Russians.

During the two weeks before Potsdam began, I made several trips outside Berlin, usually in a U.S. Army jeep made available to war correspondents. Everywhere I saw the same thing: the roads were littered with burnt-out vehicles, civilian and military. Farm animals were nowhere to be found—they had all been eaten. Cities such as Leipzig were in worse shape than Berlin, and no attempts were being made yet to clear the streets and re-establish essential services. The rivers were cluttered with sunken barges and the remains of bombed-out bridges; crossings were made on military pontoon bridges or primitive ferries. Everywhere the roads were lined with weary refugees, mostly women and children, sometimes pushing a few belongings in baby carriages or improvised carts. Some were foreign workers who had been brought to Germany to man factories and farms and were now trying to get back home to Poland, France, and Holland. Others were Germans who had been evacuated to rural areas, now returning to their former homes in Berlin, Dresden, Munich, hoping to find a roof, a family, maybe some food.

And everywhere were Russian soldiers, in their worn, discolored uniforms, using their already well-used weapons to take what they wanted.

The Potsdam conference was unfortunately not open to the press. We were briefed daily by press officers, and had opportunities to see the world leaders only by chance. One day I went down to the ruins of the old *Reichskanzlei* (government chancery) to see the remains of the bunker where Hitler was supposed to have committed suicide, and there was Churchill, lumbering over the rubble, surrounded by British security guards. On another occasion a colleague and I were sifting through a mass of discarded papers in the ruins of the old Air Ministry building, and a large Soviet patrol, commanded by a general, came through and chased us away. We left reluctantly, but looked back to see Stalin in the midst of a clutch of Soviet brass, sightseeing.

The conference was interrupted for two days by the British elections. The British do not believe in lame-duck governments and so, having lost, Churchill left office the same day, leaving the conference to recess until newly elected Prime Minister Clement Attlee could get to Berlin to take over. It was a lucky break for me, for during this unscheduled interruption President Truman decided to tour the American zone of Germany. I was one of the twenty correspondents who were lucky enough to fly along on this inspection tour. We had nearly every meal for two days with Truman, James Byrnes, General Eisenhower, and other top United States commanders. I found the U.S. zone much more orderly and presentable than the Soviet zone. Buildings were being rebuilt, as were bridges. Some trains were running, and many shopkeepers had re-opened their businesses. The U.S. military was, of course, pervasive, but the GIs were relatively well fed and no more disorderly than one would expect from any large group of young men in uniform with a few dollars in their pockets. There were stories of looting and disorderly behavior, but serious incidents were rare. Later, when I visited the British zone, I found the occupation troops even more disciplined and well behaved.

It was both interesting and touching to note the behavior of Harry Truman. He had by then been in office not quite four months, and was still frankly unsure of himself. When we questioned him about the conference and other things he said, "Boys, give me a break. I just don't know yet. President Roosevelt didn't cut me in on many areas of activity, and Germany and inter-Allied relations was one of them . . ." While inspecting he behaved a bit like a cat in a strange barn, peering around corners while whispering almost furtively to his aide, "Colonel, what do I do now?"

Back in Potsdam, at the end of July 1945, the conference was resumed, and we got consistent reports of serious disagreements. Then it was over, and the brass departed. Some important decisions had been reached. While Germany was to be treated as a single economic unit, reparations collections were to be carried out in each zone by its occupying power; the Russians were to get a few selected industrial installations from the Western zones by special agreement; an international war criminals' trial was to begin in Nuremberg in November 1945. A foreign ministers' conference was to be convened in Moscow in December to settle any outstanding problems. De-Nazification was to be carried out in each zone by the power in control, and All-German questions were to be handled by an Allied Control Council made up of the Supreme Commanders of the four powers, meeting regularly in Berlin; Berlin was to be administered by a *Kommandatura* consisting of the commandants, but decisions of both the *Kommandatura* and the Allied Control Council had to be unanimous, which meant—in effect—that these bodies could not handle controversial issues. This decision more or less predetermined the division of Germany, if not permanently, at least for a long time to come.

During the conference one event took place which was little noted in Germany at the time — the Hiroshima bomb. Later, in the contacts that I established and maintained with officers of the Soviet military administration, I learned that its effect on Soviet policy was immediate and great.

After the conference I got on with the business of trying to report on Germany to United States readers who had many other things on their minds — VJ Day, the demand to bring the troops home, serious political crises in France and Italy. I got to know General Lucius Clay, then Deputy U.S. Commander, and his political advisor Robert Murphy — both gifted and dedicated men who had more to do with shaping United States policy than anyone in Washington. Clay was from Georgia, a brilliant career officer who had spent sixteen years as a captain, then climbed to prominence largely as an administrator. Murphy was from Milwaukee, a career diplomat since the early 1920s, who had served his first post in the U.S. Consulate in Munich. A devout Catholic, Murphy once told me that his diplomatic colleague from the Vatican at the time was a man named Pacelli (later Pope Pius XII), and both had agreed that the 1923 *Bierhallputsch* was a minor incident which had little significance and would have no further consequences. In reminiscing about it long afterward, Pacelli told Murphy, "Good thing that judgment was made before I became infallible." Clay and Murphy worked well together, and it is thanks largely to them that United States interests in Germany and those of the German people were defended as effectively as they were during the late 1940s.

The Soviet high command in Germany was far removed in its headquarters in Karlshorst, and virtually inaccessible to such as me. But I got to know a number of colonels as well as several German Communists who had responsible jobs in the Soviet zone, and was able to follow events of interest in detail.

The first important issue on which policies in the Soviet zone varied radically from those in the Western zones involved currency. The Allies had printed new "occupation marks" to replace the old Nazi money, which was worthless. Since the Americans had the needed facilities, they made the plates and printed the occupation marks, which were valid throughout Germany. These were used to pay the increasing number of German civilian employees and servants, and to procure local goods when available. These marks were strictly controlled by the Finance Division of the Office of Military Government and a certain number of marks were also issued to the British and French military government authorities for similar purposes. British, French, and U.S. military personnel, however, were paid in Military Payment Certificates, in dollars or francs or sterling denominations. These certificates were used in military mess halls or PXs (military Post Exchange stores) and it was illegal for German civilians to possess this currency, which was convertible into dollars. But the Russian forces had no adequate system of mess halls and PX stores. Soviet troops lived off the land and Soviet rubles were not (and are still not) allowed to circulate outside the Soviet Union. So when the occupation marks were being printed by the United States and distributed, the Russians asked to borrow the plates and print their own. Some United States financial officials, moved perhaps by friendship for the Russians and enthusiasm for better inter-Allied relations, complied. The Soviet military government thereupon printed a very large amount of occupation currency, then lent the plates out to Soviet troop commanders, who printed even more. No accounting was ever made, but in late 1945 and early 1946 Soviet troops were being paid and given large victory bonuses in this currency while Soviet officials were using it not only for procurement of supplies and food items from their own zone, but were contriving through German intermediaries to use it to buy everything possible in the other zones. Protests produced no official response from the Soviet military authorities, but several senior Soviet officials told me privately: "We are destitute. Our country has given everything for victory. You are so rich . . ."

Another problem involved reparations. Although the French and British did take some reparations from their zones in Germany, the United States took very little, and only at the beginning. The substance of United States military government orders was to "prevent disease and unrest" in occupied Germany, which required that reparations removals be minimal, and that increasing quantities of food products, raw materials, and other items be brought into Germany to rehabilitate the economy and hasten the achievement of self-sufficiency. These items included grain, meat, tobacco, and assorted industrial raw materials unavailable in Germany. British procedures in this respect were similar to those of the United States, while for the first year French actions rather resembled those of the Russians. The Russians publicly chided the Anglo-Americans for pampering the Germans, while secretly they were delighted, because often they were able to buy items thus brought into Germany by the United States, paying in occupation currency printed from United States plates, and in some cases then sending the items to Russia as reparations. In this way the German cow was being fed at one end by the Americans, while being milked at the other by the Russians.

Another area of divergence was in de-Nazification. At the time of Potsdam very few Nazi Party members remained in the Soviet zone. Most had been shot or had fled westward. When the Russians discovered one, by denunciation or otherwise, they knew they had him in their control because if his past were revealed he could be summarily executed. Therefore, if they were technically or otherwise competent (and most competent men in Germany had had to join the NSDAP), they were put to work with the admonition: "Now you produce, and be loyal to us. If you falter, you are dead." There were undoubtedly British and United States officials who would have liked to do the same thing, but were unable to do so because of the United States and British press, which had a way of finding out about Nazis at large (often, no doubt from leaks from liberal-minded government officials) and pillorying the authorities for "shielding Nazis." In this way many competent former Nazis in the Western zones were restricted to ditch-digging jobs for many years. Most really high-level Nazis were, of course, dead, in prison awaiting trial, or had fled abroad.

The most spectacular aspect of the de-Nazification program was the series of trials held in Nuremberg during the winter of 1945–46, which I covered for *Time*. I would drive down from Berlin, a gruelling ten hours over the Berlin-Helmstedt autobahn which at the time was the only access road to Berlin that the Russians would allow us to use, then over poor roads through the British and American zones—Göttingen, Kassel, Fulda, Würzburg, to Stein, a Nuremberg suburb where an unbombed castle had been requisitioned and made into a Press Center for the two hundred or so Allied journalists, including always a dozen or more Russians. Day after day I would sit and watch the top defendants in the prisoners' box—Goering, former Nazi Foreign Minister Ribbentrop, former Deputy Führer Rudolf Hess, former Chief of Staff Feldmarschall Keitel, Admirals Raeder and Dönitz, and lesser fry such as Economics Minister Speer and financial wizard Hjalmar Schacht. They were on trial for their lives, accused of conspiring against the peace, breaking peace, crimes against humanity, and genocide. At the beginning of the trial Hess was simulating madness, and for days on end stared vacantly at the ceiling; finally he decided to change his tactics, asked for permission to speak, and said in effect: "Enough of this nonsense. I am no more mad than anyone else. I wish to take my place now and bear my responsibilities along with my comrades."

All but three of the defendants were convicted, and twelve of the twenty-four (including Martin Bormann *in absentia*) were sentenced to be executed and hanged, though Goering cheated the hangman by poisoning himself in his jail cell.

It all seemed normal to my colleagues and me at the time, but in retrospect it was clearly a victor's trial. As many Germans felt all along, the defendants were being tried as much for having lost the war as for the actions they committed in trying to win it. From the beginning the court, which consisted of four judges — British, French, American, and Soviet — applied the legal principle of *Tu Quoque* (Thou Also).[2] This prohibited the defendants from vindicating themselves by citing actions by Allied commanders or officials similar to those of which they were accused. The example that brought it to my attention involved Admiral Raeder, commander of German submarine forces, who was accused of having ordered one of his U-boats to fire on sailors of an enemy vessel which had been torpedoed and was sinking. The defense counsel tried to cite a similar case in which a British submarine commander, also fearing his vessel would be boarded by enemy sailors, had issued the same type of order. But the defense was silenced with the *Tu Quoque* ruling.

The use of this ruling in Nuremberg in trying capital crimes seemed illogical and unjust. More striking, though not used much in the main Nuremberg trial, since the defendants were almost all top-level commanders and officials, but constantly used in later, lower-level trials, was the defense's plea that the defendant had "only been obeying orders," which soldiers and officials the world round are supposed to do. Such pleas were rejected. My feelings on this were crystallized when, after the executions, one of my colleagues by accident recognized the U.S. Army sergeant hangman, whose identity had been carefully kept from the press, and asked him how he felt when hanging such prominent prisoners. He shrugged and said: "I was only obeying orders."

Still another area of divergence between the Russians' procedures and those of the Western Allies involved the formation of German government, political, and other institutions. The Russians came into Germany at the end of the war with a large group of German Communists who had been in Moscow during most of the war, being groomed to assume positions of responsibility in liberated Germany. The most prominent was Walter Ulbricht, who came in the uniform of a Soviet colonel, carrying a Soviet passport. One of his younger assistants was Wolfgang Leonard, who later defected and wrote a fascinating book about his experiences called *Children of the Revolution*. Using these men and some of the survivors from concentration camps which they had captured in early 1946 the Russians began to set up shadow German ministries and local government bodies, as well, of course, as the Communist Party. But in the first election they organized, the KPD was badly defeated in Berlin by the SPD, so the Russians used an aging and rather addled SPD leader named Otto Grotewohl to merge his party with the KPD to form the Socialist Unity Party (SED or *Sozialistische Einheitspartei Deutschlands*) which became, and today still remains, the governing party of East Germany. The SPD in West Germany protested, of course, but the Russians shrugged it off, and proceeded to invest responsibility and authority in their German stooges. I knew one of these very well—Leo Skrypcinski—a left-leaning but non-Communist survivor of the Sachsenhausen concentration camp. This brilliant and erratic man was made Commissioner of Industry in early 1946, but was unable to stomach Soviet reparations removals and the systematic milking of the East German economy by the Russians, who forced on it over-priced Soviet raw materials while taking its products at knock-down prices. He finally committed suicide.

The press in the Soviet zone was set up under Communist editors; no pretense of press freedom was made, and from the beginning the Russians took over the Nazi block leader system in cities under their control. Under this system, every city block had a leader appointed by the Party, whose job it was to report on dissident activities such as listening to Western radio programs, and to see that no clandestine activities or criticism of the Russians took place. At the beginning, Russians in civilian clothes—sometimes even in uniform—sat behind the desks of German officials, but gradually these controls became unnecessary as the German officials learned their jobs and became persuaded that, if they were loyal to the Russians, they would get remunerative and protected jobs with power independent of any unpredictable democratic elections.

In this way, by 1947 the Russians had set up a fairly competent skeleton government at all levels in what became in October 1949 the *Deutsche Demokratische Republik*, or DDR. The Russians were not popular, of course; they were and today still are feared and hated. Nor were their stooges respected or admired as was well demonstrated by the insurrection in 1953. But it worked.

The Soviet garrison, which numbered from twenty to thirty divisions throughout the late 1940s, was secure, and the Soviet Union received from East Germany a growing quantity of high-quality industrial commodities at low prices and with a minimum of trouble.

In the Western zones things went very differently. The Western Allies were dedicated to democracy, and proceeded to sponsor democratic institutions in the Western zones. Independent editors such as Erich Reger in Berlin and Axel Springer in Hamburg were licensed by the military government, and began putting out newspapers and magazines that reflected their own opinions, or those of independent trade unions or political parties. Private businessmen began to operate stores, small factories, banks, and shipping companies. Some large plants such as the Volkswagenwerk in Wolfsburg or the Hermann Goering Steel Mill near Hannover, which had been the property of the Nazi Party, were taken over and operated by the military government, but most of the old firms such as Krupp, Demag, Siemens, and Telefunken went back into business subject only to the break-up orders of the de-cartelization authorities, and to the prohibition against having any former Nazis in high positions.

The first elections took place in January 1946 and I remember the elation with which Lucius Clay watched the returns come in. "They are turning out!" he exulted. His fear had been that the Germans had been so conditioned by twelve years of Nazi government that they would not take any interest in electing a government.

By early 1946 it had become clear to nearly everyone that the Soviet zone was going its own way and prospects for getting the German economy together as a unit were small indeed. So steps were taken to begin the coordination, if not yet the unification, of the three Western zones. When the issue arose in the Allied Control Council the Russians vetoed it. But nonetheless a *Laenderrat*, or council consisting of representatives from the various German *Laender*, or states, had already been formed in October 1945 in Stuttgart. It met monthly, and I would drive down from Berlin to watch the inexperienced and still very unsure German politicians, most of them initially appointed by the military government, discuss the problems of government in very inauspicious quarters under the watchful eyes of United States and other Western civil affairs officers. It was a modest beginning, but West Germany was beginning to get together, under increasingly democratic institutions.

Also, the Western zones were beginning to come to life economically. Prisoners of war were gradually returning and taking their places in German industry and trade. The railroads were operating, and most roads and some of the autobahn stretches were passable. The Rhine had been partially cleared of broken bridges and sunken barges, enough to open the channels, and the river was becoming again a major north-south transportation artery. Smoke poured from the chimneys of the heavy industry plants of the Ruhr once more. Though the entire economy suffered from the lack of a stable currency, the occupation mark being constantly undermined by the influx of notes from the East, the Western zones were beginning to function almost normally.

During the early weeks of 1946 I decided to take a trip eastward. I had found a fine assistant by then, an efficient German bookkeeper and office manager, a competent secretary, and an excellent mechanic-driver-organizer, and now I wanted to get out of the Berlin bureau and take a look at the neighboring country, Poland. Most especially, I wanted to look into an issue that was becoming a new bone of contention between the Russians and the Western Allies — the frontiers between East Germany and Poland. So I set off in a jeep, with a trailer containing enough cans of gasoline to get me to the Soviet border and back, a heavy sheepskin coat, and a box of U.S. Army K rations.

I had heard that the Russians had simply taken the German city of Stettin and given it to the Poles, who had rechristened it Szczecin and were beginning to use the port, although it was on the right bank of the Oder River which, the Russians said, was the "natural" frontier between Poland and Germany. I was able to confirm this on my trip. Far more important, I got a casual glimpse of the utter disarray of Eastern Europe at the time. At Schwerin, just upstream from Frankfurt-an-der-Oder, I crossed the river on one of the two or three bridges then operating, and found a city utterly pulverized. One could not find a whole brick in the rubble — just chips and dust. The only traffic on the roads was the staggering refugees, heading in both directions, and some Soviet officers driving requisitioned or liberated vehicles of all kinds eastward. As I later learned, most of them were stopped at the Soviet frontier, their loot confiscated, while they were sent onward as prisoners. At the bridge where I formally entered Poland there was no sign of authority. The East Germans had no border guards or customs officers yet, nor had the Poles. The Soviet Military Police apparently had other more pressing duties. I saw them several times along the way, but I was in United States uniform, with a small flag on the front of the jeep, and they let me pass, giving a gruff salute. I drove eastward as far as Lyublin, which is a few miles from the Soviet frontier, then back to Warsaw where I visited briefly with U.S. Ambassador Arthur Bliss Lane, and the lone U.S. correspondent, Larry Allen of the Associated Press. Then I drove south to Krakow, on into Czechoslovakia through Ostrava and Prague, and through to Vienna; then back to Germany via the Soviet zone and up to Munich. It was an arduous trip but a rewarding one, for I had traveled through what Hitler had declared to be the "Heartland of the Thousand Year Reich," and seen the universal misery, the pervasive presence of the Russians, and the utter destitution of most of the population.

Back in Berlin I filed my dispatches, and then turned my attention to improving my relations and contacts among the large and growing foreign military-diplomatic community in Berlin, as well as with the Germans, some of whom—artists, actors, journalists, and politicians—were beginning to surface and try to find their way back to some degree of normalcy and security. I spent a number of evenings with Viktor DeKowa, a prominent German actor and populist philosopher and his Japanese wife, Michi, who had somehow managed to keep their house in the British sector. I met many homeless, hungry German refugees who found refuge there. Some of them later became prominent writers, actors, and politicians.

I heard from friends that Kaethe Kollwitz, one of the greatest German artists of her generation, was dying of starvation and old age in a garret in East Berlin. I tried to find her, but was too late — she had already died. I met and talked with one of the world's most distinguished chest surgeons, Professor Dr. Ernst Sauerbruch, who was still operating when possible in a hospital just inside East Berlin near the burnt-out ruins of the Reichstag.

I also met and became friendly with several of the ambassadors who, being accredited to a military government, were usually generals — among them General Palacek of Czechoslovakia, who was recalled and imprisoned after the Communist take-over in his country in 1948. I renewed my acquaintance with a number of U.S. foreign service officers who were working under Ambassador Murphy, and met some new ones, among them a tall young man named Richard Helms, who worked in a special unit based in a house across the street from mine. Helms later became director of the Central Intelligence Agency.

Most interesting perhaps, in view of what later transpired, was a contemporary named Brandt, whom I first met in Stockholm during the war when he was a political refugee from German-occupied Norway, where he had settled after fleeing Nazi rule in his native Germany. He arrived in Berlin about the same time I did, in the uniform of a Norwegian major, an information officer doubling as a correspondent for several Norwegian newspapers. I saw him a number of times in Nuremberg and later in Berlin. He was wrestling with his conscience. He had learned to love Norway. He had a Norwegian wife. He appreciated the opportunities Norway had given him after his arrival in 1933, destitute and rootless from his native Lubeck. But still, he was a

German and, moreover, a German Social Democrat, considerably wiser and more experienced than he had been when he left Germany twelve years earlier. He felt that perhaps he should leave his comfortable officers' billet as a Norwegian, and join the now-hungry and haggard German politicians emerging from prison camps and obscurity to try to organize and lead a new Germany and, hopefully, a new Europe. He argued the proposition back and forth with me and with other friends. In the early spring of 1946 he made his decision, handed in his Norwegian uniform, and went into the embryonic leadership of the SPD in Berlin. A little more than a decade later he was the Lord Mayor of Berlin, and at this writing he is the Chancellor of the Federal Republic of Germany.

3

Germany Divided

Early in 1947 General Clay invited me to go with him on an inspection tour in the southern part of the Unites States zone of Germany. We flew down from Berlin, then drove through the picturesque countryside visiting military units, industrial installations, local American commanders, and German politicians and businessmen. It was fascinating to watch the way Clay astonished local leaders by knowing more about many of their problems than they themselves did. It was also impressive to note how prosperous the German countryside and even the cities had become less than two years after the end of the war. The vineyards and fields were well tended; in the towns the streets were clean, houses were being painted, flower boxes hung outside most windows. The people on the streets were reasonably well clothed and shod, and all seemed busy. As Clay remarked: "It's very difficult to prevent the Germans from working . . ."

I was surprised and unhappy at the run-down condition of several units of the U.S. military, however. A symbolic episode sticks in my mind. On the third day of our trip around the zone, General Clay had indicated a desire to inspect a certain unit of the Seventh Army at reveille. I told him I would like to go along, and he cheerfully agreed. Accordingly, at 5 A.M. I was awakened by an orderly, who sleepily offered me coffee and disappeared. Forty minutes later, Clay and I were sitting in the back of a huge Cadillac, which was chauffeured by a sleepy sergeant from Alabama who knew the roads and took us to the assigned unit. When we arrived, an alert GI, seeing Clay's four stars, awakened the unit commander, a major, who arrived in confusion and made about every error possible in answering Clay's polite but searching questions. Mission accomplished (as Clay put it, "to keep the men on their toes"), we headed back to headquarters where we were due for breakfast at 8 A.M. Ten minutes after setting out, the Cadillac began to cough, and then stopped dead. The sergeant blushed, grinned, and then growled: "I knew it would happen. We've needed a new distributor for the last six months, but we don't have any spare parts. There's a motor pool about half a mile down there—if we could just make it."

Grinning so broadly that I afterward half suspected that he had engineered the entire episode to impress on me, as *Time-Life* bureau chief for Central Europe, the fact that the United States troops were being starved for even minor spare parts by an economy-minded Congress, Clay motioned me out of the vehicle, and together we pushed, helped toward the end by some GIs who happened along, to the motor pool.

The episode was symbolic, because the United States armed forces at the time were indeed being starved. Equipment was run down, spare parts scarce, allocations for imports cut to the bone; in effect, the United States military forces in West Germany were reduced to a shadow. As was later remarked, if the Russians had decided to attack Western Europe in late 1947 or early 1948, there would have been nothing to stop them from the Elbe to the Seine.

The Russians were, however, in no position to attack at the time, and by the end of the following year, thanks to Czechoslovakia, the Berlin airlift, and other things, Allied military posture in Western Germany had improved.

Clay was pleased to see that progress was being made in the American zone of Germany, and that cooperation among the three Western zones was beginning. Local elections were being carried out, local German political bodies were beginning to take over the functions of government. Industry and commerce were largely in local German hands and were beginning to function normally, although there were still shortages of all kinds of consumer goods and raw materials, in part at least because businessmen withheld such items from the market in the anticipation of a currency reform. Germans knew, from the bitter experiences of the early 1920s, that in a highly inflationary situation one is better off holding goods than money.

In the Soviet zone, on the other hand, as West Germans heard constantly from the refugees who came in steadily from the East, things were going badly. Continued heavy reparations removals kept the country's 17 million people constantly and desperately short of everything; the highly political administration of the Socialist Unity Party tended to put authority in the hands of loyal Communists whose technical competence was often limited; trade and industry were almost entirely in the inefficient government's hands. Wages and salaries were well below the levels in the West, which created a constant temptation to skilled workers and professionals to go westward, where their skills were needed and more highly rewarded than in the East. This created a manpower drain which complicated the Russians' tasks in administering their zone.

One factor that helped the German Communist authorities was their use of occupation marks to purchase all kinds of commodities in the West — a practice which they justified legally on the Potsdam decision that the Germany economy was to be operated as a unit. But this advantage was probably more than offset by the continued indiscipline of the nearly half million Soviet troops in Germany, who lived largely from the German economy, partly with official procurement procedures, and partly by simple seizures of property of all kinds from Germans.

During late 1947 and early 1948 one phenomenon became a factor in both East and West: the pressure from newly organized German institutions and government bodies on the occupation forces. The direction of these pressures was, however, very different. Walter Ulbricht and his SED shadow government in Pankow (a district in the Soviet sector of Berlin) pressed the Russians to squeeze the Western Allies out of Berlin or at least stop the unrestricted movement of Allied rail, motor, and barge traffic in and out of Berlin, because this incessantly reminded people under Communist government in the Soviet zone that life under Western democracy was both freer and more comfortable. The Germans in the Western zones made different demands. They wanted an end to inflation and a peace treaty so that they could begin to engage in foreign trade, and develop the industry and commerce of West Germany for the benefit of the West Germans.

I remember a spirited argument in Stuttgart with a group of German journalists after one of the *Laenderrat* meetings. "It is clear," one of them argued, "that the Russians have no intention of allowing the Soviet zone to become part of a united and democratically governed Germany. Everything points in the opposite direction. In the Soviet zone one-party government, state-run industry, collectivized agriculture, Communist-controlled press, and the subordination of the entire economy to the satisfaction of the endless demands of the Soviet Union for goods of all kinds . . . Why don't you recognize this division, and organize a West German state?" During the early months of 1948 this issue was under constant discussion among the Western Allies as well as the Russians and other occupation personnel at all levels.

My Soviet friends were often bitter in such discussions. "We Russians bled ourselves white to win the war. We lost 20 million people. Half our country was destroyed by the Fascists. Your American economy was far away, and remained undamaged. On the contrary, many American capitalists made money manufacturing arms and supplies for the war. You got richer while we are hungry. You can afford to pamper your Germans, while we must make ours pay and pay and pay as they should . . . And to make them pay we must impose controls and Socialist institutions which in any case we believe in and practice in our own country. Your liberalism corrupts our system." These points were well taken. I had lived for nearly ten years in the Soviet Union, and knew very well that socialism functions effectively only in isolation from freer societies. This fact was made even more evident by developments in Eastern Europe after it was occupied by Soviet forces in 1944. Some Soviet idealists thought that the Bulgarians, Rumanians, Hungarians, Poles, and Germans, if freed from evil capitalist influences, would elect Communist or pro-Communist governments. But the opposite happened. Early elections in Rumania demonstrated overwhelming strength for Juliu Maniu and his anti-Communist peasant party, and the first post-war election in Hungary gave the Communists only a tiny percent of the vote. Everyone could see during the referendum in Poland in 1947 that without flagrant election rigging, the country would have elected a Centrist Social-Democratic (PSL) or perhaps even a nationalist (NSZ) government — nor was this surprising, since Poland was then and remains today overwhelmingly Catholic, and bitterly anti-Russian for ancient historic reasons.

Even if the Soviet government had been so inclined, it could not have permitted free elections or a free economy in East Germany or in East Europe, without seeing the entire area — 100 million people — become a bastion of anti-Soviet reaction and a threat to Soviet military security. The Soviet government *had* to divide Germany and Europe in defense of their own national interests as they saw them.

There is also every evidence that Soviet government personnel, dedicated as they are to the Marxist-Leninist-Stalinist ideology which has been drummed into them as children in school and, later, in relentless political indoctrination courses at their places of work, believe that communism is the wave of the future, bound to triumph over a moribund and decadent capitalist system.

"We are having trouble now," said a brilliant and convinced Communist Soviet correspondent whom I got to know well, "but in the long run we will win. You have been both lucky and skillful in contriving that the main destruction of this war fell on our shoulders while you profited. You have a vast and rich country, and have taken the technology created by Europeans and put together a highly productive industrial machine. Using the raw materials you squeeze for a pittance from the less-developed countries, you flood your country and the world with your cheap automobiles and ballpoint pens and radio sets. But your system has no real substance. In the long run you will drown in your surpluses and we will win."

The inconsistency of this orthodox Communist position was clear then to most German and indeed most European intellectuals, and has since become clear also to millions of people in the Soviet Union itself, as witnessed by the popularity at this time of the new voices of freedom within the Soviet Union.

But it was not clear in 1948 to some West European and American liberals who believed that the United

States, British, and French military governments were betraying their war-time Russian allies and violating the pledges made at Yalta and Potsdam by not cooperating with the Russians. Some of these people blamed the neo-Nazi Germans for preventing Allied harmony. "In Berlin the Germans have divided the Allies into four sectors," a British liberal told me seriously.

While these arguments were being waged in Berlin and elsewhere, I decided to make another trip around East Germany and Czechoslovakia, where there were rumors of trouble. My family (which had now joined me) and I set out with the required travel permits, which were getting more and more difficult to obtain from the Soviet and East German authorities. We drove around for several days — Dresden, Leipzig, Weimar, and into Czechoslovakia, where we were the guests of Ambassador Laurence Steinhardt, whom we had known well in Moscow just before the war. In talks with him, and with Jan Masaryk, then foreign minister, I learned that the situation was indeed serious. The Communists had reached a peak strength of 38 percent of the votes cast in the elections in February, and had begun to lose strength. Many Western-minded Czechs and foreign observers feared that, anxious to score the first "legal" Communist takeover in the world and egged on by Soviet Ambassador Zorin and Czech Communist leader Klement Gottwald, the Communist Party might precipitate a crisis and seize power while it still enjoyed a substantial plurality. And this is indeed what happened in June, soon after we returned to Berlin.

For weeks, German friends had been telling me that a currency crisis was imminent in all of West Germany.

They had been trying to get more exact information from me. I was even more curious on this score than my Russian friends were. "What kind of action would American, British, and French finance authorities take?" I made inquiries among my many friends and Allied functionaries, and drew a blank. In retrospect I am rather pleased about this, since it indicates that the security on this issue was pretty good. At the time I was miffed at not having known in advance of the event which took place on June 20, 1948. In an action undertaken simultaneously by the British, French, and United States military governments, the currency circulating in Germany was declared invalid and a new currency was introduced. To put this complicated procedure in simple terms: every resident could change forty invalid marks for the new D-marks at any bank. All the rest of the money in circulation was simply annulled.

This radical move aroused consternation among some Germans who had made fortunes in speculation and in legitimate business and were left with forty marks like everybody else. But the majority of the population breathed a sigh of relief. "Endlich haben wir eine anständige Währung . . ." ("At last we have a real currency . . ."). And, as many economic experts had predicted, within hours "scarce" commodities began to appear, and within several days the entire West German community experienced a burst of economic activity. Materials suddenly became available. Labor power, which had already been present in some surplus, was quickly absorbed in a variety of productive activities. Farmers sent their products promptly to market rather than holding back some for more remunerative semi-surreptitious sale. More important, perhaps, some 47 million inhabitants of the three Western zones, encouraged by the currency reform to believe that more general political cooperation by the Western Allies in their German policies was imminent, suddenly began to feel optimistic about the future, glad to be alive, and in some cases even pleased to be Germans.

The reaction to the currency reform among the Russians was, predictably, negative, but few expected the burst of vituperative attacks which came from the Russians and the Pankow authorities. The action was in clear violation of the Potsdam agreement, the Soviet authorities trumpeted, and in violation of the spirit of many other agreements, including the Charter of the United Nations, which assumed and specified friendly cooperation between the Soviet Union and the Western Allies. By this action, the Russians asserted, the Western military governments in Germany had deprived themselves of the benefits of such by-products of cooperation with the Soviet Union as the privilege of access to Berlin across the territory of the Soviet zone.

The Pankow government and the Russians were in trouble. They had not anticipated so rapid and radical an action from the West, and had not printed any new currency for the Soviet zone, where the population immediately lost all confidence in the old currency, since it was no longer legal tender in the West. In an embarrassingly slipshod operation, the Soviet zonal authorities called in all currency and affixed a poorly printed tiny validation stamp on each bank note. This, they bravely asserted, gave it the equivalent value of the new West German currency. But it was an empty assertion, and very rapidly the true value of the two currencies became expressed in the black market rate of one West mark for three East marks—an exchange rate which fluctuated very little during the next generation.

But the Soviet authorities and their German subordinates in Pankow had other modes of retaliation as well. As might have been predicted on the basis of the initial Soviet reaction, they moved to squeeze the Western Allies on access to Berlin. First the bridge over the Elbe near Magdeburg was closed for "repairs" and all traffic was re-routed via an axle-breaking and time-consuming detour over a temporary pontoon bridge a few miles downstream. Special tolls were instituted to pay for the upkeep of the 110-mile autobahn stretch from the Berlin checkpoint to Helmstedt, and the Soviet guards began to inspect vehicles for contraband or illegal passengers. Concurrently, a series of obstructions began on the canals, which virtually stopped barge traffic from West Germany to Berlin. Rail transportation was halted for bridge repair and other "technical" reasons.

This harassment culminated on June 24, with the formal imposition of the Berlin blockade. I myself was involved quite by accident. I had traveled the Helmstedt autobahn many times, but this particular trip was an important one personally, as I had been transferred home and was leaving the city with my family. Our heavy baggage and furniture had already been packed and sent by rail, and we were leaving by car—my wife and I, the two children, and a dog. We got through the Berlin checkpoint after an hour's delay, and drove across the zone, through the outskirts of Magdeburg, to Helmstedt. But there the answer was a firm "*Nyet*." We waited for several hours, and then went back to Berlin. The Berlin blockade was on.

It was not so bad for us. Several days later I was able to arrange air transport to Frankfurt. But for Berlin it was serious. General Clay and his British and French colleagues, of course, protested most vigorously to the Russians. But they received no satisfaction. The unilateral Western currency reform had invalidated former procedures, the Russians said. The only thing for the Western Allies to do was to go to the newly constituted East German government and make arrangements, which no doubt would involve the placing of all Western installations and operations in Berlin under the jurisdiction of the East Germans.

This was clearly unacceptable to the Western Allies. We were in Berlin by agreement with the Soviet government as victors in an occupied country. We had not recognized any Communist governmental authority in East Germany, nor, at this writing a generation later, has such recognition been extended. Although the position of the Western governments was somewhat weakened by the absence in the agreements reached by the European Advisory Commission in London during the war, or at Potsdam, of any specific written guarantee of access to Berlin, the position taken by General Clay and his French colleague (the British were somewhat more cautious) was very positive. An Allied column of Western troops, headed by General Clay and his colleagues, or even perhaps by President Truman and Prime Minister Attlee, if they were willing to do it, should move across the zonal frontier at Helmstedt, and proceed to Berlin, stopping only long enough to repair the bridges on the

Elbe, something which could have been done in a couple of hours, our engineering officers told me. Clay was convinced that the Russians would not shoot at such a column. If they mined the autobahn, we could sweep the mines.

This audacious plan was turned down in Washington and the other Western capitals. Instead, it was decided to institute an airlift.

The Berlin airlift was one of the most extraordinary enterprises of its kind ever undertaken. It involved the movement of almost one and a half million tons[1] of assorted freight by air from half a dozen West German airports in 200,000 flights.[2] Most of the planes were American, with symbolic and logistic help from the British and French over a period of eleven months. There were crashes, of course, and sixty-one Allied airmen died, but the operation succeeded. Berlin was supplied with all the essentials. Even heavy items of equipment, such as bulldozers to lengthen the Berlin runways, were cut into pieces, flown in, and reassembled. During the foggy weather in November and December the planes kept flying, and West Berlin suffered no important shortages of food or fuel, or even industrial raw materials. Perhaps more important, the operation inspired the imagination of people all over the world, and astonished and impressed the Russians, who had not thought this kind of massive air operation possible.

During the airlift, Russians could still come to West Berlin, though they were not popular either among the Allies or the West Berliners. Several Soviet friends of mine came for lunch one day in November, and at their request after lunch we went down to Tempelhof, in the

American sector, one of the three airports in West Berlin used during the airlift, and stood for a while near the end of the main runway. Though the weather was not good, we watched for an hour as planes landed, one after another. My Soviet friend Alexei took out his watch. Sixty seconds — fifty-five seconds — seventy seconds — fifty seconds. In they came, moved to the ramp where they were unloaded by enthusiastic German teams, and were back on their way to Frankfurt in a turn-around time of as little as twenty minutes, depending on the type of cargo. Near us on a little hill of rubble right under the flight path of the incoming planes we noticed a group of German children of various ages. They would wave at the approaching planes and then, as the planes passed only a few feet over their heads, they would dive to the ground as though picking something up, then cheer. We went to investigate. They were picking up chocolate bars, dropped by the incoming pilots. Alexei was torn between admiration and rage. "Imperialist devils," he growled. "Devil-Heroes."

We went back to the house for a drink before Alexei returned home to the East. He was shaken. "You bastards. You're going to make it," he said.

And make it we did. The Russians could have shattered the airlift with an attack on our aircraft. But the Western powers had flown fighter cover on some missions just to show that if attacked we would fight, and it would mean war. At the time the United States had a near-monopoly on the atomic bomb, and Soviet leadership was apparently unwilling to risk a confrontation.

In late winter, the Soviet government, realizing that the airlift was going to be able to supply West Berlin almost indefinitely, invited talks and made a settlement under the terms of which Western access to West Berlin of both civilian and military shipments and personnel, over rail, canal, and autobahn were orally reasserted. The West had spent $170 million on the airlift, and emerged with the *status quo*. Some observers thought we should have insisted on a better deal — on a corridor, or at least specific written guarantees of access. More cautious military and government leaders in Washington and London and Paris were glad to settle for a return to the previous status.

But Germany had been divided, and much to the disadvantage of the newly formed German Democratic Republic, or DDR, the initials of its German name. It had suffered in the first place from the halting of food and other exports from the Soviet zone to West Berlin, and through West Berlin to Western Germany, exports which had previously constituted a substantial source of foreign exchange used by the DDR to pay for needed imports. It continued to be hurt by its inability to use its currency for procurements in the West. Finally, the leaders were deeply disappointed that the Soviet government had not been willing to undertake more risks in backing up the DDR's insistence on sovereignty over West Berlin. All these factors were well known in East Berlin and in East Germany, and they tended to encourage East Germans who had been wavering to go west and seek new careers and lives in an increasingly booming West Germany.

Before getting into a discussion of the gradual evolution of the DDR and the tensions between the two Germanies that exist today, I want to deal with a problem which cuts right across the East-West division lines, and also across the chronology of post-war German developments. This is the problem of the German Jews. Here, as in so many other issues, the policies of the two Germanies grew apart, and today stand almost diametrically opposed to each other.

One of the most damaging of the self-inflicted injuries which resulted from Hitler's anti-Semitic policies was felt by Germany only in the heat of the battles of World War II and afterward. This was the "brain drain" caused by the extermination and emigration of most of Germany's Jewish population, many of whom had been leaders in the country's scientific, artistic, and cultural life up to and during the Weimar Republic.

Quite aside from the physical destruction of millions of Jews in Germany, Austria, and Poland who had not been able to emigrate, or who had refused to believe that Hitler was aiming at total destruction of the Jewish people and did not even try to leave until it was too late, there were hundreds of thousands who, as early as 1933, took a perceptive look at the future, and gathered up their families and whatever possessions they could move, to seek relative safety and security in Holland, Scandinavia, the Soviet Union, France, Latin America, Palestine, and the United States. In the field of science, particularly, losses were serious. Both the United States and the Soviet Union welcomed these talented refugees with open arms, offered them asylum, put laboratories at their disposal, and offered the material security to make possible their optimal output. The gains for the West can be symbolized by the work of Albert Einstein, who had already won the Nobel Prize in 1921, and became a United States citizen in 1940. Some top Jewish scientists preferred to go to London, as did Sigmund Freud. Of those who went to the Soviet Union, many later fell afoul of the witch-hunting of Stalin's secret police, who ruthlessly persecuted tens of thousands of top-level intellectuals because of their real or imagined hostility to Stalinism.

Germany's cultural life, too, suffered great losses. Jewish creative artists and writers, and often their non-Jewish colleagues, felt oppressed and mentally shackled by the anti-intellectualism imposed by the Nazi regime, and emigrated to other countries where they could breathe and work more freely. The magnificent artists and architects of the Bauhaus were dispersed. Walter Gropius, Mies van der Rohe, and many others, for example, came to the United States. The painter Oskar Kokoschka emigrated to England. Stephan Zweig also went to Britain, and then to Brazil. Arnold Zweig went to Palestine, but later returned to East Berlin where he joined a vigorous group of former emigrants including Hans Eisler, Bertolt Brecht, Anna Seghers, and many others. Communist leaders hoped that from this group in East Berlin would come a great cultural revival, but unfortunately Brecht produced no major works after 1945, and the others found that the Communist government of the DDR and the Soviet occupation authorities imposed restrictions almost as stifling as those of the Nazi regime before them.

Either through emigration, or death in gas chambers or in dark cellars, or starvation, Germany's Jewish population almost completely disappeared. Nazi persecution of Jews was more severe in Poland than in other occupied countries in Eastern Europe. In 1931 the Jewish population of Germany was more than 560,000; by 1933 it had already dropped to around 500,000, and by 1955 in West Germany it was only 27,000, of which 18,000 were German Jews, the rest displaced persons from farther east. By 1965 the Jewish population of the Federal Republic of Germany was 25,000 or about .04 percent of the total population.[3] Estimates of the total number of Jews who perished in Nazi concentration camps during the war vary between 3 and 6 million, most of whom were Polish Jews.

For the friends and relatives of the millions of Jews who perished the contrite attitude of the West German government since the war is meaningless or even insulting. But reparations have been paid by the Bonn government to those Jews who were lucky enough to escape from Germany, or who were liberated by the Allied armies. An agreement signed in Luxembourg on September 10, 1952, between the governments of Israel and West Germany provided that the latter pay 3 billion German marks (about $750 million at the time) to the State of Israel over a period of twelve years and another 450 million marks (about $112 million) to the Conference on Jewish Material Claims Against Germany. In addition to this, several large German firms which had employed "slave labor" from the concentration camps during the war made individual settlements with their former employees. The three companies that together formed I.G. Farben Industries agreed to pay each surviving Jewish employee of its plants 5,000 marks ($1,200). A similar settlement was sought from Krupp, but because of poor administration and poor records some of them received $750, some $500, and some nothing at all.[4]

I know several German Jews who were children during the war and had been hidden by sympathetic non-Jewish friends, or camouflaged as "Aryans." Two of them received "compensation" from the government for the loss of educational opportunities they had suffered. In one case the sum was 6,000 marks, enough to buy a Volkswagen. In the other case it was slightly more. Two very prominent American journalists — Max Frankel and Henry Kamm, both of the *New York Times* — were Jewish children in East Germany during the war, were hidden, and emigrated to the United States only in the late 1940s. I do not know whether they ever applied for or received any compensation.

The West German government has continued until the present to prosecute Nazi war criminals when it discovers them, and to cooperate with the attempts of the government of Israel to find and punish the persecutors of the Jews in Europe under the Nazis. The most spectacular example of this activity was the prosecution and execution of Adolf Eichmann in Israel in 1962. The Federal Republic has carried out an active trade and tourist exchange with Israel, and has vigorously prosecuted the perpetrators of occasional anti-Semitic incidents in West Germany, such as the desecration of a Cologne synagogue on Christmas Eve, 1967, and occasional anti-Semitic slogans used in local elections by the NPD (the right extremist party of West Germany).

At the same time, because of quirks in international law respecting double jeopardy and the statutes of limitations on certain categories of crimes, several former Nazi officials who were convicted *in absentia* in courts in other countries such as France, but were not "major war criminals," surfaced in Germany where they received pensions for their military service, and retired in relative tranquillity. This has, of course, caused some criticism on the part of Jewish organizations in Germany and elsewhere.

The attitude of the East Germans was essentially different from the earliest days after the war. The East German authorities offered no individual or collective reparations or compensation to Jews in East Germany or to the State of Israel. They claimed that the Communists had always opposed the Nazi *Endlösung*, or liquidation of the Jews, and had worked to frustrate it in the Underground. They further asserted that there were no Nazis in East Germany, since all had fled westward, where they were working actively although sometimes surreptitiously to carry out Nazi anti-Semitic policies, and that therefore it was only right and proper that the West German government compensate individual Jews and the Israeli state, but entirely inappropriate for anyone to suggest that the East German government do the same. Underneath this public position, the East German government has followed closely the attitudes and actions of the Soviet government in breaking diplomatic relations with Israel on the outbreak of the Six-Day War in 1967, and in aiding and supporting the Arab states in carrying out their anti-Israeli actions both diplomatically (although, since it is not a member of the United Nations, the East German government cannot in this respect be very useful), and in the extension of economic and military aid, in which respect the DDR has contributed more per capita than most of its East European neighbors. Although no official figures are available, it is estimated that the current number of Jews in the DDR is less than ten thousand.

I have often wondered why some twenty-five thousand Jews still live in West Germany, although all are free to emigrate if they choose. I asked several Jewish friends, and the answer I received was essentially this: "I am a German Jew. I do not want to go to Israel. I was never a Zionist. Maybe there are enough Jews now in America. But in any case I feel more at home in Germany than anywhere else, in spite of everything . . ."

One of the most touching and powerful books to come from Germany since the war was the *Diary of Anne Frank*. In play form, it was produced in many theaters in Germany about 1950. It is based on a real diary, written by a young Jewish girl during the war. The principal characters in the play are all Jews, and all the action takes place over a three-year period in an attic in Amsterdam, where a sympathetic Dutch family had hidden them from the feared Gestapo. Often hungry, suffering from frustration and claustrophobia, the group of Jews, including Anne Frank, who is eleven when the play begins, display many of the varied traits for which the Jews are known: individualism, ethnocentrism, intellectual curiosity, ambition, sensitivity, and faith. In the last act they are discovered: there is a heavy pounding on the door, the harsh German word *"Aufmachen!"* is heard, and the curtain goes down. In the epilogue in front of the curtain, Anne's father, the only survivor of the little group, reads the last lines of Anne's diary, which she finished just before she died of starvation in a concentration camp during the last days of the war. They were: ". . . but I still believe in the goodness of people."

I saw the play once in Berlin and once in Düsseldorf, and on both occasions the audience of all ages and both sexes left the theater convulsed with sobs, ashamed to look at one another.

I am convinced that the Germans in general and particularly those in the West are deeply ashamed of and contrite about their actions against the Jews under Nazi leadership. I would guess that for at least one more generation this will form a major factor in the formation of German attitudes and policies.

4

The Soviet Zone Bids for Nationhood

The German Democratic Republic (DDR) was officially launched on May 30, 1949, and the constitution was enacted on October 7 of the same year. Wilhelm Pieck, Otto Grotewohl, Walter Ulbricht, and other functionaries were duly elected and appointed according to the by-laws of the newly established republic and set up shop in the East Berlin district of Pankow. Although the leaders were all Germans, and the operation of the fourteen new ministries was nominally under their control, in fact the administration of these ministries, and the governing of the provinces and cities in the DDR was initially almost entirely in the hands of Russian officers of the Soviet Military Administration. This group was based in Karlshorst, a Berlin district lying in the extreme eastern part of the sprawling city, while many important aspects of the administration of the Soviet zone were in the hands of the command of the Soviet garrison, a force of about twenty-five divisions in 1949, headquartered in Potsdam.

The Soviet Military Administration, commanded in the late 1940s by Marshal Vassily Sokolovsky, was directly associated with the British, French, and United States military governments in the Allied Control Council in Berlin, which met regularly under rotating chairmanship. On the Berlin level the comparable quadripartite body was the Kommandatura. The Soviet troop commanders in Potsdam were associated with their Western opposite numbers, though no regular meetings on this level occurred. There was, however, by mutual agreement, a system of missions from each occupying power accredited to each of the others. For example, there was constantly resident in Potsdam a United States military mission, usually commanded by a colonel, and consisting of a dozen or so officers competent in artillery, communications, transportation, and other aspects of military activity. These men had their own vehicles, operated in uniform at all times, and were authorized to travel at will all over the Soviet zone, which they did except for a few occasions when they were molested or interfered with by Soviet Security authorities, actions that were vigorously protested by the United States command at the highest level.

Similarly, the Soviet Union had a mission resident in Heidelberg, with similar travel rights, which they also used constantly. This arrangement really worked to the advantage of the Western powers because, after the airlift, access to the Soviet zone—the DDR—became increasingly difficult for all categories of Western personnel, and information about developments there was hard to get. The Western zones were relatively wide open, foreigners of all kinds traveled freely, the German and foreign press, including pro-Communist publications, were free to ferret out stories and publish them, although they were often embarrassing to the Western authorities.

The Soviet government even maintained a large, officially accredited repatriation commission with offices in Frankfurt and Munich and elsewhere. Its job was to encourage the many thousands of assorted Soviet defectees, non-returnees, deserters, and former forced laborers who had found their way to Germany or been brought there from the Soviet Union during the war, to return home — which many were reluctant to do — to the Soviet Union, and then to arrange for their transportation. Since it was well known that those who returned were sent directly to distant prison labor camps, often without being allowed to communicate with their relatives, few of these men and women returned after about 1947.

But the Soviet missions were active long afterward, gathering information about events in the Western zones, and using local German Communists and other recruits to penetrate Allied and West German organizations of all kinds. The Soviet military missions accredited in the Western zones did not add much to what the Soviet government learned from other sources, whereas the Western missions in the East were an invaluable source of information which, unhappily, the Western military rarely if ever shared with the press for fear of "blowing" the operation.

The United States and other Western governments had no official communications with the new DDR government in Pankow. Indeed, until the present time Washington does not regard the DDR as a state. Its citizens—such as sports teams and journalists—are occasionally admitted to the United States, and U.S. businessmen, journalists, and ordinary citizens visiting relatives may use their United States passports to travel to the DDR if they are granted visas. But it has been the position of the United States, and also the British and French governments, that the DDR elections have been consistently spurious, and the government is not representative of the 17 million residents of the area. And indeed, as we shall see, many incidents suggest that if the Soviet military garrison had been withdrawn from East Germany at any time, the Pankow authorities would have been overthrown almost immediately by a restive people.

This situation was embarrassing and distasteful for the Soviet government, which made repeated efforts to "legitimize" the Pankow government. In addition to the predominant SED, three other political parties were permitted to function in East Germany, and to run candidates for office in periodic elections. One or two representatives of these parties usually were to be found in the Pankow cabinet.[1] A small number of "private" companies were permitted to function in East Germany, particularly in retail trade and the service industries.[2] Heavily subsidized theatrical groups in East Berlin and elsewhere in the DDR tried to, and indeed did compete with West Germany in the quality of their productions, which they were sometimes allowed to perform in the West.

Beginning about 1950, the DDR began to take an active part in international trade, exporting its goods to Asia and Africa where they benefited from the prestige of being "Made in Germany." They also undertook increasingly ambitious economic aid activities in the Arab states, and in such less-developed Asian countries as the Mongolian Peoples' Republic, where I saw a sizeable East German construction team at work building a machine shop.

But these efforts met with little success internationally, as very few nations of the non-Communist world recognized the DDR. Even more serious and embarrassing to Walter Ulbricht and his sponsors was the fact that they were not successful with the East German people. The relentless pressure of Soviet reparations collections, and after about 1950 the Soviet demand for high-quality East German optical equipment, chemical industry components and products, automobiles, radio sets, typewriters, and other such items at low prices, concurrent with the exports of Soviet raw materials at prices above what the DDR could have paid on the world market — all these factors kept the DDR living standards well below those of the West Germans. This was well known throughout the area, for Berlin was right in the middle of the DDR. All an East German had to do was to go to East Berlin and take the subway across to the Western sectors to see the relative affluence there, in spite of the blockade and periodic harassment of transport and communications.

And if that had not been enough, the United States authorities in the American sector of Berlin had organized a powerful radio station — RIAS — which bombarded the entire DDR with long-wave, all-but-unjammable radio signals around the clock. The result of all this was that large numbers of skilled and professional East Germans continued to emigrate westward, and thousands of young East Germans made use of the educational opportunities in the DDR, which were free and of reasonably good quality, with the intention of going west after graduation.

This situation became more serious and awkward for the DDR after the end of the blockade in 1949, when the Western Allies and West German authorities extended substantial subsidies to West Berlin to help the economy and its roughly two million citizens overcome the problems created by the blockade. West German companies got tax advantages to set up businesses in West Berlin and transportation costs were subsidized for both passengers and freight. West Berlin, which had still had some problems of unemployment before the airlift, began to boom, and East Berlin and East German workers and others became more unhappy with their lot.

Though by the early 1950s the East Germans had set up a reasonably competent criminal and political police, and the SED was directly represented in every industrial and commercial organization in the country, subversive groups began to appear. They were, no doubt, in some cases advised and guided by the East Department of the SPD, and perhaps by Allied functionaries who were more than usually anti-Communist, and anxious to make trouble for the Russians and their friends. The demands of these groups were simple: higher wages and a free election. The DDR authorities found it impossible to deal with these demands effectively: higher wages would have meant reducing shipments of all kinds to the Soviet

Union—something the Russians would not tolerate—while most observers believed that a free election would have produced an anti-Communist and anti-Russian government.

So the DDR authorities dealt with the rising discontent the way police states usually handle such matters. The more articulate leaders were identified, arrested, and sent to prison, or to Siberian exile; informers were given secret bonuses and promises of rapid advancement in payment for their cooperation with the secret police; everyone was endlessly harangued with promises of the ultimate benefits of communism, the immense debt owed by all Germans to the Soviet Union for their liberation, and the iniquities of the revanchists* and neo-Fascists who were climbing to power in West Germany. But the discontent increased, and led to the explosion on June 16 and 17, 1953, in East Berlin.

For months, East German workers had been chafing under the demands made on them to work harder and harder in order to fulfill their norms—their planned minimum output or performance. As more and more workers and farmers fled to the West, it became increasingly difficult to fulfill these norms, and the officials, to offset the man hours and production time lost, set the norms for 1953 even higher, at 10 percent above those of the preceding year. Workers in East Berlin decided to go on strike. Their demand was simple enough: that the work norms be reduced again to a level which, although high, could be fulfilled. On the morning of June 16, they laid down their tools and began parading through the central

---

*Revanchists: people seeking revenge; in this case West Germans willing to start a new war to win back territories lost to the Communists.

part of the city. Within hours, a spontaneous demonstration began: the workers were joined by thousands who for years had been secretly hoping that they would be able to decide their political future for themselves.

By noontime, thousands of people had gathered in front of the Ministry House in the Leipzigerstrasse. The soothing words of Minister Selbmann regarding the work norms now were not enough; the crowd demanded that the present government retire, that Ulbricht disappear, and that the future of Germany be decided by the Germans — that is, the Russian "power behind the throne" be removed. Ulbricht and Grotewohl promised again that the norms would be reduced, but it was too late. The workers declared a general strike for the next day.

By the morning of the 17th, the population was up in arms. "Up in arms" is not quite correct; they had no arms to speak of, only stones and pitchforks. The People's Police (called Vopos) were unable to deal with the crowds demanding "freedom" and "free elections"; Ulbricht, probably fearing for his life, vanished from Berlin.

If the Soviet Army had not been at hand, it is unlikely that the Pankow government could have survived. But by noon of June 17, without invitation from the frightened leaders of the shadow government, Soviet troops moved in. Two motorized divisions, replete with tanks, began rolling through the streets of Berlin. A few of the workers chose to die a martyr's death, but in short order everyone saw that stones against tanks was not a fair fight, and the "revolution" was ended by evening.

The Berlin uprising had been suppressed with little

bloodshed, thanks to the restraint of the Soviet troop commanders and the fact that the East Berlin workers had no arms. And there the matter might have ended, an unpleasant but not very serious episode, simply somewhat awkward for the Russians because of the presence in Berlin of Western journalists, which caused some unfavorable publicity. At no point had the Russians been in any military danger. They had absolute control of the territory of the DDR. The East German troops with arms were in isolated units, out of touch with one another, so that even had some unit been inclined to help the insurrectionists, they would have been contained easily by the Soviet troops.

But one important factor was not entirely in Soviet hands, and that was control of information. RIAS in Berlin had a regular and all but universal audience all over the DDR, an audience built up over several years by broadcasting high-quality entertainment and interesting features over its powerful facilities. Under the able guidance of Gordon Ewing, a U.S. information officer who at the time was director of RIAS, that station broadcast a blow-by-blow description of everything that happened in Berlin: how the demonstrations were organized; their slogans; the way in which they coordinated their actions; and finally the way in which Soviet troops and tanks were brought in by the Russians. RIAS was careful not to urge insurrectionary action on its listeners, and certainly not to promise any outside aid from United States or other sources, which in any case could not have been made available without a direct military confrontation with the Soviet Union. It simply reported. And as some observers like myself expected, and as top-level Russians feared, within hours demonstrations began in Halle, Leipzig, Magdeburg, Erfurt, and other cities.

The result was that the DDR underwent a two-day nightmare of insurrectionary activity. Complete figures are unavailable because no Western journalists were able to get to the areas outside of Berlin, and of course nothing was ever printed on the subject in the East German press, but few people were actually killed in the street fighting; in some cases, Soviet troops had refused to move against demonstrators when ordered to do so, and several local SED organizations had proved themselves "unreliable," by cooperating with or actually joining the insurrectionists. Retaliations came later. As far as can be established, approximately 1,100 people were brought to trial; of these about 100 were sentenced to death, and about 100 more to life imprisonment.[3]

And so the Soviet Union survived its first major difficulty in administering the hundred million people, in six allegedly sovereign states of Eastern Europe, which constituted (and at this writing in 1972 still constitute) for the Soviet Union a contiguous empire and a defense perimeter on which all Moscow's foreign policies for the past generation have been based. It survived the test without any significant military losses. Thanks to good information control inside the Soviet Union, there were no unpleasant internal political complications. The Western world was momentarily struck, and many nations noted that they had been wise in not recognizing the DDR, which had now demonstrated itself to be a mere puppet of the Soviet Union. But the memory of the Western world is short, and, bombarded as it is with daily sensations from all over the planet, it was probably little affected by the East German insurrection of 1953.

But the Berlin confrontation had gotten on my nerves and I was glad to return to the United States. I continued to travel widely for *Time*, not only around Europe, but to many other major problem areas in the world.

And so it was that I found myself, late in 1953, in Moscow, in deep conversation with two Soviet officials whom I had first met in Berlin. Though Stalin's death had given us much to discuss of immediate significance and fascination, we found ourselves commenting on the German events earlier in the year. One of my friends, then a lieutenant colonel, ruminated: "We learned a lot from those German events. We learned that governments friendly to us outside our own borders depend in the last analysis on our military power. Let the ideologists say what they want, but particularly in Europe most people don't want a Communist government. Maybe it is a measure of the stupidity of most people. And, of course, people can be persuaded, or bribed or bought. But people don't stay bought. In the last analysis we must have troops on the ground. Not too many, and not conspicuous. But just enough . . . "

I could comment, as I did then, by saying that communism was not popular because it is not a very efficient system and deprives most people living under it of something they prize, namely their personal freedom to speak, to write, to travel as they wish. My Soviet friend shrugged and said, "So what? This is our system. We intend to make it work as best we can, and to ensure our own security. We had no real alternative in Eastern Europe but to put Communists in control. If it had been possible, we might have been better off to do there what we did in Finland, which has worked pretty well. However, the Finns are dumb but honest. The others in Eastern Europe are too smart for their own good, and most of them are dishonest or at least unreliable. And anyhow, the Finns had a 'state in being' in 1945. None of the others had . . . "

I remembered these remarks over the next few years, as Soviet control in Eastern Europe continued to be based more and more on military power on the spot.

During the next seven years I visited East Germany usually twice a year, frequently for the Leipzig Fair, or for a transit trip through by car or train, from Czechoslovakia to Scandinavia or from the Soviet Union to Western Europe. Transit visas were and are still not difficult to obtain, and the roads and other transportation facilities in the DDR are well above the average for the Communist world. During these seven years, after a short clean-up period following the insurrection, the economy continued to grow in size and in productivity. The Soviet garrison was gradually dispersed and hidden away in well-constructed, strategically situated permanent bases. Officers were permitted now and then to visit cities in civilian clothes, but the troops were kept on base except for occasional bus excursions under supervision. In this way defections were kept down, and so were awkwardnesses such as marriages between Soviet soldiers and German girls.

The DDR developed a booming trade with West Germany, which the Bonn government called "interzonal trade," consistent with its position that the DDR was not a state, but simply a slightly Germanized administration for the Soviet zone. They carried out the trade in order to maintain some contact with, and perhaps to be of some help to the millions of East Germans, who were the brothers and sisters and fathers and sons of as many million West Germans. The East Germans found the trade most useful as a source of foreign exchange with which to purchase rare materials and spare parts for Western equipment still operating in many of the DDR's industries, and other things which they could not buy with the rubles they earned from their large and ever-mounting exports to the USSR.

The DDR put together a substantial army, complete with natty uniforms, goose-step marching routines, and good modern mechanized equipment. They organized an international airline named Interflug, and East German vessels began to sail the high seas.

But the domestic situation remained poor. East German workers and intellectuals wanted to get out, and they left in a constantly growing stream. In 1955, for example, there were 382,000 migrants from East Germany, including East Berlin, to the Federal Republic; by 1957 it had risen to 385,000; in 1959 there was a slight decrease with only 174,000, but it swung upward again to 225,000 in 1960.[4]

In spite of periodic squeezes applied by the DDR authorities or by the Russians on access to Berlin, the city remained an open highway for the refugees. Nikita Khrushchev swore that he would get rid of this "bone in my throat," and the issue almost led to war in the 1961 Vienna confrontation between President Kennedy and Khrushchev. But Kennedy stood his ground, then made political capital on his action in his famous Berlin speech when he told a huge crowd outside the Schöneberg City Hall: "Ich bin ein Berliner. . . ."

Kennedy had more than his courage to stand on, however. During this period the Western garrisons in Berlin were small, but they were well selected and well trained, and could have protected West Berlin from anything short of an all-out Soviet assault. And that, of course, would have meant war.

In 1960 I was in East Berlin, and had a long talk with one of the few East German functionaries with whom I established and maintained any but the most casual contacts. I found him furious, not so much at us "imperialists" or at the "war-mongers" in Bonn, but at the Russians.

"I have been in the Soviet Union since I last saw you," he said. "I know the kind of security they maintain around their country. Try and sneak an unauthorized man or woman into or out of the Soviet Union! It would be impossible. The Russians know you can't operate an efficient state without an efficient frontier. Well, damn it, let them give us a frontier. With Berlin the way it is, with the West German monopolies practically recruiting skilled labor and technicians from our factories and technical schools, Western agents wandering in and out of our country at will . . ."

We discussed the possibility of a wall across the city, but he was unenthusiastic. "It would be messy. All those canals and cellars and sewers. And our young people are as foolish and romantic as any others. They would try to climb over, and we'd have to shoot them . . . No. That is not the solution. We must at long last realize the fact that Berlin is in the territory of the DDR!" he said, repeating the formula endlessly repeated by Soviet representatives at all kinds of meetings for the previous decade. "Perhaps West Berlin could have some sort of autonomous status; perhaps it could even use D-marks instead of our money. But this uncontrolled wandering in and out. It is impossible, and the Russians must do something about it."

But it was easier said than done. As had been made amply clear on several earlier occasions, the Russians were not prepared to start World War III over Berlin. On the Western side, the governments in Washington and London and Paris had allowed the Berlin position to become seriously eroded, by allowing DDR authorities to take over the policing of the Helmstedt autobahn, with the right to examine all Allied vehicles, even though *all* Berlin was supposed to be under quadripartite administration. On the air corridors Soviet fighters periodically buzzed Allied planes to make them stay under 10,000 feet, and they complied. Under Soviet protest, we had persuaded the West Germans to exempt West Berliners from military service and withhold the right to vote in Federal elections, although East Berliners were fully franchised citizens of the DDR. In many other ways, the Western Allies had given way to Soviet demands, but on the fundamental issue of free access, we had stood firm.

And so, on August 13, 1961, the Russians took the step that divided Berlin and sealed the division of Germany for many years to come. They ordered the construction of the Berlin Wall. Typically, they acted cautiously, not knowing what the reaction of the West would be. The first stones were placed by an East German task force which could have been easily and quietly withdrawn. Berlin was a quadripartite city, all of whose citizens were supposed to be free to travel at will anywhere in the city. Thousands of East Berliners held jobs in the West, and a few vice-versa. Soviet military and civilian officials daily went across the sector boundary to their jobs in the Four-Power air traffic and safety control center in Tempelhof, and to the Allied Control Authority building on Potsdamerstrasse in the American sector. Many West Berliners and Western Allied personnel frequented the opera and the theaters in the East. It seems likely that if one or all of the Western commandants had reacted vigorously, for example, by sending a detail of West Berlin policemen to remove each stone as the East Berlin detail put it up, or by driving a truck or bulldozer through it when this was still possible, the Communists would have desisted.

But the Western Allies were indecisive, and after unsuccessful attempts to get high-level reaction from the Western capitals, local officials decided to "wait and see." It took only ten days to build the wall and to reinforce it in such a way that it could have been dismantled only by explosives.

The wall, a solid mass of bricks and concrete more than six feet high, topped with barbed wire, runs straight through the city for forty-five kilometers. Houses that lay in its path were evacuated, the windows blocked up, and the walls reinforced to form a part of the Berlin Wall. At first there were eighty-one crossing points, which were then reduced to thirteen, and now there are only seven, all heavily guarded.

At the same time that the wall was built, the Russians

and the East German authorities went to work to improve the barrier which had already been constructed along the five hundred miles or so which form the frontier between the Soviet zone and the American and British zones. An area about one hundred yards wide was ploughed, and in some places mined; along the center three barbed wire fences were installed, about ten feet high. The center fence was electrified. Farmers on the Soviet side of the boundary were subjected to strict security checks, and the border zone was closed to all others. Germany had been physically divided, from the North Sea to the Czech frontier.

Then the shooting started. The first incident was on August 17 when Peter Fechter, an eighteen-year-old East German, tried to climb over the wall from East Berlin, and was shot by an East German border guard. Vigorous protests were made by many governments, but the DDR authorities shrugged them off. From that time on, they said, people would enter and leave the territory of the DDR only at authorized points, and with appropriate documentation. And the DDR police and transportation authorities proceeded to install the equipment to enforce this position. Most subway crossings from East to West were closed. One was left open for the use of the few citizens of East Berlin who were authorized to work in the Western sectors. For this purpose, the first station on the eastern side of the wall—Friedrichstrasse Station—was completely encased in meshed wire, so that people coming in or out had to pass through a checkpoint where their documents could be examined.

I went through this procedure on several occasions: the traveler presents his documents—in my case my passport—through a tiny window, and then waits for perhaps fifteen minutes, during which the document is presumably scrutinized by East German officials, and the individual checked against their lists. Then the passport is pushed through another window, the wire mesh gate is opened, and the individual is permitted to pass. If he has baggage with him, it is opened and inspected. Going into East Berlin he must make out a currency declaration, stating how much of what kind of money he has, and on leaving he must return the declaration and present his money and receipts for any he might have changed while in the East.

At railroad crossing points a simpler procedure is followed. Trains are sealed at the border of the DDR, and an armed sentry is placed at each end of every car. No one is permitted to leave or enter the car during its presence in the territory of the DDR. The last time I made such a trip I boarded the express train in Prague, and for some eight hours was in East German territory until the train arrived at the Baltic seaport of Rügen where it pulled up beside the Swedish ferry which plies across to Trelleborg. This pier was also enclosed in wire mesh. During the trip the passengers were offered sandwiches and coffee, brought through the car by a waitress accompanied by a DDR border guard. Payment was accepted in foreign currency only.

Berlin's numerous canals were carefully laced with underwater and above-water barbed wire entanglements. East German barges and sea-going vessels were subject to strict security controls. Only the air traffic continued to operate without restrictions, and with heavy West German subsidies. In order to avoid any diplomatic controversy, Lufthansa (the West German airline) did not fly to Berlin; the traffic was handled by BEA, Air France, and PanAm. Traffic was heavy. Today these three airlines operate 103 flights daily from Berlin's three commercial airports to a dozen cities in West Germany. Soviet and East European traffic goes in and out of Schoenefeld, just east of East Berlin in the Soviet zone.

Particularly at the beginning, the wall, and the shooting of people trying to cross it, aroused a great deal of emotion in Germany and elsewhere. Militant anti-Communist organizations in West Berlin began keeping records of the DDR border guards who had shot attempting wall-crossers, in anticipation of being able to try these individuals for murder at some future time. Accusations were not difficult to make, since the border guards were often publicly decorated for their vigilance, and the procedure may have been instrumental in getting a number (about 8 to 10 percent of the total number of defectors each year) of the East German policemen to defect themselves, in fear or shame or both. But the net effect of these activities was not impressive, and in recent years they have been discontinued.

I have seen no reasonably reliable estimates of how much it cost the DDR to build the Berlin Wall and the other obstructions, or what the manning of them involves in annual expenditures for guards and other running costs. But it must be substantial. The cost in human life is more easily measured. During the first year of operations, in Berlin alone the Vopos fired 282 times on those attempting to escape, resulting in 10 deaths and 89 wounded. Others died in unsuccessful attempts to crawl over the wall and over the barbed wire, or by jumping out of windows, hoping that their momentum would carry them to the western side of the wall. On the other hand it is a back-handed tribute to German organizational ability that this security system has been made to work without interfering with East Germany's large foreign trade amounting to some 12 billion East German marks, which is handled by rail, truck, and ship.

And the wall has been effective in virtually stopping emigration from the DDR. Whereas more than 180,000 refugees left that unhappy area in the first seven months of 1961 before the wall was installed, the number fell to 21,500 in 1962, although a few more may have escaped and left no record.

Whereas the wall stopped all DDR travel to the West, and West Berliners were entirely prohibited from visiting East Berlin and the DDR, except for some special holiday deals worked out in subsequent years, other West Germans were permitted, with appropriate visas, to travel to the East to visit relatives. And Western Allied personnel in Berlin visit the East regularly, often in excursion buses. Citizens of countries other than Germany may and often do travel to the DDR, once they have their passports duly visaed by the DDR consular authorities. All vehicular traffic from East to West Berlin normally passes through "Check Point Charlie" on Friedrichstrasse, where a formidable array of reinforced concrete barriers makes any crash entrance into or exit from the DDR, with anything short of a heavy tank or bulldozer, utterly impossible.

The wall rapidly became a tourist attraction on the Western side. Many "neutrals"—Arabs, Africans, and

Asians — visiting Germany go to look at it, probably with mixed feelings. Many democratically minded men and women no doubt find it repulsive — a symbol of coercive imprisonment of millions of people. Others probably regard the wall as I do — a cruel but realistic measure undertaken reluctantly by the Russians and the DDR government. As my East German friend remarked, "Communism functions effectively only behind walls." The Soviet Union is fortunate in being geographically situated in such a way that the walls are not obvious. The DDR was more exposed, through no fault of its own. And from the standpoint of its leaders, the wall accomplished very effectively the purpose for which it was built, as we shall see in Chapter VII.

The Federal Republic of Germany

The currency reform in the three Western zones and in West Berlin, as we noted earlier, triggered not only a burst of economic activity, but also a wave of pressure from West Germans for the unilateral unification of the three Western zones into a German state. This would have given the 47 million West Germans the framework within which to work for their own long-range interests in the community of the Atlantic nations.

The British, French, and United States governments agreed that since Soviet policy made a united Germany impossible in the foreseeable future, and in any case the French and the Russians as well as the Dutch and the Czechs were almost certain to oppose the formation of a new Greater Germany, the founding of a West German state might be the optimal way to allow the Germans to become strong enough to be self-sufficient and able to play their part in a free and prosperous Western Europe, but not so strong as to be able to become again a threat to their neighbors.

In line with these decisions, the Western Allied military governments allowed locally elected German bodies in their three zones to gradually take over the functions of government in cooperation with one another, and in June 1948 a constituent assembly was elected for all three zones. This body went to work, with juridical and political advice and guidance from the occupation authorities, and produced a constitution which borrowed much from the Weimar constitution, leaving a substantial area of authority to the states, but provided for a Federal government responsible to an elected Bundestag, or Federal Parliament, headed by a chancellor selected by the party or coalition of parties commanding a majority in the Bundestag. The constitution was approved by the constituent assembly and formally by the Western Allies on May 23, 1949 and on that day the Federal Republic of Germany was declared to have been created.

The constitution contained one provision that many later thought to have been unwise, namely the assertion that the Federal Republic embodied *all* Germany, including the Soviet occupation zone, whose residents, because of continued Soviet occupation, were temporarily unable to assume the responsibilities or enjoy the benefits of citizenship in the Federal Republic. This provision reflected the general desire of Germans — East and West — for reunification, a desire kept at a high pitch in West Germany by the actions of the powerful associations of refugees from the East. Gradually it became clear to most West German politicians that reunification under conditions the Russians might possibly accept would burden the entire country with heavy reparations payments to the Soviet Union, and flood it with Communist subversives; it would also reverse in the new unified Germany the present slight majority of Catholics over Protestants, and Christian Democrats over Social Democrats. But in 1949 and for several years thereafter *Wiedervereinigung* (reunification) was something favored by nearly everyone. And from this general consensus there flowed the Hallstein Doctrine, named after the State Secretary of the Federal Republic from 1951 to 1957, which declared that the Bonn government would not establish or maintain diplomatic relations with any nation that recognized the DDR. Though an exception was made for the Soviet Union, this doctrine limited the flexibility of the Bonn government for years, until Willy Brandt more or less invalidated it in 1970 by engaging in direct talks with top leaders of the DDR.

As soon as the Federal Republic was promulgated, the electoral procedures provided for in its constitution were put in motion, and on September 15, 1949, President Heuss proposed Konrad Adenauer as the first Federal Chancellor.

Dr. Adenauer was at the time seventy-three years old. A staunch Catholic, he was a long-time Christian Democrat, and he had served for years as lord mayor of Cologne as representative of the old pre-war *Zentrumspartei*, many members of which became Christian Democrats after 1945. During the occupation of his native Rhineland after World War I he had toyed with the idea of Rhenish separatism under French tutelage, but nothing ever came of the idea, and it was forgotten by all but several of Adenauer's political enemies. During the Nazi period Adenauer had refused to cooperate in any way with Hitler or his henchmen, and as a result was hounded from office in Cologne, and held in jail for several months. He was too old for military service in World War II. An accident as a young man had left Adenauer's face scarred and frozen into a stony imperturbability which the public was quick to identify with his authoritarian political behavior, his fierce rejection of any concessions to the Russians on the Berlin issue.

I talked with Adenauer on several occasions, once when I accompanied him on his election train during a trip to Germany in 1957, once in Washington, and once in New York. I found him not nearly so authoritarian and didactic as he looked. In response to critics who accused him of hindering German reunification by refusing to cooperate with the Russians, he stated that one could deal successfully with the Russians only from a position of power, and that Germany could be strong only in alliance with the West. This simple and logical position, along with his personal preferences, conditioned Adenauer's consistent support of assorted Western organizations and associations: the office of European Economic Cooperation (OEEC) beginning in June 1947, with the Marshall Plan; the North Atlantic Treaty Organization (NATO), which came into existence in August 1949 in the aftermath of the Berlin blockade and the Communist takeover in Czechoslovakia; the Western European Union later in the same year; and later, during the 1950s, the EEC (European Economic Community, usually referred to as the Common Market).

When Adenauer took office the Federal Republic was not yet a fully sovereign state, and was still heavily dependent on United States aid to help rehabilitate its industries and institutions. Of the $13 billion appropriated by the U.S. Congress for the Marshall Plan, about $1.5 billion[1] went to Germany. This economic effort was enormously successful. Whereas in 1947 the Western European countries' industrial production stood at only 87 percent of the pre-war level, by 1951 it had jumped to 34 percent above the level of 1938.[2] In 1950–51, Western Europe — which was hungry and utterly dependent on UNRRA (United Nations Relief and Rehabilitation Administration) and other U.S. aid in 1945 — was producing food at a rate 11 percent above the pre-war level. Naturally, the rate of growth of all kinds of production in West Germany was even higher. The GNP (gross national product) of West Germany in 1949 stood at 81 billion marks; by 1952 it had risen to 136 billion marks; and in 1957 it had jumped to over 200 billion marks.

German industry went to work with vigor. I made two trips around the Ruhr, and one in southern Germany in 1952, and was astonished at the activity. The huge chemical cartel I. G. Farben had been broken up by the Allied decartelization authorities into three daughter firms: Hoechst, Bayer, and BASF (Badische Aniline und Soda Fabrik), and although its plants had been badly damaged by bombing during the war, I found them busy installing new equipment and beginning to export. The large Daimler-Benz plant in Stuttgart, where the justly famous Mercedes trucks and automobiles are built, had dug itself out of the rubble, and was back in production and expanding. Siemens, AEG (Allgemeine Elektrisitäts Gesellschaft), Telefunken, and other electrical companies were back in business in Munich, Berlin, and elsewhere. Countless smaller companies were hard at work.

The equipment and raw materials needed for this industrial revival in many cases came initially from Marshall Plan aid, but after about 1950 increasingly from German sources. The German banks began to have money again, and to lend it out judiciously for industrial reconstruction and expansion. One of the country's most powerful bankers, the long-time chairman of the Deutsche Bank, Dr. Hermann Abs, commented to me at the time on this subject: "I continue to exercise some judgment in putting German capital to work for industrial expansion and, of course, the competitive pressures have been heavy: everyone wanted money, but the supply was limited. I use fairly consistently a rule of thumb: plants that were bombed out, or whose equipment was removed as reparations get money first; plants still using their old equipment get money last."

This judgment was pragmatic and sound. Within a few years after the war, American and British exporters were complaining that their German competitors underbid them because the Germans' equipment was newer and more efficient, thanks to aid financed by taxes which the American and British companies had paid. There was more than a little justification for these complaints. In retrospect, if the United States had extended aid more sparingly, or if it had been extended not as grants but as long-term credits, even at low interest rates, the United

States balance of payments problems of the early 1970s might have been much less severe. But at the time it was United States policy to get Europe back on its feet, so that it could pay its own way and defend itself against its own domestic dissidents and eventually against a possible Soviet attack; and in carrying out this task an increasing input went into Germany, and a growing responsibility was placed on German shoulders.

This process was directly reflected in the political developments of this period. Britain, France, and the United States officially terminated the state of war with West Germany in 1951; the Soviet Union waited until 1955 to follow suit. In 1955 the Federal Republic became officially a sovereign and independent country, though still bound by prohibitions promulgated at the Nine-Power Conference in London in 1954 against producing submarines, military aircraft, biological and chemical weapons, and nuclear materials.

All of these developments were attacked by the Soviet press and Soviet government as revivals of German militarism, revanchism, and neo-Nazism.

After the Berlin blockade the Western governments proposed to the Russians that new free elections be held in all of Germany as a measure that would reduce the tensions produced by the insurrection in East Germany. At the time United States State Department friends of mine felt that this proposal was unrealistic, amounting only to a snide dig at Russian ribs, and that Moscow would ignore it. But the Russians did respond. In early 1954 Soviet Foreign Minister Molotov rejected the proposal politely and suggested instead the formation of an All-German government to consist of representatives of the two existing German governments — Bonn and Pankow. This suggestion was, of course, unacceptable both to Bonn and to the Western Allies. Why should a group of stooges in Pankow, who did not even command the support of its own 17 million Germans, have a fifty-fifty representation with the government in Bonn, which had been elected by 47 million Germans, none of whom had challenged the fairness of these elections?

I learned later that this Soviet proposal was the result of a policy dispute in Moscow on the German question. I do not know to this day which Soviet leaders favored which position, but I have been told by friends, who were in a position to know, that the "hards" in Moscow, who had favored extreme pressure to force the Western Allies from Berlin in order to secure Soviet control of East Germany, and who had hoped that West European Communists would be able to seize power in France and Germany, now had insisted on a political power play involving the DDR, in a last-ditch attempt to penetrate and destroy or subvert what could be seen as an emerging and potentially powerful anti-Communist West German state. The majority agreed, suspecting that the effort would not succeed, and that the Soviet government was going to have to do what it had several times done in the past — recognize an unpleasant reality and make the best of it.

And this is what occurred. In June 1955, the Soviet government informed the government in Bonn that an official visit to Moscow by Chancellor Adenauer would be welcomed by the Soviet government as conducive to a peaceful settlement of outstanding problems.

Adenauer leaped at this opening. It would, theoretically, have been more desirable if the Russians had sent a high-level official to Bonn. But after all, the Soviet Union had won a war only a decade earlier, and besides, Adenauer had one very important issue on which he would have to appeal to the Russians; namely, the German prisoners of war still believed to be in the Soviet Union in work camps, working to complete the $10 billion reparations payments the Soviet Union had demanded from Germany in goods and services. On the evidence of those German prisoners who were released, careful research had been carried out, on the basis of which the German government estimated that 1,731,668 German prisoners in the Soviet Union were still alive, and were waiting impatiently for repatriation. The Germans are a sensitive people in such matters, and Adenauer was subjected to constant pressures to do something about these prisoners who were still awaited by loved ones in Germany, although in many cases no mail had arrived for many years.

Consequently Adenauer went to Moscow with an adequate staff in September 1955. They were received politely, even impressively—Prime Minister Vyacheslav Molotov and Foreign Minister Andrei Gromyko both were present at the airport to meet the entourage—but with almost no publicity; and after seven days of talks, agreements were reached which provided for the establishment of diplomatic and trade relations between the two countries and for the repatriation of the German prisoners still in the Soviet Union. Nothing was decided on Berlin, to no one's surprise. The Soviet position was and has since remained that West Berlin, as a part of the territory of the DDR, concerns that country, and because of wartime agreements is the legitimate subject of discussions with the Western Allies, but that it is no concern at all of the Federal Republic of Germany. Adenauer returned to his residence on the Rhine feeling that he had opened the way for further negotiations with the Russians without having compromised the interests of the Federal Republic by accepting the Oder-Neisse frontier between Poland and East Germany.

Adenauer remained at his post as Federal Chancellor until 1963, when he somewhat reluctantly resigned at the age of eighty-six. During his term of office Germany had made immense strides. Anglo-German trade doubled between 1953 and 1959. In that year the consumption of the average German worker's family had increased by 70 percent over 1950, and total industrial production had risen to two-and-a-half times the 1936 figure. Also in that year the Federal Republic overtook the United Kingdom to become the second largest exporter in the world, just behind the United States.[3] During this period unemployment was completely eliminated from the German economy, which began to suffer from an acute labor shortage. This was dealt with in the first place by re-employment of pensioners and the employment of housewives, and the beginnings were made for what later became the massive importation of foreign labor.

During Adenauer's chancellorship his country took its place as a respected member of the Western community of nations. German participation in the Common Market was vigorous, and although Adenauer was a good friend of Charles deGaulle, he consistently supported the suggestions to enlarge the Common Market. He would have liked to include the British and perhaps others, and to implement those paragraphs in the Treaty of Rome that provided for the harmonization of procedures and the creation of supranational institutions and, later, government bodies to be jointly administered by the European Community.

During these same years the Western military presence in West Germany was drastically reduced. Foreign troops remained, of course: in the U.S. Seventh Army, with some 140,000 men in uniform, the British Army of the Rhine, and the far smaller French forces. But neither they, nor the remnants of Allied military governments, took any important part in the life or the government of the country, except in Berlin. In Wiesbaden, the headquarters of the U.S. Air Force, in parts of Frankfurt and Heidelberg, and in smaller German towns with large Allied installations, such as Kaiserslautern or Oberammergau, foreign troops were still in evidence in substantial numbers. But more and more off-duty personnel were dressing in civilian clothes, and since the Germans were, by the 1960s, as well dressed, shod, housed, and even well wheeled as the British or even the Americans, the foreigners were almost unnoticed.

German armed forces, on the other hand, began to be noticed. Under direct NATO command, the German army, air force, and navy began to take their places in the defense plans of Western Europe. Between 1955 and 1956 the forces were volunteer, but in 1956 the draft system was established. The armed forces numbered 67,000 in 1956, and ten years later had climbed to about 438,000, broken down into army with 278,000, air force with 97,000, and navy of 35,000, with an additional

36,000 serving in the "territorial defense." In 1960 nine billion D-marks were earmarked for the military in the Federal Republic, and five years later the amount had doubled.

One remarkable characteristic of the new German armed forces was their democratic discipline. Anxious to get away from the traditional image of the stiff-backed and regimented Prussian soldiery, the new German troops were relaxed, a minimum of saluting was required, there was freedom of speech and political discussion, and the public criticism of officers by soldiers was not only permitted but encouraged.

During these same years West Germany produced a bountiful cultural harvest. Theaters and opera houses, as well as witty political cabarets appeared in a score of German cities. In Munich alone four theaters for serious plays were in operation, including the stately Prinzregententheater and the much smaller Cuvillies Theater, a restored classical German small opera house. Bayreuth's Wagnerian opera house became a Mecca for European Wagnerian admirers. The music festivals in Würzburg, Munich, Ansbach, Darmstadt, as well as the opera houses in many smaller cities thrived, while art exhibitions abounded in Kassel, Düsseldorf, Cologne, and Berlin. A generation of post-war German writers appeared and produced some excellent books. Heinrich Böll and Gunther Grass were perhaps the best-known on an international plane, but there were many others such as Uwe Johnson, Carl Zuchmayer, and Martin Walser.

In short, the fourteen years under Konrad Adenauer were good years. When "der Alte" died in April 1967 at the age of ninety, the crowds that filled the immense

THE FEDERAL REPUBLIC OF GERMANY

Cologne Cathedral to hear the organ and choir toll out Bach's *St. John's Passion* shed genuine tears of respect and love for the shrewd and stubborn old man who had played such a vital part in giving some 50 million men and women some reason to be again proud that they were Germans.

Before proceeding to the spectacular story of the phenomenal economic developments in West Germany during the decade of the 1960s, I would like to devote a few paragraphs to an aspect of German reality which, like the German Jews, transgresses lines of both chronology and geography.

During the Middle Ages, German knights had wandered eastward into lands traditionally inhabited by Slavic, Urgo-Finnish, and other Baltic peoples, and had established themselves in what later became East Prussia and the Baltic States. In the seventeenth century, large groups of German artisans and farmers left their country to settle elsewhere. Then, in 1764, Catherine the Great of Russia requested some German settlers to move into the Volga area and introduce more modern methods of agriculture and home industry. Several hundred thousand German settlers arrived (in 1939 the colony numbered 400,000), plotted out their land, built houses, established their own churches, maintained their own language and, indeed, introduced new skills and customs into Russia. At about the same time, but in different ways, an even larger number of Germans, mostly from southern Germany, settled in Transylvania, that oft-disputed Balkan crossroads which lies now largely in Rumania, but which during earlier generations was governed by Hungarians, Turks, Austrians, and Russians.

During later years, further waves of German emigrants went southward and established themselves along the Danube and Sava rivers in Hungary and Yugoslavia, and on the northern slopes of the Riesengebirge (the mountains in what became known as the Sudetenland in post-World War I Czechoslovakia) and along the southern slopes of the Alps around Trento and Bolzano in northern Italy.

In most cases these German colonies prospered, generally enjoying a higher level of education and more discipline and diligence than many of the indigenous residents. Understandably, in the late 1930s the Nazi government tried to make use of these groups — perhaps altogether eight or nine million strong — of what they called *Volksdeutsche*, or ethnic Germans, many of whom carried the citizenship of other countries, and had done so for several generations, but most of whom still spoke German at home and considered themselves Germans. Thousands of these *Volksdeutsche* were carefully cultivated as Nazi agents, and became the spearheads of German invasion in the countries where they lived. Many became active and enthusiastic volunteers in the various German military and para-military organizations. In the course of carrying out these functions, they aroused the hatred of the indigenous peoples in the areas where they lived, so that, after the German collapse in 1945, many were driven summarily from their homes, "back" to Germany, although most of them had never been in Germany, and had neither homes nor jobs to go back to.

This hungry and destitute wave of humanity, which found its way in some fashion to Germany at the war's end, overlapped with another group, the residents of German territories occupied by others during the final phases of the war, such as eastern Prussia, much of Silesia and Pomerania, western Poland around the city of Posnan, and several districts in Holland.

And finally, there were the prisoners of war, who straggled back to Germany as late as 1964 from the Soviet Union, also—in most cases—homeless, destitute, and hungry. A few of those who returned went back to their homes in East Germany, but the overwhelming majority of them ended up in the more promising and secure Western zones.

Thus, the total number of Germans who flooded into the Western zones of occupation and the Federal Republic of Germany numbered perhaps 14 million. Most were exhausted, spiritless, beaten men and women, glad to get a crust of bread and a place to sleep. But some were angry irredentists who proceeded to organize committees and initiate campaigns aimed at their "return" to lands which in the meantime had become incorporated into other countries.

It is a tribute to German organization and efficiency that most of these refugees were given housing and job opportunities by the rest of the West German community, which with little complaint paid a substantial capital levy (by 1963, the total amount of money devoted to solving this problem was nearly 47 billion D-marks) to raise money for this purpose. It is also significant that, within the next twenty years, most of these returnees had found jobs and careers, and had integrated themselves into the West German economy with little thought of ever going back to Transylvania or East Prussia or wherever they had come from.

The second general category of foreigners whose presence in Germany at the end of the war created various problems were the foreign laborers whom the Nazis had imported into the country from German-occupied countries to work in industry and agriculture. These included perhaps a million Soviet citizens, and substantial numbers of Poles, Frenchmen, Italians, Greeks, Yugoslavs, and others. In addition, there were the prisoners of war — Russians, Balts, Frenchmen, Poles, and others — who found themselves on German territory as the Allies moved in. Some of these had been incorporated into the German armed forces during the war, or into foreign legions under German command. The largest of these was the Russian Liberation Army under General Andrei Vlasov, which consisted of some four divisions, and had fought with distinction on the German side. Most of the Frenchmen, Belgians, Dutchmen, and other Western Europeans who fell into this category were repatriated within several months of the end of hostilities and reabsorbed with little difficulty into their former homes and jobs. But the men and women from the Soviet bloc were in most cases unwilling to go back. Indeed, they had good reason to believe that return would mean execution[4] or, at best, long sentences in prison camps. They therefore sought assorted methods of avoiding repatriation. If they found themselves in East Germany, they fled west as soon as they could. As a result, almost no foreigners remained in the Soviet zone and the few who were rounded up were summarily and, if necessary, forcibly repatriated. Many of those in the Western zones destroyed their documents, registered themselves as Greeks or Finns or Eskimos, and tried to get jobs in the German economy, even though this was difficult right after the war. Others got semi-legal jobs as servants with the occupation forces. Still others registered as displaced persons, and requested evacuation and resettlement in the United States, or in Canada or Australia where labor power was needed.

When I began inspecting my beat in Germany in late 1945 many of these displaced persons (DPs), as well as the growing number of East Germans who were fleeing across the borders, were living in camps such as Schleissheim on the southern outskirts of Munich, or Giessen near Frankfurt, or in one of the several camps in and around Nuremberg. They were patiently awaiting resettlement, meanwhile living on meager rations provided by the occupation forces. Eventually most of these people were evacuated and resettled and by now have become diligent and loyal citizens of Manitoba or Texas or Queensland.

But a few thousand, out of idealism or political opportunism or a combination of both, launched into anti-Communist political activities directed at the establishment of free and democratic regimes in the nations of Eastern Europe. Some formed their own organizations, such as the NTS (National Labor Union) or Solidarists, a Russian anti-Communist organization which had cooperated with the Nazis during the war, and ran several newspapers and magazines and a radio operation based in Limburg (later in Frankfurt) with funds which probably came from U.S. Army sources. A number of Ukrainian, Uzbek, Kalmyk, and Baltic nationalist organizations were formed, in some cases supported in part by fellow countrymen now resident in the United States or elsewhere in the West, and also possibly by United States government funds. But most of these politically minded DPs wound up working for, or in connection with, one of the two American-supported committees organized in 1948 and 1949, and based then in Munich.

These two organizations were the American Committee for Liberation, and the Free Europe Committee. As was later revealed, both were financed at least in part by the United States government, the funds being channeled through the Central Intelligence Agency. The principal function of these committees, in addition to trying to find jobs for anti-Communist refugees from Eastern Europe, was the operation of two radio broadcasting facilities — Radio Free Europe and Radio Liberation (which was later renamed Radio Liberty). Although the actual transmitters for most of these operations were later moved to Spain and Portugal, and the central headquarters to New York, the bulk of the editorial work and much of the technical planning was carried out in Munich where over a thousand East Europeans and nearly as many German technicians and other personnel were employed. Radio Liberty (at this writing) broadcasts in twenty languages of the peoples of the USSR, around the clock (forty-eight program hours a day in Russian alone), and Radio Free Europe broadcasts in Bulgarian, Rumanian, Hungarian, Czech, Slovak, and Polish to those countries, 540 hours per week. The transmitters of these operations are very powerful, totaling more than 4 million kilowatts. Most of the actual broadcasting and much of the writing was and is done by Russians and East Europeans, who were encouraged to regard the stations as theirs and to speak to their listeners as fellow countrymen. The total budget of these two operations, when it was disclosed to the U.S. Congress early in 1971 that they were being surreptitiously financed by the CIA, was about $35 million a year, and the total number of employees in both organizations was some three thousand. Both had gone into associated operations—distribution of books and magazines, the operation of research institutions putting out scientific publications, and the operation of extensive news gathering and audience research networks.

Both these organizations, which are presently under close governmental scrutiny as a result of pressure from the U.S. Congress, operate in Germany on licenses from the government of the Federal Republic, which, however, is somewhat nervous that the existence of foreign-financed and directed propaganda and/or political warfare operations on German soil and without German control might constitute a violation of German sovereignty. But at this writing top German statesmen have declared that the operations constitute a necessary and important part of the East-West dialogue, and that if Radio Free Europe and Radio Liberty were not doing this work, then the Germans themselves would do it, since Germany is the logical place from which to carry on such activities.

It is entirely possible that within the next year or two precisely this will take place as a part of the growing independence and affluence of the Federal Republic, and the reluctance of many U.S. legislators to support a vigorous dialogue with the Communist states as a part of a progressive forward United States foreign policy.

The third category of foreigners in West Germany is the extraordinary phenomenon of the foreign workers, who now number something like two and a half million. But this falls into the next chapter. In this respect again, as in others mentioned earlier, the Federal Republic found itself involved in operations and beset with problems which had no parallel in the DDR. The two Germanies were growing further and further apart.

The Economic Miracle

General Lucius Clay tells a story about a conversation between himself and roly-poly Ludwig Erhard, the one-time professor of economics and economics minister who succeeded Konrad Adenauer as Chancellor of the Federal Republic. It was in the late 1940s, when Clay was trying to decontrol the German economy so that the initiative and the creativity of the free enterprise system could operate. Erhard was describing the salutary effects of a greater degree of *laissez faire* which he had introduced into the Bavarian economy, and urging Clay to proceed more boldly and rapidly in lifting the bureaucratic controls which had been used by the Allied military governments. Though Clay was very much in sympathy with Erhard's ideas and actions, he was meeting stiff resistance from his own military bureaucrats in Berlin and Frankfurt, and right on up to the Pentagon and the Department of State. He summarized his problem by telling the burly Bavarian: "Dr. Erhard, my advisors oppose such radical decontrolling . . . " "Don't let that bother you," said the maverick, Protestant Bavarian. "So did mine . . ."

The first factor responsible for the burst of economic activity, which brought West Germany so rapidly from complete economic dependence on the victorious Western Allies to the forefront of the world's industrial powers, was without question the currency reform of 1948. This gave the country a sound currency which is essential for the functioning of a market economy. Most observers would agree that the loosening of the mechanisms created by the military government to see that the Germans lived up to the restrictions imposed on them at Potsdam and elsewhere was also most useful. I would add a third specific measure: the *Mitbestimmungsgesetz* or co-determination law, which was incorporated into German law in 1951. Under its terms representatives of the trade unions whose members worked in a particular plant were given seats with votes on the advisory board of the corporation running the plant. Introduced initially in the steel industries of the Ruhr, this procedure was later adopted in other industries, and created a community of interest among German industry, labor, and the public, which was one of the most important ingredients in the *Wirtschaftswunder,* or economic miracle.

These factors became fully operative during the decade of the 1960s, with results of economic growth which were equaled only by Japan among the world's larger nations. The GNP of West Germany increased at a rate of about 10 percent annually in the late fifties and early sixties,[1] export trade leaped from 37 billion marks in 1958 to 114 billion marks in 1969; and exports and imports paralleled this phenomenal rise, to make West Germany in 1969 the world's second largest exporter. Industrial production rose 45 percent between 1960 and 1968, and was particularly astounding in the chemical industry which grew 128 percent in that eight-year period. For the individual German citizen, the felicitous results of the *Wirtschaftswunder* were immediately noticeable. In 1960 the average West German worker's monthly paycheck showed a gross pay of 510 D-marks; nine years later, it was 1,007 D-marks, an incredible increase of 97 percent. Taxes and the cost of living were rising too, but at a markedly slower rate than income and, in fact, due to the increased volume of production, many household items, such as television sets, stoves, typewriters, vacuum cleaners, and refrigerators actually dropped in price, some by as much as 27 percent.

The companies that produced these results were diverse. They included famous family firms such as Krupp, the new daughter companies that emerged from the decartelization of such pre-war industrial giants as I.G. Farben; old and experienced German companies such as Siemens, Daimler-Benz, and AEG; new companies that had their origin during the short period of Nazi control, such as Volkswagen; government-owned companies such as the German airline, Lufthansa; and brand new enterprises founded by post-war businessmen, many of whom were schoolboys during World War II. Among these are such men as Axel Springer, whose publishing operations, based in Hamburg and active all over the country, approach the scope of Time Inc. in the United States.

The labor force at work in all these diverse plants was essentially the same. It was made up of German workmen with strong trade union traditions and a sense of common interest with industry, firmly based on an efficient welfare state and widespread worker participation in management. These German workers shared the experience of losing a war, and realized that it was their labor that could make possible national recovery and a better life for all. This sentiment was in large measure responsible for the low level of industrial strife during the 1960s. As late as 1960, only 38,000 man-days of labor were lost by strikes and lockouts in West Germany, compared to almost half a million in the Netherlands, 3 million in the United Kingdom, and 19 million in the United States in that year.[2] It is important to note that this diligence, this willingness to work, was not shared by the British or Italian working class to nearly so high a degree. For millions of British and Italian and even many French workers, the employer was the class enemy, and it was the class-conscious worker's duty to demand and get a maximum of pay for doing a minimum of work. This attitude, fostered by Communist or Communist-controlled trade unions in Italy and France, was notably absent in West Germany where, not at all by accident, Communist influence was so small as to be negligible. German workers in uniform had seen communism at work during the war years and immediately afterward and most of them wanted no part of it.

During the decade of the sixties the labor shortage in

West Germany became acute, and industrial enterprises attempted to solve their problem by introducing labor-saving devices and equipment of all kinds, and by the widespread use of foreign labor, recruited from Portugal, Spain, Iran, southern Italy, and the Balkans. By the middle 1960s about one million foreign workers were busy in German plants, and as I write these lines the figure has risen to about two and a half million.

Many of these men have now brought their families to Germany and settled down. Some have gone into other areas of employment such as the railroads and the post office. Many of these foreign workers rapidly adjusted themselves to the higher wages and more highly organized industries of Germany. Their children, of course, are in German schools and many if not most of them are taking their places in German society as Germans, as did the sons and daughters of immigrant labor in the United States a generation or more earlier. Some of these foreign workers intend to stay only long enough to qualify for pensions, and then return home to wherever they came from, with a car, a TV, and savings in desirable D-marks. Some German economists fear that in a decade or so these workers will create a balance of payments problem for the Federal Republic by sending millions of marks out of the country, but there is every indication that the German balance of payments will be able to afford this expense.

Most of the foreign workers in Germany had no Marxist revolutionary tradition or training and fit into the work-oriented, disciplined West German industry painlessly and effectively.

One of the most remarkable things about the *Wirt-*

schaftswunder was the fact that it did not depend to any appreciable extent on rearmament. Whereas German economic revival in the 1930s had been based to a large extent on Hitler's rebuilding of the country's armed forces, in the 1960s German industry remained almost entirely out of military manufacture. In part, of course, this was imposed by the Potsdam and other international agreements which prohibited Germany from manufacturing chemical warfare equipment, submarines, most types of military aircraft, and heavy weapons or ordnance. But in addition the German industrialists themselves, including such famous traditional arms-makers as Krupp, wanted no part of the business. The result was that the substantial armed forces built up during the 1960s by the Federal Republic[3] used weapons made by others. The German air force flew F-111s and other U.S.-made aircraft, armored units used British-made tanks, and even some hand weapons were of British, French, and U.S. manufacture. I visited two German aircraft manufacturing plants in 1968 and watched the production of experimental, newly designed helicopters and of an airbus, both of which could have military application, but the operation was on a small scale, and not a money-making proposition.

The shipyards of Hamburg and Bremen were, of course, capable of making large naval vessels, but stuck stubbornly to the construction of merchant ships and a few small naval patrol boats. The chemical companies and experimental and research laboratories, which could have gotten into chemical and nuclear weapons development, stayed strictly out of such efforts. The *Wirtschaftswunder* was solidly based on the production and sale

THE ECONOMIC MIRACLE 117

both at home and elsewhere of automotive vehicles, a wide range of machines, and other producer and consumer goods from cameras to women's wear to heavy bulldozers.

During this productive period, I visited Germany at least once a year and every time was shown around industrial enterprises of various kinds. On two different occasions I visited the Volkswagen plant in Wolfsburg. Lying only about five miles west of the zonal boundary which now separates the Federal Republic from the DDR, Wolfsburg is an undistinguished town, most of whose residents work for or in connection with the VW plant. The company was begun by the Nazi Party in 1938 to make a "people's" car, and raised its initial capital for the purchase of equipment by collecting money — 990 marks[4], or about 400 dollars — from loyal Nazis, on the promise of delivery of a Volkswagen as soon as the company started producing them. The vehicle was designed by Dr. Ferry Porsche, but almost no vehicles were made because the war broke out in September 1939, and from then until the bitter end the plant turned out tanks and other military equipment for the Nazi war machine. The plant suffered heavy bomb damage during the latter months of the war, and in July 1945, when I first saw the place, it was a complete shambles. But Dr. Porsche's design was still there, and so were some of the jigs and dies which had previously been made. The British military government authorities (Wolfsburg was in the British zone) got together some materials and local labor, and production began. The question of the ownership of the plant was simply ignored, and never finally settled until 1960, when VW workers and executives, and later the public, were permitted to buy shares of stock in what was made into a private company.

If Dr. Porsche had been available, he might have become the director of the plant in 1945. But he was at that time a prisoner of war in France, where he was given facilities and told to design a new civilian vehicle for the Renault company, which was owned mainly by the French government. The result was the 4-CV or Quatre Chevaux, the sturdy little workhorse of the French passenger car industry for half a generation. By the time Dr. Porsche was released and came back to Stuttgart to work, Professor Heinrich Nordhoff had taken over the top executive job at Wolfsburg, and ran the company well for the next decade. Under his leadership the sturdy little "beetle" grew to dominate first the domestic German market, and then to become an export phenomenon. Air-cooled, simple, tough, and efficient, the VW in 1967 had 75 percent[5] of the imported car market in the United States, and made major contributions to Germany's balance of payments during years when this was very important. A good share of the profits of the company were spent on workers' housing and plant improvement, and, later, the construction of VW plants in other parts of Germany and of the world — Brazil, South Africa, Ireland, and Belgium.

During the late 1960s a huge percent of the labor force at VW was foreign. Every sign around the plant was in five languages, including Greek. The organization of the plant I found exemplary. VW had a major advantage over Detroit in that the VW design changed practically not at all from one year to another, saving the costly and time-consuming design change through which

THE ECONOMIC MIRACLE 119

United States manufacturers try to increase their share of the market. I tried unsuccessfully in Wolfsburg to get cost figures on the "beetle." The reason for the company's secrecy on this point was obviously the high profitability of the operation. For years the company did little advertising, relying on word-of-mouth reports of millions of satisfied customers. When the competition got more difficult, however, in 1969 or so, the VW company found funds, without apparent difficulty, for an immense advertising campaign in the United States and elsewhere. Today, heavily pressed by Japanese competitors, VW still maintains a very respectable share of the market in Germany (about 20 percent) and elsewhere.

Having worked in a steel mill as a very young man, I have ever since followed steel manufacturing in various countries, and so I visited several mills in the famed Ruhr valley. Here German heavy industry was born in the first half of the nineteenth century, thanks to the presence of large quantities of coal and iron ore on that excellent inland waterway, the Rhine River. In some cases the coal mines were right within the gates of the mills, and the iron mines only a short distance away, while the manufacturing and construction industries which used the Ruhr steel products were also close by. Heavy expenditures were made on research and development, and even when Ruhr steelmen had to import high-grade Swedish iron ore to meet quality standards, the German steel industry was competitive. Right after World War II, some far-sighted German economists and steel men were unhappy about the fact that the country's steel industry was all in the middle of the country, many miles from tidewater, while newer steel mills in Italy,

France, and Japan were being built right on deep water in order to be able to make use of high-grade imported raw materials at lower costs. "If we Germans had had real vision in 1945, we would have rebuilt our whole industry in Bremen or Hamburg," one top executive of the Phoenix Rheinrohr Company told me. But the industry did well nonetheless.

Two new radical developments in steel technology have occurred since World War II. The first was the Basic Oxygen or LD furnace for making steel out of iron; the second was continuous casting. The former process was patented by Sir Henry Bessemer in England in 1855, but was never used commercially because of the high cost of oxygen. During the last two years of the war, however, the Germans had built a large steel mill in Linz, Austria, while a few miles away in Munich they constructed a huge and improved plant for the manufacture of large quantities of oxygen needed as fuel for the V-1 and V-2 rockets with which the Germans so mercilessly bombarded London and other cities. During the closing months of the war, the plant in Linz was heavily bombed, and most of the open hearth furnaces were knocked out. The blast furnaces, on the other hand — far sturdier installations — were relatively undamaged. Consequently, when the Austrian government took over the Linz plant and put it into operation again, they found they had a heavy surplus of iron-making capacity not nearly matched by their equipment to make steel. And there, just a few miles down the Inn River was Munich with its monster O_2 plant intact. As the newly formed Austrian government steel trust VÖEST (Vereinigte Österreichische Eisen-und Stahlwerk AG) began operating, several of its engineers realized they had a "natural". For Sir Henry Bessemer's patents were in the public domain, there was a large capacity of hot iron production at Linz, and there was a source of O_2 at a lower cost than ever before. They went to work, and in eight years developed the LD process, after Linz-Donowitz, usually called BOF or Basic Oxygen Furnace in the United States. During the next fifteen years the LD had replaced the open hearth furnace at most of the world's modern mills, including those in Germany. The effect this new development had on the economy is measured in many millions of dollars.

Continuous casting was developed in Lucerne, Switzerland, a country famed for its precision technology, but not a producer of basic steel. The process consists in taking hot steel in a ladle directly from the LD or the open hearth, and pouring it into an oscillating mold sprayed with water, producing directly either slabs or billets, eliminating the soaking pits, the ingot molds, the blooming mill, and at least one expensive reheating of the steel. Today Japan's steel industry, which is probably the world's most modern, produces nearly 90 percent of its steel by LD, and nearly half its billets and slabs from continuous casting. The Soviet steel industry, which is today the world's largest producer, is just behind Japan in technology, and West Germany is in the third spot, with most of its mills working now on LD and continuous casting.

The two Ruhr mills that I saw in operation in the late sixties had already installed LDs and were working hard at the continuous casting of rimming steel, something that the Russians and Japanese claim to have done, but which at this writing the United States steel industry has not yet perfected.[6]

On several occasions during the 1960s I was in Poland, and twice visited the Poznan Fair. Poznan, or Posen, still looks very German, although along with another old German city, Breslau, it has for the past generation been incorporated into Poland, and most of the original German-speaking population who survived the war have been repatriated to Germany. It is not surprising, therefore, that German companies, large and small, who are anxious to do business in the East, try to present a good image at Poznan every year. One of the companies that was most prominently represented with heavy machinery and equipment of all kinds was Krupp.

Talking with the suave, multilingual engineers and salesmen representing the ancient giant of the German arms industry in the large Krupp building, I learned that "business was good." The Poles wanted German equipment for the industries they were developing, shipbuilding in Gdynia and Gdansk (formerly Danzig), steel production near Cracow—and although they had perennial problems with foreign exchange, they skimped heavily on consumer goods imports in order to be able to spend a maximum on importing machinery. Chatting further over lunch with several of these German businessmen, I heard a story that I found fascinating, and also symbolic of German industry's *Drang Nach Osten*, or drive to develop business in the East. It was also symbolic of the frustrations that await anyone, perhaps especially any German, who seeks trade with Eastern Europe.

As I have several times indicated, beginning about 1950 West Germany began to suffer from a severe labor shortage, which it dealt with in part by importing foreign labor. Several German industrialists and economists noted in the early sixties that Poland's centrally planned Socialist economy suffered from the opposite difficulty. There was an unemployment problem, an embarrassment to the Poles, since a centrally planned Socialist economy by definition cannot suffer from unemployment. The Polish government tried to deal with the problem by sending several thousand Polish mine workers and laborers to work in northern France and Belgium on government contracts and by allowing a few Polish workers to take jobs in West Germany on contracts. But several Germans and one or two Polish officials realized that a more radical and promising possibility beckoned: rather than send Polish workers to Germany, why not take German industry to Poland?

One of the most audacious and enterprising of postwar German industrialists was Berthold Beitz who, as general manager of Krupp, made many of that company's key decisions. Beitz worked out a complex proposal under the terms of which Krupp was to build in Poland — in the neighborhood of Poznan, where competent and even German-speaking labor was available — a large plant for the manufacture of assorted electronic equipment — tape recorders, radio sets, and so forth. In an ingenious triangular deal, these products then were to be sold in hard currency markets by the West German firm Grundig, which had built up large export markets for its excellent products but was unable to fully supply the demand because of labor shortages in its own plants in Bavaria. Krupp would build and run the plant, and of course supply its heavy equipment; Polish labor would be employed making products which would earn hard currency; Grundig would make money selling more tape recorders in North America and in Western Europe. The problem, of course, was: who would put up the money to build the plant? Poland's constitution, like those of all the Communist bloc states, provides clearly that the means of production belong to the people, i.e., to the government, and Poland's government therefore was not empowered to offer or make available any share of equity of any factory or other productive installation in Poland to any foreign company. What the Poles therefore told Dr. Beitz was: "Fine. You go ahead and build the plant. We will own it; you can run it on a management contract, and we will allow Grundig, for a fee in hard currency, to market the products." The German banks took a look at this proposal and turned thumbs down, probably reasoning: "If we are going to finance a German plant abroad, let's do it where the German companies involved can own the installation or at least a substantial share of equity in it — as in Brazil, Thailand, the United States or Spain." Without the financial backing of the German banks, the deal fell through. Shortly after that (although I do not think the two events were related), Krupp had serious financial problems, and had to go public; that is, offer its shares for sale to anyone who had the money to buy them and wished to do so.

The problem of doing business with Communist states is not limited to West Germany and Poland. At this writing major U.S. companies are signing deals with the Soviet Union, so far on a non-equity basis. Among the more or less Socialist states, Yugoslavia is the only one that has modified its constitution in such a way as to make equity deals possible, and that only in the service industries. On the capitalist side it is possible that the big banks will eventually relax their traditional insistence on equity or collateral to secure investments. The arguments in favor of such a change of attitude are strong ones. Equity deals can be violated by sovereign governments, as we have seen with the seizure by Fidel Castro of roughly $1 billion worth of U.S.-owned productive property in Cuba, the nationalization of oil properties by the governments of Algeria, Peru, and Iraq, of U.S.-owned mines by the Allende government in Chile, and many more. It is my guess that in the years ahead management contracts will begin to be accepted rather than equity or collateral to secure developmental investments made by United States or West German companies abroad. But for the moment East/West trade is consistently hampered by the incompatibility of the desires of Socialist governments to acquire developmental investments from capitalist states without surrendering ownership, and the reluctance of the capitalists to give equipment and technology away.

In their activities in many non-Socialist countries German industry has gone full steam ahead. In Brazil, Argentina, Australia, Japan, Thailand, Indonesia, Canada, and many other countries, Germans have built plants which are turning out Volkswagens, Mercedes trucks, electrical and electronic equipment and consumer products, Olympia typewriters, heavy and light chemicals, and diverse machinery and consumer goods for local markets. These plants, partially or wholly owned by Germans, are making profits which contribute to Germany's spectacular performance in maintaining a consistently positive balance of trade, and a heavy balance of payments surplus in spite of two upward revaluations of the D-mark—one in late 1969 of 8 percent, the other in August 1971 of 12 percent.[7] Thanks to these revaluations, a West German traveling in the United States can today buy almost 25 percent more for his money than he could four years ago.

I have been dealing so far with the *Wirtschaftswunder* as an expression of the performance of German manufacturing industries. But for millions of Germans, and hundreds of thousands of foreign visitors to West Germany, other aspects of the *Wirtschaftswunder* are far more important.

Let us take a look at German cities. Most of the big ones—Berlin, Frankfurt, Munich, Hamburg, Düsseldorf—were in large measure destroyed during World War II. Some of the smaller cities suffered proportionately even more. One example is Kassel, a city of about 210,000 in Hessen. When I first drove through Kassel in 1945, I couldn't get my jeep through most of the streets. Now a new city has been built. Some old buildings were repaired, of course, but many more new ones have been erected in and around a central downtown area from which cars and trucks are barred except for deliveries that must take place at night. Attractive squares, parks, and shopping arcades have been built near the collection of buildings that house the *Dokumenta*, the Kassel art exposition held every four years. I have walked and driven around in the outer areas of Kassel, and I did not see a street or a building I thought of as a slum. Many private houses and apartment houses have garden plot areas where residents grow flowers or vegetables, and where children play in well-planned parks enjoying sunshine and fresh air.

And it is not just Kassel. Even in traditionally tough towns like Hamburg and Bremen, or parts of Düsseldorf and Berlin, Germans feel secure, night or day. There is some crime in Germany, of course, but assault and battery, murder and rape are far less prevalent than in most large United States cities.[8]

I have a friend living in the Düsseldorf suburb of Gräfenberg. Most of the buildings there are old ones, rebuilt or at least fundamentally repaired after the war. Rapid, efficient street-car service takes the Gräfenbergers to their jobs or offices in downtown Düsseldorf, about four miles away, or to the Deutsche Oper Am Rhein or any of the several excellent repertory theaters in this city of nearly a million inhabitants. Within five minute's walk of my friend's house is a city park — the Gräfenbergerwald — which offers lovely walks, saddle trails, a tennis club and, perhaps most important, a sense of space, although it is within five miles of the center of one of Germany's most important industrial cities.

When one goes a few miles away from the central parts of Cologne or Düsseldorf out into the coal mine and steel mill area which extends from Cologne through Leverkusen, Düsseldorf, Essen, Duisberg, Wuppertal, and right on north to Dortmund, one finds an area in which hundreds of thousands of industrial workers live in their own houses with their own gardens, and go to work on foot or by bicycle, though most German skilled workers now have automobiles. Some large shopping centers have sprung up in these areas, but most housewives still shop from a small, family-run store at a nearby crossroads. Schools, churches, clinics, recreational areas are within walking distance or certainly bicycle distance of most of the population. When one compares this area with Cicero, Illinois, or New York's Bronx, or parts of Washington within a mile of the White House and the Capitol, one gets a measure of what the German *Wirtschaftswunder* has meant to millions of Germans.

Another aspect of any modern society that can help make the lives of its citizens miserable or pleasant is transportation. The foundations of the German autobahn road network were designed under the Weimar Republic, and construction was begun under the Nazis during the 1930s. But since the war it has vastly improved, and today is a very efficient transportation network. About 14 million privately owned cars roll incessantly over the 4,000 kilometers of autobahn, and although Germans are notorious for their maniacal driving, the accident rate is actually not very high—in 1967, for example, West Germany had 28.3 traffic accident deaths per 100,000 population while the United States had 26.7 deaths. On Sundays commercial vehicles are allowed on the autobahns only in emergencies. In principle these highways are reserved for Germans to go on picnics in the family car.

Millions of Germans still take pride and pleasure in riding in their trains. Though not as fast as the newest Japanese trains, the TEE or TransEuropeExpress trains which operate in West Germany, France, Italy, Belgium, Switzerland, and Austria are consistently punctual and clean, with good, efficient service. For many frequently traveled runs such as Frankfurt-Düsseldorf, or Cologne-Hamburg the downtown-to-downtown running time by train is well below the comparable time by air.

One of the most interesting and beautiful train rides in the world is that along the Rhine from Cologne to Heidelberg. The mountain tops on both sides of the river are encrusted with ancient castles, some rebuilt and being lived in by mountain-climbing Germans, some mere heaps of crumbled stone. Below on the slopes lie some of the world's most famous and productive vineyards; along the banks, quaint towns built by the merchants and artisans of the Middle Ages are now busy, thriving communities servicing the river transport and catering to tourists. And the river itself teems with barges and passenger vessels flying the flags of the four Rhine nations—Germany, France, Holland, and Switzerland. On Sundays the commercial traffic on the river is tied up along the banks, and small pleasure boats take over, along with fishermen trying to catch the delicious but diminishing Rhine salmon.[9]

Though beautiful from a distance, the Rhine is badly polluted, making both swimming and fishing neither pleasant nor safe. Also, industrial use of the river's water has cut the level so much that in dry years shipping is seriously inhibited. For example, in 1972, the boat cruises from Rotterdam to Basel and back were cancelled due to the low water level. Measures are being taken to improve these conditions, but not nearly up to the level that many German conservationists and sportsmen would like to see.

Many nations have had bursts of economic energy and high growth levels which have added little to the quality of the lives of the people who worked in these industries: the factory towns of England after the repeal of the Corn Laws; the industrial slums around the coal and steel districts of Pennsylvania during the years after the Civil War, or Chicago or Cleveland or Detroit a few years later; the congested and unsanitary slums within and around Osaka or Kobe or Yokahama right up to the present. Most recently some countries have succeeded in beautifying and humanizing their industrial areas — Holland, Scandinavia, parts of the suburban areas around Paris and Lyons. And the Japanese have become conscious of their problems and are making plans with all the passion with which those extraordinary people throw themselves into new activities. In the Soviet bloc efforts have been made. I saw the results when I lived in Magnitogorsk, and more recently while visiting friends in industrial suburbs near Moscow, Leningrad, and Bucharest. But the facilities available are limited, the quality of the buildings poor, recreational facilities meager.

Thanks to the *Wirtschaftswunder*, and perhaps the chastening influence of the twelve years of Nazi domination and then defeat, in the past twenty years the West Germans have surpassed every other country in making their booming steel mills and industrial plants first of all the instruments of a better life for the people who work in them rather than the source of profit for their owners, or of power for their government.

7

The DDR's Coercive Economy

The construction of the Berlin Wall, beginning on August 13, 1961, and the other security work done at roughly the same time along the frontiers between the German Federal Republic and the DDR, as well as the manning of these installations with a firm determination—called Socialist discipline on the DDR side and cruelty on the other—opened up a new and creative period for the DDR.

Nor is this surprising. For in spite of Marx's no doubt sincere assertions that socialism would give real freedom to the individual, it is a hard fact that the Socialist societies of the Soviet bloc today are all coercive societies. Economic policies such as the collectivization of agriculture are decided by small, Communist elitist bureaucracies, and then implemented, or put through, to use the useful Russian verb *provodit*, with whatever measure of administrative pressure is required, up to and including the execution of those who resist. In these Socialist states the allocation of material resources, the product line and price structure, the channeling of the national product into consumption and production and defense are all carried out by tightly controlled state and party organs and never submitted to any kind of plebiscite or referendum. They are simply carried out, and when their implementation requires more work for less pay, the controlled press, the cultural superstructure — the theater, the cinema, the educational system, the radio and TV, and thousands of staff and volunteer propagandists and agitators — goes into action to prove that what the Party has decreed is what the people really want. Dissidents are severely punished, and loyalty is handsomely rewarded — and so the system works. This has been demonstrated for half a century by the Soviet Union. The system works, provided there is a well-guarded frontier to prevent people from leaving, provided there is a wall, a physical obstruction, to prevent the citizens from going to some other land where regimentation and coercion are less severe.

Many Western statesmen and observers regretted that the Western Allies were booby-trapped at the European Advisory Council in London into accepting a Western presence in Berlin without written guarantees of access through a corridor or at least well-defined transit rights. Thoughtful Soviet officials regretted even more having accepted a Soviet zone of Germany with an open frontier through Berlin. And their apprehensions proved to be well founded. The constant departure of highly qualified men and women to seek a better life in the West made the administration of the Soviet zone, and the maintenance of industrial efficiency there most difficult. During the late 1950s and early 1960s the DDR economy fell steadily behind the standards set by the Federal Republic, even before the *Wirtschaftswunder* really got started.

So the wall was built. And it worked remarkably well. Though a trickle of adventurous East Germans continued to find ways to leave the DDR—through tunnels dug under the wall, by swimming the canals obstructed with barbed wire, by jumping from coastal ships and trying to reach Scandinavia, or by the ingenious falsification of documents—the total manpower leakage was negligible. During the first seven months of 1961, just before the wall was constructed, almost 200,000 East Germans arrived in West Germany, 16,000 of them during August 1961 alone; during the twelve months after the wall, the figure had shrunk to a mere 20,000.[1]

The lesson was rapidly learned in East Berlin and East Germany. The Vopos had orders to shoot to kill at all wall-crossers. Liberal friends of mine, such as James P. O'Donnel, who still lives in Berlin and does pieces for the *Reader's Digest*, is indignant about the slaughter on the wall, and is perennially trying to arouse interest in a campaign to make the Vopos stop shooting. Well meaning though his efforts are, they are quite illogical. Without the shooting there would not be an effective wall. For the structure is only some four meters high, and along the zonal frontier there is no wall at all, but only a barbed-wire entanglement which can be clipped through in a few minutes. It is the fear of being shot that makes the wall work. If the shooting stopped, this would be tantamount to dismantling the wall, and undoing its major contributions to the economy of the DDR.

And these contributions have been extraordinary. Knowing now that they were not going to be able to leave the DDR, the East German labor force by-and-large decided to make the best of it, and to make their industries more efficient so that they would reap higher rewards.

In 1968 I drove through the DDR from Poland and then, after several days in both East and West Berlin, out through Leipzig and Dresden and into Czechoslovakia. It was early June, and the universities were winding up their examinations. Students were heading home for their summer vacations, or for summer jobs. Like students in many countries, these East German young men and women had limited funds, and they lined the entries to the autobahns outside several cities, hitch-hiking. I gave rides to more than half a dozen during three days driving some four hundred miles. One couple I remember particularly: he was studying chemistry, she was studying architecture. They were engaged, and planned to work in Leipzig after their graduation in another year. They had hopes of getting an apartment, and perhaps a Trabant, the small East German two-cycle engine sports car which sells for the equivalent of about three thousand dollars. They were enthusiastic about the work they would begin, he in the chemical plants in Leipzig, and she in the planning and construction of a new inner city. During a long and relaxed talk they did not even mention the West. So I asked them whether they ever thought of traveling or perhaps working abroad. Both shrugged: "Naja, dass wäre schön," ("Sure, that would be very nice,") but "es kommt nicht in Frage" ("it is out of the question"). If they try very hard, and are very lucky, they said, they might manage a year of graduate study in Moscow. But the West? No. It was another world. I asked whether they realized that some young East Germans did contrive to leave the country. "Ja, es gibt doch sicher Verbrecher" ("Yes, there are certainly criminals"), they said, slipping into the use of the word "criminal" which is applied by the East German press to anyone seeking to leave the country. But they had no interest in such activities. They were about to complete a good higher education. They had challenging work to do in their chosen field, and a secure future.

Of course, if the wall were to be dismantled, if emigration were permitted, and if the subject could be freely discussed in the press, there is every evidence that many citizens of the DDR would indeed leave. But in the immediate future this is highly unlikely. The East Germans by and large are adjusted to the wall, and to remaining productive citizens in their coercive but relatively affluent economy, as compared with other Communist countries.

For ten years after August 1961 production in the DDR increased rapidly. The DDR quickly passed Czechoslovakia to achieve the highest GNP in the Soviet bloc—about 275 billion East German marks in 1970. Thanks in part to the rupture of economic and most political relations between Communist China and the Soviet Union in August of 1960 and also to a trade agreement between the USSR and the DDR,[2] the DDR rapidly rose to become the Soviet Union's largest trading partner, the trade balance between the two countries growing from about 1 billion marks in 1949 to almost 8 billion in 1960, and more than doubling (to over 15 billion marks) in 1970.

Using raw materials—iron and other ores, coal, gas, petroleum, agricultural raw materials, forest products, and other important ingredients—shipped in from the USSR at stiff world market prices, the DDR factories and mills produced a stream of high-quality machine tools, automotive vehicles, railroad equipment, components for the chemical and petro-chemical industries, optical equipment, and precision instruments of all kinds, most of which went to the USSR at prices well below what the Russians would have had to pay the Swiss or Scandinavians or British or West Germans for similar goods. In Moscow offices, for example, one could see DDR typewriters, calculators, and inter-office communications equipment; Soviet department stores carry East German radios, TV sets, tape-recorders, sewing machines; in Soviet pharmacies, there are assorted medicines and cosmetic goods from the DDR.

The quality of these products was in general not good enough to compete successfully in Western markets, with the exception of the Zeiss cameras and binoculars. The East Germans could, of course, have exerted themselves and improved the quality of their products so as to make them competitive in the West. But the political association of the DDR with Moscow was so close that no DDR official ever suggested an attempt at drastic penetration of DDR goods into the West, as did the Czechoslovaks in 1968. And the Russians were most pleased with the performance of their East German associates. "Oni rabotayut," a Soviet friend in Moscow's Academy of Sciences told me in the late 1960s, referring to the East Germans. "They work. They don't get drunk like the Poles, or make fiery, empty speeches like the Rumanians. They work." On the other hand, the Russians—from top officials to ordinary people—continued to feel for the Germans, both East and West, the mixture of fear, admiration, and loathing of a people whose country has been twice invaded and partly devastated within the memory of many Russians now alive. I do not think that the very top Party leaders, or the top military commanders in Moscow seriously believe that Germany, East or West, has either the intention or the capacity to invade the Soviet Union again at least during the rest of this century. But the popular fear, and the use of the Germans as a scapegoat to explain away assorted shortcomings, remain strong elements in Soviet attitudes to both Germanies.

As the DDR moved ahead in industrial production and technology, it began a series of important activities in the field of foreign economic aid. In the Mongolian People's Republic in the late 1960s I saw teams of East German technicians working at industrial construction projects. In Africa and the Middle East, East German trade and aid missions appeared, using "Made in Germany" as a symbol of quality, and offering assorted industrial products along with technology in a mix of aid and trade controlled by the leadership in Berlin and their superiors in Moscow. Although the total of DDR economic aid was not significant in comparison with that of the United States or the Soviet Union, nonetheless it attracted attention, and along with political efforts resulted in the establishment of diplomatic relations between some thirteen nations and the DDR, as well as commercial representatives in thirty-two other countries.³ In many cases this success brought a bonus to Pankow thanks to the Hallstein Doctrine, according to which the Bonn government had bound itself to break diplomatic relations with those nations which established them with the DDR, as was the case with Egypt, Yugoslavia, and others.

The DDR has made a strong effort to enhance its international reputation by concentrating heavily on foreign aid and trade with the under-developed countries of Asia and Africa, as well as instituting a broad program of scholarships and educational opportunities for students from these countries within the DDR itself. Between 1960 and 1970 the amount of export/import activity between the DDR and the under-developed countries rose from 791 million marks to 1.5 billion marks. A typical example is the trade with Iraq, which in that ten-year period rose from 14.5 million marks to 48.5 million marks. Exports to the less developed countries concentrated heavily on machines of all sorts—electric and mechanical, office machinery, generators, motors, transformers, cranes, trucks, and tractors. Although no statistics are available concerning the amount of money spent on the education of foreign students in the DDR, the portion of the national budget dedicated to education is fairly high. Indeed, in the fields of science, the training received in the DDR is good (in the liberal arts and fields such as political science and philosophy the education garnered in the DDR is considered tendentious by

THE DDR'S COERCIVE ECONOMY

most Westerners, since it is highly propagandistic) and scholarships are made readily available for students from the less developed countries. A regular campaign is made to recruit such students, and they are offered stipends to cover their living expenses, given suitable housing and, of course, free tuition.[4]

During the 1960s the DDR also moved to build up its armed forces. It put together a force of about half a million men: 150,000 in the National People's Army, a modest navy of about 11,000, and a respectable air force of 15,000, with 400 planes and heavy technological dependence on the Soviet Union. The army is equipped with 2,500 tanks (mostly Soviet T-54), 300 self-propelled guns, and 1,800 other artillery pieces including AA and anti-tank guns. The navy in the mid-60s included 4 frigates, 39 patrol vessels, 93 patrol boats, 22 fleet minesweepers, 50 motor torpedo-boats, 87 minesweeping boats, 3 surveying vessels, 3 oilers, 7 tugs, and 2 training ships, while the air force was flying MiG-15s, 17s, 19s, and 21s in the fighter and fighter-bomber divisions, and other units included a wing of Mi-1 and Mi-4 helicopters and two squadrons of IL-4 and An-2 transports.[5]

In addition, there are 34,000 Vopos, 8,500 transport police, and about 320,000 militiamen organized into combat groups and trained under the aegis of the People's Police.[6]

I first got a glimpse of this military force in Berlin in 1964 when I watched a company of DDR infantry goose-step across the Marx-Engels-Platz in East Berlin in front of a reviewing stand of Communist bigwigs from many countries. During the past decade East German units have regularly taken part in Warsaw Pact maneuvers in Eastern Europe, and units from the DDR participated in the occupation of Czechoslovakia in August 1968. Western military experts believe that the East German units would prove the most reliable and efficient in the Warsaw Pact in case of war. This is not because of political viability of the DDR (indeed this has been and remains in the early 1970s signally low); it is because Germans make good soldiers.

The DDR racked up another achievement behind its protective wall during the 1960s: it adjusted itself to the economic reform movements in the Soviet Union and other members of the Comecon.[7]

Under Stalin the Soviet economy maintained high levels of capital investment and of production, while consumption remained low. Popular discontent with this much-work-for-little-pay regime was nipped in the bud by cruel police pressure, and centralized economic planning maximized the use of the country's resources for the fulfillment of the targets of the sequential Five-Year plans: the construction of heavy industry as the base for world-wide military and economic power.

But after Stalin's death in 1953 his successors found it expedient to make some concessions to the unorganized but very real popular demand for more consumer goods and more leisure time for the workers. And these developments triggered a series of problems. It is fairly easy to plan an economy heavily concentrated on the production of steel and tanks. But when the economy began to produce a diversified line of consumer goods of various qualities, colors, sizes, and styles, the work of the central planning authorities in Gosplan (the State Planning Commission) became much more complex. Under a centrally planned economy each product had to be launched by a plan which specified where it was to be made, and from what raw materials, how much it was to cost, where it was to be shipped for distribution, and who would be its ultimate consumer. Even if Gosplan had had modern computers, of which there are still very few in the Soviet Union, the formulation and then the implementation of these decisions — decisions which are made impersonally in the West by the market factors born of the laws of supply and demand — would have required immense expenditures of effort. And the apparatus of Gosplan and its regional branches all over the Soviet Union did proliferate enormously during the late 1950s and early 1960s. Noting this, the Soviet theoretical economic magazine *Voprosy Ekonomiki* remarked on several occasions that if this proliferation continued, within a few years most Soviet adults would be engaged in planning, and there would not be enough workers to staff production lines.

Other problems made themselves felt. Factory directors and heads of assorted enterprises, aware of the difficulty of getting supplies and materials without which they could not fulfill their plans, began to find shortcuts through and around the increasingly muscle-bound official bureaucracy. They stashed away materials and equipment for use in unofficial and unplanned barter with other executives, and highly paid expediters began to be essential to carry out the unofficial procurement.

This predictably led to nepotism, the use of bribery, and the development of booming black markets in deficit items. The job security and bonuses and promotions of high executives began to depend increasingly on *blat*, a ubiquitous Russian word meaning pull or bribery.

These serious problems were accompanied by a continued failure of the Soviet economy to compete with the more advanced countries of North America and West Europe and Japan in the production and distribution of goods of all kinds. Soviet economists began searching for ways in which the Soviet economy could improve the efficiency of its operations and become more competitive. One such economist was Evsei Lieberman, Professor of Economics at the University of Kharkov. In the early 1960s he began writing articles proposing certain economic reforms, and it is a tribute to the late Nikita Khrushchev that he allowed these articles to be printed not only in the technical and theoretical journals, but also in the daily press, as a basis for discussion. Others joined in this polemic from which several clearly defined reforms were proposed:

1. The planning of the Soviet Union must be decentralized, with greater authority in the hands of local and regional officials in closer touch with the consumer.

2. The profit motive must be used along with or perhaps eventually in place of centrally planned production targets as the basis for the rewards or punishment of executives and production workers at all levels.

3. Interest must be charged on both fixed and working capital as a means of preventing the hoarding of materials and equipment and their informal barter.

4. In order that all these measures be implemented it was necessary to restructure Soviet prices in such a way that they be reflections of unit costs, rather than the arbitrary result of some planner's political judgment.

Implicit although unstated in all these suggestions was the realization that capitalist market factors — that is, the flow of goods and materials and the price structure according to the law of supply and demand rather than as the result of some bureaucrat's arbitrary decision — could and should be useful in making the Soviet economy more efficient.

These reforms were embodied in a resolution passed by the September Plenum of the Central Committee of the Communist Party of the Soviet Union in 1965, and their implementation was ordered within two years. With this decision a great wave of reform suggestions swept the Soviet bloc. Reforms were "in." In Czechoslovakia and Hungary, in Rumania and even in Bulgaria, polemics were carried out and suggestions made for the de-centralization, and even the humanization of socialism in those countries.

But from the very beginning of this reform movement of the 1960s, Walter Ulbricht was skeptical and very careful. Ulbricht realized earlier than many of his associates in other parts of the Soviet bloc that there was a fundamental contradiction between Party control and a market economy. He realized that if the basic decisions of any economy — the allocation of resources — were to be transferred in total or in part to market orientation, it would take power away from the Communist Party *apparatchiks* — those several hundred thousand Party hacks, in the case of the Soviet Union, whose privileges and power depended precisely on their monopoly of power to make those decisions.

So for several years, while Soviet officials were talking about reforms, were shaking their heads over the misdeeds of Stalin and talking about de-Stalinization, while Khrushchev and his successors tried to de-centralize the Soviet economy through the organization of 102 regional economic councils and then abolished these organs when they did not produce any positive results — while all this was going on in the Soviet Union and by reflex action in other parts of the Soviet bloc, Walter Ulbricht maintained a quiet Stalinist leadership structure in the DDR. There was no talk of economic reforms in the controlled East German press. Indeed if there were any changes they tended to be in the direction of greater emphasis on the tested German traditions of centralized control, discipline, and paternalism which had come down from the kaiser's time and then been used with some distortions but with great effect by Hitler. While Soviet and Polish and Hungarian writers attracted some attention with demands for more literary freedom, less censorship, and more ready access to foreign travel, East German writers and other intellectuals were mercilessly and efficiently regimented, and foreign travel outside the Soviet bloc remained severely limited.

What Walter Ulbricht *did* do, was to seek to increase the efficiency of the DDR economy through improvements of his own. Ulbricht had no intention of relinquishing any significant element of power held firmly in the hands of himself and his SED (Socialist Unity Party, the official name of the East German Communist

Party) into any other hands. But he saw to it that the *apparatchiks* of the SED were technically competent and able to make decisions with an eye to the efficiency of the entire economy rather than just as an expression of Party control. He was able to do this, in part at least, because of the German traditions of diligence and relative freedom from corruption, and because of the high German standards of literary and technical training.

The economic reforms ordered by the September Plenum in Moscow were never carried out. Nor were they repudiated. They were simply ignored, drowned in irrelevant words in the public press, buried in obscurantist bureaucratese at Party meetings. The reason was clear: The half million or so Soviet middle- and upper-level *apparatchiki* who owed their chauffeured Volgas and summer suburban houses to their control of decision-making, were not prepared to surrender these advantages to upstart factory directors and market researchers, many of whom were not in the Party at all.

And because the reforms were not carried out in the Soviet Union, Moscow felt that it was clearly undesirable for them to be realized in the junior Socialist states. In Czechoslovakia, the Soviet Union had to use military force to suppress the reformers who, Moscow said (with some justification) were planning actions which would lead to a capitalist restoration in Czechoslovakia. Janos Kadar in Hungary, a far more subtle and flexible man than his Hungarian predecessors or his Czechoslovak contemporaries, managed to introduce substantial reforms into the economy of Hungary in a manner that was well enough camouflaged to avoid trouble with Moscow.

From the entire episode Walter Ulbricht emerged with top marks in the books of Soviet leaders. His leadership of the DDR had been unswerving. It had been effective. He had built up a country with limited resources and only 17 million inhabitants into the eighth country in the world in industrial production. And he continued to make available to the Soviet Union the products of this economy at preferential prices, while at the same time rewarding his citizens well enough on the one hand, and keeping them sufficiently terrorized by his secret police on the other so that there were no problems.

There was only one trouble with Walter Ulbricht as seen by Moscow. He was getting old.

Brandt Assumes Power in a Troubled Federal Republic

Willy Brandt worked for twenty-five years to prepare himself for leadership of the Federal Republic, but his progress toward this goal was by no means even. On two occasions he suffered serious setbacks—in the elections of 1961 and 1965—when he failed to win the support he and his party had hoped for. On both occasions he was disheartened and discouraged, and this reflected itself in some bitterness and, according to Brandt's political opponents, in occasional lapses into an over-consumption of brandy, of which Brandt had always been fond.

But the lapses were brief, and Brandt continued to pursue the rigorous program of self-education he had followed for years in a concerted drive to make up for his lowly, illegitimate birth and his modest formal education. And he continued to work systematically within the Social Democratic Party to secure a base from which he hoped to move to power at the appropriate time.

The time approached in 1966 when an electoral deadlock between the SPD and the Christian Democratic Union led to the formation of the government of the Grand Coalition, in which Dr. Kurt Kiesinger assumed the position of Chancellor and Brandt became Deputy Chancellor and Minister for Foreign Affairs.

Using this position to present and pursue his objectives of a new approach to the East—to the DDR and the Soviet Union—while maintaining firm ties with NATO, the Common Market, and the United States, Brandt proceeded to initiate a series of innovations in foreign policy. In so doing he used the talents and energy of Egon Bahr, who was to become a sort of Henry Kissinger for Willy Brandt.

Egon Bahr was born in Thuringia in 1922, and moved to Berlin with his schoolteacher father in 1938. The fact that he had a Jewish grandmother barred him from university entrance and in 1942 he was drafted into the Luftwaffe, where he entered fighter pilot training school only to be dishonorably discharged, again because of his one-quarter Jewish blood. He went to work in the Borsig Locomotive Works which was then producing Tiger tanks. He thus survived the war much better than many contemporaries; he remembers thoughtfully that of twenty-five male members of his high school graduating class, only seven are alive today.

After the fall of Berlin he found work as a cub reporter on the newly organized *Neue Zeitung*, then moved to RIAS for which he became Bonn correspondent in

1950. He joined the SPD soon afterward, and made the acquaintance of Willy Brandt. Shortly after Brandt became mayor of West Berlin in 1957 he offered Bahr a job as press officer. In this capacity, for nearly a decade, Bahr was Brandt's confidant and advisor, and participated in countless conversations and studies largely concentrated on the need to break away from the one-directional westward orientation of Konrad Adenauer and to open windows to the East.

When Brandt became Foreign Minister in the Kiesinger government in 1966, he made Bahr head of the Foreign Office Policy Planning staff. In this capacity Bahr acted as a trouble-shooter and as special envoy to make contacts and carry out preliminary arrangements for what was to become Brandt's *Ostpolitik*, or Eastern policy.

Since Brandt's thinking and his policies have become a most important element in the current history not only of the two Germanies but of Europe, it is necessary to devote a few paragraphs to this subject, basing my remarks on several talks with Brandt and Egon Bahr during the late 1960s, and also on Brandt's public speeches and writings, particularly his book, *A Peace Policy for Europe*, published in 1969.[1]

Brandt's thinking on Germany begins with the historic fact of German responsibility for two disastrously destructive wars which Germany initiated and then lost. To quote: "In this century Germany has lost two world wars for which she was either partially, or very largely solely responsible . . . Thoughtful and responsible governments could have avoided both wars . . ." Forced to flee his country by the actions and policies of the Nazi government, Brandt has a deeply rooted sense of the need for Germans to recognize the disastrous errors of the immediate past and dedicate themselves to the creation of a new national conscience, coupled with a determination to avoid any repetition of past crimes and blunders. Again, from Brandt: "As far as it depends on us, never again will murder be wrought in the name of Germany, never again will a dictator be able to blind the people, never again will a war be waged by Germans or a government formed that is not elected by the people . . ."

Brandt places great emphasis on Germany's relations with the Western democracies which constitute fellow members of the North Atlantic Treaty Organization and of the European Economic Community (EEC). As he put it: "It is no small matter for Germany, the instigator and loser of World War II, to be accepted into this alliance as a full and equal member . . ." Particularly with France, Brandt believes, Germany must develop close and cooperative relations, for ". . . without an intimate and trusting relationship between Germany and France no European peace order is thinkable . . ."

On the other hand, Brandt did not agree with all of the ideas of Charles deGaulle, nor did he go along with every twist and turn in French policy. On the subject of the expansion of the Common Market to include the British, Brandt consistently oppposed the French view, and urged British entry. While serving as Foreign Minister he wrote that he ". . . would much regret casting a vote [on British entry into the EEC] that was different from that of [his] French colleague . . . However, I must be allowed to refer to Article 5 of the Rome treaty which enjoins every member state to desist from any measures that might jeopardize the realization of the aims of the Treaty, [among which] the enlargement of the Community [is one] . . ." And in this connection, Brandt's attitude toward the British has been consistently friendly. He wrote: "As a European I must ask myself, somewhat bewildered, why Great Britain must knock. Did it not prove, in Europe's darkest hours, that it belonged to it?"

While supporting the Common Market and applauding its achievements, Brandt expressed frequent criticism of the attempts of Adenauer (and some current critics and historians) to give the EEC a Christian Democratic or even "Carolingian"[2] character. This tendency invites the risk that at some point in the future this concept might be counterposed by a Social Democratic ideology for Europe. European cooperation must include all democratic forces. "The great goal of a United States of Europe should not slip away from us . . ."

On this basis Brandt moved to formulate German policies conducive to the realization of peace for Europe.

To begin with, Brandt insisted, German policy must be positive, rather than negative. It must stand *for* something rather than *against* something or someone. Implicit in this position was a criticism of Adenauer, who was consistently against communism, and often quite clearly against the DDR and the Soviet Union. Brandt considers himself a non-Communist rather than an anti-Communist. He is convinced that the European states must cooperate in seeking prosperity and security as common interests in spite of having different kinds of governments and social structures. On the other hand Brandt fully recognizes that the governments of some

European states, such as the DDR and the Soviet Union, are not based on free elections, and Brandt points this out consistently, without making it sound provocative. He firmly asserts that in the Federal Republic, on the other hand, democracy has put forth strong roots, "and we are now strong enough to protect these roots."

With the millions of refugees and deportees who found themselves in West Germany after the war, with the hunger and despair which until so recently were so common, it is indeed a miracle that a democratic state could evolve, Brandt points out. But having achieved certain successes in this respect, it is essential, he believes, not to override democratic procedures. "An 'ideal' foreign policy may be easy to devise. But if it is not supported by a Parliamentary majority, if it contradicts the conscience of the people, it is worth nothing because it cannot be realized."

So, stone by stone, Willy Brandt formed the structure of his peace policy: that any general European policy must involve an integrated German participation was axiomatic; that German attitudes must start with a recognition of German responsibility for the world's two major wars in this century, Brandt felt to be obvious. The meticulous observance of democratic procedures and the close cooperation of those states that maintained these procedures, Brandt felt, were fundamental to guarantee peace and security.

But beyond these basic tenets, Brandt felt it necessary to deal realistically with those states ruled by authoritarian governments which did not pretend or aspire to be freely elected by their citizens. In the first place, this pertained to the DDR, whose government depended heavily on the presence of some twenty-two divisions of Soviet troops and whose citizens were treated consistently by their government as children or criminals, locked up behind a wall and deprived of any opportunity to decide or even discuss such fundamental issues as the desirability or viability of the Socialist system. But there the DDR was, for nearly a quarter of a century. Its industries, its theaters and athletic teams, architects, scientists, and educators were winning substantial recognition even in the West. How long could the West German community continue to act as if the DDR were only a Soviet invention, and assert that the government in Bonn was the only legitimate German government? How long could this continue, particularly in light of the obvious Soviet determination to support the East Berlin government and the increased pressure for its international recognition? How long, in the light of the fact that millions of citizens of West Germany desired and hoped for some arrangement, perhaps far short of reunification, but under the terms of which West and East Germans could visit, telephone, write each other freely? Brandt was convinced that the time was more than ripe to attempt such an arrangement, which would have to be pursued with the governments of both Moscow and East Berlin.

From the beginning, Brandt made it clear that he would not deal with East Germany as a foreign nation. The East Germans were, after all, Germans.

But he could accept the concept of two German states within one German nation. And although he opposed "any recognition under international law of the [East Berlin] regime . . . because it does not represent the will of the people, because without Soviet troops it could not have maintained itself, and because it prevents the exercise of the right of self-determination . . ." he began direct negotiations in 1967, soon after he became Minister for Foreign Affairs, aimed at a personal meeting with an East German government official of equivalent rank. It was not surprising that he chose Egon Bahr to carry out preliminary talks in East Berlin. It was also not surprising that from the beginning Walter Ulbricht opposed any direct contacts with Bonn officials until the West German government extended formal recognition to the DDR as a separate and equally sovereign state.

Moreover, Ulbricht and his colleagues demanded that the first step in any rapprochement be based on a recognition by the Western powers that West Berlin was an independent political entity "on the territory of the DDR" and had no right to claim any organic association with the Federal Republic. Implicit in this demand was the understanding that all access routes to West Berlin be turned over to the DDR, that Western garrisons be ousted from West Berlin, that the use of West German D-marks in West Berlin be terminated, and that West Berliners give up their West German passports. These questions constituted the most important barrier to any *detente*. But they could not be decided by the West German Foreign Minister, since they involved four-power agreements concluded in 1944 and 1945 which were still — at least nominally — in force. Brandt therefore urged four-power talks, which took place intermittently in Berlin among the ambassadors of the USSR, France, the United Kingdom, and the United States. The arguments were bitter, and bore no immediate fruit.

Indeed the four powers had been bickering about Berlin since 1945. The Russians had won a great victory in that the issue had been gradually changed from Berlin to West Berlin. Gradually, by constant repetition, the Communists succeeded in establishing at least the semantic recognition of East Berlin as the capital of the DDR and after the construction of the wall, arguments of access, of economic and political control, centered around West Berlin.

A nerve-jangling sort of merry-go-round began to revolve around West Berlin. The DDR insisted periodically on putting the squeeze on the city by clamping down on road, railroad, and barge traffic, to the vast irritation of the British, French, and Americans, who protested to the Russians, who in turn advised them to go directly to the East Germans, which on principle they refused to do.

I wish all the readers of this book had a chance to savor the exasperation caused by these harassments. As a poor substitute for the actual experience, let me tell you about a trip I took in 1968.

I had bought a SAAB in Stockholm and had driven into the Soviet Union through Finland. There were no serious problems or delays, and even though the Soviet authorities are not used to dealing with large numbers of automobile tourists and require far more documentation than is needed when crossing frontiers in Western Europe, they were polite, and the longest delay I had — on the Soviet side of the Finnish-Soviet frontier — was about twenty minutes. I happened to arrive at the Soviet-Polish frontier at the same time as a large Soviet motorcycle convoy on its way to a rally somewhere in Czechoslovakia, and could have been delayed for some time, but the Soviet officer in charge took me aside, along with a Frenchman in a Peugeot who had happened along at the same time, and cleared us through, five minutes ahead of the convoy. At the Polish-East German frontier, on a new bridge across the Oder, there was little traffic; formalities lasted about ten minutes, and I was speeding along over the autobahn toward Berlin. The road was well maintained, speed limits were clearly marked, and patrols enforced the limits — usually 100 kilometers per hour, or about 62 mph. Signs were clear and frequent, and I was beginning to feel comfortable, and thinking what a vast improvement this was over Poland or the Soviet Union.

Then I reached the Berliner Ring, the circular two-lane highway that circles Berlin just outside the city limits. There, clearly marked, was a detour: all vehicles other than those with DDR registration or specially authorized vehicles must proceed southward around the Ring and enter Berlin from the west. Whereas I could have been on the Frankfurterallee in fifteen minutes and at Alexanderplatz in half an hour, I had to drive nearly an hour around the Ring, the traffic getting heavier as I encountered other non-DDR vehicles coming to Berlin from Czechoslovakia and Bavaria in the south; then we all converged with Scandinavian vehicles coming in from the north on the main autobahn at the Soviet check point near Steinsdorf. There I found myself in a jam of some five hundred vehicles in a huge parking lot, awaiting clearance. Passengers had to get out of their vehicles and take their passports and automobile papers to a large waiting room, where they were surrendered through a small, high window to a surly Vopo. Someone told me that the wait for the documents would be about an hour, so I took a walk around the area, where arrogant Vopos dressed in uniforms reminiscent of those worn by the Nazis were inspecting vehicles. About forty-five minutes later I went to the other side of the waiting room, where a large crowd was standing and waiting for a Vopo to emerge from an inner office with a handful of documents. He would call a name, the individual would come to the front, the Vopo would examine him or her carefully to make sure the individual corresponded with the photograph on the document, and give him his papers with a number indicating where he was to present himself and his vehicle for inspection. In my case it took another hour before I could drive into the assigned inspection area.

"Get out of the car," said a Vopo with a scowl. I did. He opened the hood, looked under the seat cushions, poked into the tool kit. Then he took a gadget which is standard equipment at all DDR borders: a 12-inch × 18-inch mirror mounted on two small wheels with a handle about 4 feet long. Using this, the Vopo could examine the underside of the car thoroughly without getting his uniform dirty. I had only one suitcase, the contents of which he examined carefully. He noted the number of my typewriter. When all this was finally done, he gave me my documents and waved me on to the final clearance area. There, after another fifteen-minute wait my turn came; I was given one last perusal, and cleared through the heavy iron gates and around two concrete buttresses constructed to prevent anyone from literally crashing the frontier. At last I was off down the autobahn to Zehlendorf. Total time consumed in this crossing — just over two hours. With the delay caused by driving around the Ring — nearly half a day.

And this was a normal day. When the DDR authorities were staging one of their periodic slow-downs, the delay could have taken days.

The harassment was similar on trains that operate from West Berlin to West Germany, although few passengers chose this method of travel.

Only air traffic is unobstructed by the arrogant authorities of the DDR, who find this lack of power intolerable, and constantly raise the demand for DDR control of West Berlin's three airports. Periodically Russian or East German fighter planes buzz Berlin-bound aircraft, which must stay within one of three ten-mile-wide corridors, and below ten thousand feet, but so far no accidents have resulted from this outrageous practice.

A second complex of issues between the DDR and the Federal Republic which has caused much exasperation was the restriction on visits to the DDR by West Germans. Most citizens of the Federal Republic have become accustomed to the fact that East Germans are not permitted out of the country, nor are they likely to enjoy foreign travel privileges any time in the near future. But the West Germans failed to see why the Pankow government was so adamant in restricting their visits to the DDR except in unusual circumstances. As for West Berliners, they were unable to visit the DDR legally under *any* circumstances, since the DDR authorities did not recognize their use of Federal Republic documents. There was great pressure in West Germany for an attempt to negotiate some sort of relaxation of these restrictions. This pressure gave Willy Brandt the public support he needed when he began his efforts to establish official contacts with the DDR.

General elections were scheduled to be held in West Germany in the autumn of 1969, and the business recession that had set in led to a growing discontent with the Kiesinger government. Brandt's party, the SPD, formed a coalition ("The Little Coalition") with the FDP (Free Democratic Party) and with a paper-thin majority in the *Bundestag*, Brandt became Chancellor, and took office on October 21, 1969. His efforts as Foreign Minister to establish some sort of working relations with the DDR had been widely and usually favorably reported throughout West Germany. In the meantime, he had maintained good relations with the United States and the other Western Allies. The climate was good and the time ripe for him to push further his *Ostpolitik*.

Brandt quickly put his ideas into action and began to arrange for visits to Warsaw and Moscow, with the aim of signing treaties with Poland and the USSR. Egon Bahr, meanwhile, had been meeting fairly frequently with Michael Kohl of the DDR in East Berlin and Bonn, and gradually arranging for small concessions which would make day-to-day life between the two Germanies more viable, such as increased visiting privileges for West Germans to East Berlin (the DDR, of course, would not agree to allow the East Germans to visit West Berlin freely), speedier telephone communications, and less harassment at the border crossings.

But the most important result of the preliminary talks was the arrangement for Willy Brandt to meet personally with DDR Prime Minister Willi Stoph. The first meeting was to take place in Erfurt, in the DDR, the second in Kassel in the Federal Republic.

The substance of the talks in both meetings was neither well publicized nor particularly significant. But demonstrations that took place around both meetings were both widely reported and most interesting.

Brandt arrived in Erfurt on March 3, 1970 by private train. His official welcome by the DDR authorities was cool, and the East German police had taken measures to prevent any spontaneous demonstrations by residents of the city, including the fact that no public announcement had been made of the time and place of the talks. But the measures were inadequate, and as Brandt's train arrived, a huge crowd had assembled at the train station. They broke through the barriers, and were shoved back by Vopos, at whom they screamed: "Why can't we stand here? We're not criminals!" Brandt was whisked away to his room in the Erfurter Hof, but here, too, a crowd of about two thousand had gathered and called him to his window. When he appeared on the balcony, they started cheering and shouting, "Long live Willi Brandt! Success! Courage!" More Vopos were brought in to keep the crowds in order, there was shoving back and forth, the crowd began to split up into discussion groups, and "for a short time, Erfurt was the capital of Germany."[3] The East German authorities, embarrassed, arranged for demonstrators to be brought in from the factories to stage a "spontaneous" demonstration in favor of Willi Stoph. They were instructed to call out slogans showing their support of the SED, and were relieved every two hours by new groups of "spontaneous" demonstrators.

In the afternoon Brandt was scheduled to visit Buchenwald, and on his return from the site of the notorious concentration camp, thousands of East German citizens lined the highway, waving and cheering. Some of these demonstrators were beaten and carried away, and later two thousand of them were "identified" and handled accordingly by the East German authorities. That evening, Brandt left again by train, as planned, accompanied to the railroad station by Stoph, where again a crowd had assembled. But as the train pulled out, the cries were suddenly in *favor* of Willi Stoph, who raised his hand like a winner.

Later, both leaders were asked for comments about the Erfurt happenings. Brandt smiled: "The day enriched my life." Stoph, more coolly: "The meeting was useful."

But the demonstrations in favor of Brandt had been most embarrassing to the DDR, as they so vividly demonstrated the lack of popular support of the Pankow government among the people. Some West German observers were apprehensive that Ulbricht, who was known to have opposed the meetings, would force the cancellation of the second meeting. This was not done. Instead the East German authorities made quiet preparations in cooperation with West German Communists for a counter-demonstration which turned out to be nearly as spectacular as the performance in Erfurt.

The number of loyal Communists in West Germany is not known officially, but is estimated to be very small, because in the past few years (since the Communist Party has become legal again in West Germany) the Communists have not been able to muster up even enough votes to place their candidates on the ballots in national or regional elections. But among the Federal Republic's 61 million citizens there are, nonetheless, several tens of thousands of sympathizers. A number of these were quietly mobilized and organized, and thanks to the unrestricted freedom of travel in the Federal Republic converged on Kassel on the eve of Willi Stoph's arrival on May 21, 1970. They carried folded placards and banners, and even erected a beer tent replete with DDR music and propaganda.

On the next morning, Stoph arrived as scheduled, and was escorted with his delegation to the rooms reserved for them at the Kasseler Schloss hotel. Now the crowds started converging on the hotel. Although Stoph did not appear at the window, the demonstrators started calling his name and generally creating a ruckus. Suddenly, a group of young people of rightist leanings (theoretically members of the NPD, or Neo-Nazi Party, although some observers felt that they were really Communist Party members disguised and brought in for the purpose of creating havoc) began marching toward the hotel in a *Schweigemarsch* (silent march). Fighting immediately broke out, and shortly before lunch the DDR flag was torn down from the flagpole in front of the hotel.

Inside the hotel, the meetings had been continuing regardless, and Stoph and his delegation, unperturbed, appeared at lunch. After lunch Stoph was scheduled to make a trip to a monument in Kassel, which had been erected shortly after the war to remind the Germans of the crimes of the Nazis, where Stoph was to lay down a laurel wreath. But he and his aides now retired to their quarters in a huff, claiming that the West German police were not giving them adequate protection, and refused to carry on with their plans until Willy Brandt cajoled them by saying he would accompany them on the trip to the monument. All along the route in both directions, demonstrations both for and against the DDR continued, but by now the police had them enough under control so that no serious incidents occurred, and the DDR delegation was brought safely back to the hotel. Toward evening, Brandt accompanied Stoph to the railroad station, where a group of pro-DDR demonstrators had gathered to give Stoph a send-off. The train was a bit late, but Brandt maintained enough presence of mind to tell a few jokes and then shake hands with Stoph as he headed off home.

Later, the East German press used the Kassel demonstrations to add fuel to the fire, and claimed that they showed "new evidence of the Fascist, war-mongering, revanchist nature of the government of the Federal Republic, perhaps most of all its allegedly Marxist Chancellor, Willy Brandt" and the "inability of the Federal Republic to keep peace within its own land."

But the dialogue between the DDR and the Federal Republic had begun, and although Brandt was deeply upset by the disorders in Kassel, another force was at work in his favor, namely the Soviet preoccupation with the Chinese, which followed the serious military conflicts along the Ussuri River and in Central Asia in 1969 and 1970. The Soviet government mounted a substantial military build-up of perhaps a million men along the Chinese frontier, and even the Soviet public press expressed concern for the security of such cities as Vladivostok, Khabarovsk, Chita, and even Alma Ata, all of which lie within a few miles of the Chinese frontier, not to speak of the strategic Trans-Siberian railroad which runs along the frontier for hundreds of miles. In view of this conflict with the Chinese, the Russians wanted quiet in Europe. They did not want any confrontations with the West Germans or their allies. And their impatience with the abrasive intransigence of aging Walter Ulbricht finally reached the point where, in May 1971, they forced him to resign, on grounds of poor health and advancing age, in favor of Erich Honecker.

At the end of November 1969, Bonn had already proposed meetings between West German officials and Polish and Russian officials. In January 1970, Egon Bahr traveled to Moscow, now with the title of State Secretary, representing Chancellor Brandt, who had just moved into his new office. He went to arrange for Brandt to pay an official visit to Moscow and to lay the foundations for a new policy of peace and cooperation between the Soviet Union and the Federal Republic of Germany.

During this and subsequent visits he found the climate favorable. The Russians wanted a *detente* with Germany in order to be able to deal more flexibly and decisively with the Chinese. They wanted technological and financial support from West Germany in developing those many areas of industry in which the Soviet Union lagged behind the more developed capitalist countries — automobile manufacture, chemical industries, certain kinds of machine manufacture. In return, the Russians were willing to stop using West German revanchists and neo-Fascists as a devil image, on whom the blame for assorted Soviet failures and shortcomings was placed. The Soviet press did indeed stop its vicious attacks beginning in early 1970, and well they might, since Moscow had acquired in China a more up-to-date, more real, and more plausible devil image.

In his official visit to Moscow in August 1970, Brandt was well received, the talks proceeded productively. In a later, less formal, but much more revealing visit, which Brandt made at the personal invitation of Leonid Brezhnev to spend a few days with him in his official summer house in the Crimea, Brandt was given a rare view of the way in which Soviet policy decisions are made.

Nor did Brandt neglect his Western allies. He paid regular visits to London, Paris, and Washington, and managed to establish close personal relations with Richard Nixon, perhaps because Nixon, like Brandt, started at the bottom, from a lower middle class and undistinguished milieu.

These efforts, backed by a large part of the German business community which was suffering a recession and wanted to increase trade and cooperation in Eastern Europe, and by a substantial part of the West German intelligentsia, which was disillusioned with the United States because of the Vietnam War and wanted Germany to have a more even-handed foreign policy, bore fruit in the Moscow Treaty, signed on August 12, 1970.

The main points in the Moscow Treaty were the following:

1. Both parties will seek to bring continued peace and security to Europe and the world; they will try to "normalize" the situation in Europe and give their support to the growth of friendly relations between European nations.
2. Both parties will follow rules laid down in the charter of the United Nations. They will solve mutual problems by

> friendly means, and will refrain from using force or the threat of force to achieve their aims.
>
> 3. Both parties agree that to achieve peace in Europe, the present boundaries now established must not be touched. They agree to observe the territorial integrity of all nations in Europe, they agree that neither side has any further territorial claims to make, and they regard — today and in the future — the frontiers of all nations in Europe to be unchangeable, including the Oder-Neisse Line, which forms the western border of Poland, and the border between the Federal Republic and the DDR.

Now the way was paved for making a Polish treaty. Discussions with Poland had been conducted since February 1970, and, following Moscow's lead, the Polish authorities finally arranged for Brandt to come to Warsaw in early December 1970, to sign the treaty which, like the Moscow Treaty, had been worked on laboriously for months in advance. On December 7, Brandt traveled to Warsaw, and in addition to the signing of the treaty, one of the most striking episodes of his career occurred when he was being shown around the city. In front of the dignified monument built on what used to be one of the entrances to the Warsaw Ghetto, where thousands of desperate Jewish insurrectionists were slaughtered by German troops in 1944, Brandt stood in silence as assorted Polish dignitaries watched. Then he sank to his knees and bowed his head for a long minute of symbolic shame for the misdeeds of other Germans and of tribute to their victims.

The Warsaw Treaty was duly signed, and the main points of this treaty were:

> 1. The Oder-Neisse-Line,[4] as it now stands, forms the western border of the People's Republic of Poland. Both

parties agree that now and in the future this border is unchangeable, and they pledge themselves to mutual respect of territorial integrity. Neither party has now, nor will raise in the future, any territorial claims.
2. Both parties, in the interest of security of Europe, agree to abide by rules laid down in the charter of the United Nations. They will solve mutual problems by friendly means, and will refrain from using force or the threat of force to achieve their aims.
3. Both parties will take further steps to "normalize" their relations, and it is agreed by both parties that cooperation in the fields of economics, science, technology, culture, and other relations would be to the advantage of both parties.

Further, Brandt managed to get the Poles to agree to allow ethnic Germans living in Poland to leave the frontier provinces and go to Germany, an agreement which was made official and public by the Polish government on November 18, 1970, and which began to go into effect, with the help of the German Red Cross, after the Warsaw Treaty had been signed.

But the most unique and significant thing about both the Moscow and the Warsaw treaties was the fact that Brandt specified publicly at the time that he would present the treaties for ratification to the Bundestag *only* after a satisfactory Berlin settlement was made.

The responsibility for reaching a Berlin agreement rested, of course, on the Allied powers. After renewed and often bitter negotiations, the ambassadors of the United States, the Soviet Union, France, and the United Kingdom finally did formulate a settlement[5] which guaranteed access to West Berlin by rail, road, air, and canal; which provided for periodic and regular holiday visits to the DDR by West Germans and West Berliners, whereby there would be no harassment on the border, cars and suitcases would no longer be subject to search, and tourists would no longer be required to pay a visitor's fee; which accepted the *de facto* integration of West Berlin in the economy of the Federal Republic. On the other hand, the West Germans were to avoid holding demonstrative or provocative political meetings in West Berlin. The Russians agreed to force the government of the DDR to accept these conditions and crush any stubborn resistance to the implementation of the settlement which die-hard Ulbricht followers in East Berlin might make.

Having thus forged the main elements of his policy for peace, Brandt, his parliamentary majority pared to as little as one vote on several occasions, faced the Herculean task of winning ratification of the *Ostverträge,* and preparing to defend himself and the SPD in the elections anticipated for early 1973, and of dealing with economic recession and the financial problems growing out of the awkward strength of the D-mark.

But Brandt had made a good start. He had won wide approval from the most diverse elements among the German people, far beyond the blue-collar workers and liberal intellectuals who form the mass of the SPD. A close friend in Düsseldorf, a baron of aristocratic Schlesian origin, a tank officer for four years during the war, twice wounded on the Russian front, a congenital conservative, and bitter anti-Communist confided to me: "I voted for Brandt in 1969, and I probably will do so again. The CDU [Christian Democratic Union] has nothing to offer the country . . ."

9

Soviet Policy On Germany

Before taking a look at the state of the two Germanies today, it seems useful to examine briefly the role of the Soviet Union in the evolution and the future of both the DDR and the Federal Repulic.

Today, Soviet troops sit in solidly built, permanent barracks less than fifty miles from Hamburg and Kassel and only slightly more than one hundred miles from the Rhine. Soviet forces in Germany constitute the largest military establishment in Europe, and—particularly since the reduction in forces of the U.S. Seventh Army in West Germany—the Soviet military enjoys clear *de facto* control of all of Central Europe, limited only by Moscow's preoccupation with China, and the deterrent of nuclear stalemate between the United States and the USSR.

So it is necessary to ask: what do the Russians want in or from Germany?

To begin with, the Russians — indeed all the Slavs — fear and distrust the Germans for reasons going far back in history. In the early Middle Ages, Slavic tribesmen and peasants inhabited not only the territory of today's Poland, but large areas to the west. The Wends — a Slavic tribe — are still in evidence today in much of Mecklenburg, an area west of Berlin, although their Slavic language has all but disappeared and most Wends consider themselves, and are considered, Germans. But in the aftermath of the Crusades, German knights pushed eastward and established their control over most of Silesia and East Prussia, then founded cities on the Baltic Sea, conquering and vassalizing the local Latvian, Lithuanian, and Estonian peasants. The progeny of these German conquerers became the ruling class, the landed gentry, of what is today western Poland and the Baltic states, though the basic population of most of these areas remained Slavic. During the seventeenth century another wave of Germans moved eastward, this time not as conquerors but as skilled artisans and settlers, often invited by local rulers who were anxious to use German proficiency and diligence for the development of their own countries. Such a group was the Volga Germans, invited by Catherine the Great (see Chapter 5, page 103).

These historic circumstances led to a combination of admiration and respect for German skill and efficiency with envy, distrust, and dislike for these wooden-minded foreigners who were always working and trying to regiment others.

Then came three invasions. The first was organized

and led by Napoleon under the tricolor of France, but a large part of his armies consisted of Hessian and other German mercenaries. Then, in World War I, German armies took over most of the Ukraine, created a puppet regime, and did their best to exploit the country for more than two years. Finally, in 1939, German armies overran much of Poland, and in 1941 invaded the Soviet Union, going as far as the Volga and the North Caucasus, inflicting enormous losses on the Soviet forces, and causing the death of perhaps 18 million Soviet people.

It is important to remember that thanks to Stalin's forced collectivization of agriculture, his paranoid purges, and the fact that communism was resented by many religious Russians, millions of Soviet citizens were bitterly antagonistic to the Soviet government. They waited eagerly for a German invasion which, they hoped, would liberate them from Communist tyranny. If Hitler and his government had followed rational policies — dissolved the collective farms, allowed free local elections, cooperated in a religious revival — they could have had overwhelming popular support, particularly in the Ukraine. But they did not. Arrogantly confident of military victory and dedicated to the thesis that the "master-race" Germans were destined to rule over the inferior Slavs, the Germans permitted no local self-administration. Because the Germans were desperate for food, they left the collective farms intact, hoping to use them to squeeze out of the rich Ukrainian and Russian farmlands enough to fulfill their needs. Otherwise, the invading Nazis did everything to antagonize and embitter the local population.[1] As a result, although nearly a million Soviet prisoners of war more or less voluntarily joined General Vlasov's Russian Liberation Army or even regular German army units, and fought on the side of the Nazis until the bitter end, the overwhelming majority of the Soviet population backed the war effort of their own government. Thus at war's end millions of Soviet citizens hated and feared the Germans for historical reasons, added to which was the resentment growing out of the fact that they had hoped for liberation by the Germans, and had been bitterly disappointed. In addition to that, of course, hardly a Soviet family had not suffered immediate losses at the Germans' hands, and millions of families had lost everything.

These facts were cleverly used by the propaganda organs in the Soviet Union, and by the authorities in charge of the repatriation of Soviet prisoners of war and civilians and of the rotation of Soviet occupation forces in Germany. As a general rule, any Soviet citizen who had been in Germany under Nazi jurisdiction was assumed to have been a traitor to the Soviet Union and was sent off to distant labor camps in Siberia, from which few returned. Soviet soldiers and others who came into Germany as victors, but who might have formed sympathetic feelings for the Germans, were likewise isolated from the Soviet population on their return home.

Although the government in Moscow already in 1946 began cooperating with and supporting the German Communists and helping them create a government and even an army, this was given little publicity in the Soviet Union. Every medium of Soviet propaganda worked night and day on the drumbeat theme of the "iniquity of the Germans," the "neo-Nazi warmongering and revanchist character of the West German government," and the "ever-present danger of another German invasion of Eastern Europe" if due precautions were not taken. This went on from the late 1940s until 1970, and conditioned an entire generation of Soviet citizens.

This anti-German sentiment among the Soviet people was in part the result of real German crimes and actions, historic and recent; but it was also in part the conscious creation of a Soviet government wrestling with increasingly difficult economic and political problems, desirous of presenting a plausible and convincing "devil image" to the people, which could explain to them their assorted woes.

On several occasions I have had the chance to talk with senior Soviet military men, and have read carefully some military publications from Moscow, and am convinced that Soviet military leaders are not worried about another German invasion of Russia any time in the forseeable future. In the last third of the twentieth century the Germans lack the population, the resources, and the political power to undertake an invasion even of some small neighbor, particularly as long as Germany is divided into two antagonistic states.

Top Soviet leadership realizes full well that the great threat for the Soviet Union in the future is China, particularly if that country should form an alliance or association with the United States. For these leaders, the Germans and the two German states are not something to be feared, disliked, admired, or envied; they are something to be *used*.

In dealing with almost any open society, such as France or Sweden or even India or Japan, one could expect that popular attitudes and predispositions would play a significant role in determining policies with reference to other states or nations. But the Soviet Union does not fall into this category. Soviet policies are determined by the leaders of the Communist Party. When Stalin was alive, this leadership rested almost solely in his hands. Since his death the base of power has been broadened to include perhaps a dozen men, of whom at this moment Leonid Brezhnev is number one, followed closely by Alexei Kosygin and Nikolai Podgorny. These men consult technical experts, of course, and also work with other members of the Politbureau such as Mikhail Suslov and Dmitri Polyansky; and in defense matters they certainly consult with Marshal Grechko and other military commanders.

Decisions are made by the top two or three men. But no attempt (or even pretence of one) is made to consult with the public which, indeed, is often not even informed of the nature of decisions being studied or made.

So, it is top Soviet leadership that uses the two Germanies in the interests of furthering the objectives of the Communist Party, namely the establishment of a worldwide Communist system controlled as far as possible by Soviet leadership, and the realization of traditional historic Russian interests: security against invasion from either East or West; access to the Mediterranean and the Persian Gulf; as large a share as possible of the world's resources; a maximum of technical and financial support in building up the Soviet economy and making it self-sufficient and strong.

In making its plans to use the two Germanies, the Soviet leadership must and does take into consideration external factors. One is the fact that most of Germany's neighbors—the Netherlands, Belgium, Denmark, France, Austria, and even Czechoslovakia, which is to some degree still an open society—fear Germany and do not want German reunification no matter what kind of government is in power there. With nearly 80 million Germans in the DDR and the Federal Republic combined, and several more millions of German-speaking, German-thinking men and women in Austria, northern Italy, and the Balkans, the Germans are by far the most numerous ethnic group in Europe. And they have a bad record in recent times of trying to impose their will on their neighbors. Thus, by blocking German reunification, the Soviet government finds support among both the governments and the people in western and central Europe. Because of this factor, I believe that even if Moscow thought it possible to manipulate a German reunification which would bring the Communists to power in a new Greater Germany, they would not do it. The Soviet government prefers to maintain its present amicable relations with most of Germany's neighbors, and, on its own account, would fear competition sometime in the future from a united, even though Communist-led Germany.

A second fact is that the Soviet economy is still less developed than the leading capitalist states in many areas of industry, science, and technology, and both Germanies can be useful in helping the Soviet economy catch up.

The Soviet Union's natural resources are immense in nearly every category. The population is numerous and diligent, and now fairly well trained in industry and technology. But the system is top-heavy, over-centralized, and inefficient. Furthermore it is subordinated to political power plays and the realization of Marxist objectives. Also, certain fields of endeavor take priority over others. In those areas such as space research, military engineering, and certain branches of metallurgy to which the ablest people and most valuable resources have been assigned, the Soviet Union has done very well. In 1971 the USSR built 18 nuclear submarines, the United States built 4. In 1971 the Soviet Union produced 134 million ingot tons of steel, the United States 120, Japan about 90, and the two Germanies combined about 51. But in vast and important areas of production the Soviet Union is far behind the most advanced nations of Western Europe, North America, and Japan.

A good example is the automotive industry. At the present time, the United States has about 90 million registered passenger motor vehicles, the Soviet Union about 1 million. The DDR and Czechoslovakia both have many more automobiles per thousand population than have the Russians, while the Italians, British, and French have far more.[2]

Furthermore, in styling, design, and quality Soviet motor vehicles are some twenty years behind those made by the more advanced nations. What does one do when faced with this kind of situation? One thing to do is to dig in, spend money on research and development, and make up the gap by concentrated effort. The other thing one can do is to try to get advanced technology from those who have it. But the Soviet Union is shockingly short of investment capital and of foreign exchange, and as we shall see, had to try to get foreign technology on credit.

Soviet exports consist largely of primary commodities—ores, fossil fuels, grains in good crop years, forest products. Even with their East European fellow Socialist states and fellow members of Comecon, the Soviet Union has a colonial trade structure, importing manufactured goods and exporting raw materials. As the prices of primary commodities tend to fall and those of manufactured goods to rise, the Russians become increasingly the victims of this deterioration in the terms of trade. In dealing with the East European states, which are militarily and politically under Soviet control, through bilateral trade agreements the USSR has been systematically able to overcharge for its exports and underpay for its imports, thus easing the strain on its own economy. But with the capitalist states, the Soviet Union must sell for what it can get, and pay the market prices for purchases, making the Soviet economy consistently short of hard currency, in spite of the fact that all Soviet imports are controlled by the Ministry for Foreign Trade—that is, by the government—and practically no luxury consumer goods are imported.

This shortage of foreign exchange is visible in the black market in foreign currency which runs about three to one against the ruble both in Moscow and in foreign money markets. The Moscow black market is, of course, illegal. And if you ever go to Moscow, I advise you not to use it. Police provocations are frequent; if caught, you go to jail, and unless you have a diplomatic passport, the Embassy cannot help you. The money markets in London, Vienna, and Zurich are also illegal as far as the ruble is concerned, because it is illegal to take a ruble out of the Soviet Union. But rubles in all these free markets fetch about one third of their legal value, which is about $1.25 per ruble. In order to secure hard currency needed to buy the things it wants from the capitalist states, the Soviet government has set up an elaborate network of foreign currency stores, bars, and restaurants in nearly every city and international airport in the Soviet Union. In these stores, a traveler with dollars or sterling or D-marks can buy items such as black caviar — now almost unavailable in the Soviet domestic market because pollution and desiccation of the Caspian Sea have cut production to something like one-third the level of a generation ago.

These stores and restaurants are the cause of much critical comment from Soviet citizens and travelers from other Socialist states. I remember going to the foreign currency bar of the Astoria Hotel in Leningrad one evening, where a large sign above the bar stated: "Payment accepted only in dollars, pounds, marks, French, Swiss, and Belgian francs, shillings, guilders, yen," and so forth. An East German came in, tried to buy a drink with East German marks, and was curtly refused. He made quite a scene, but got nowhere, nor did any of the other patrons sympathize with him. I have seen Soviet citizens shout and hammer on tables when their rubles are refused in these stores and restaurants, but to no avail.

The reason for this situation is of course simple: the Soviet bloc economies, on the average, are much less efficient than the free market economies, and this reflects itself in high prices and often simple unavailability of consumer goods. Does this necessarily have to be so? No. Theoretically, if the Soviet Union would decentralize its economy, allow normal incentives to operate unrestricted by political dictation and by several hundred thousand Party *apparatchiks* who now use their control of the allocation of resources to maintain their own power and privileges—in short, if the Communist Party gave up a centrally planned economy in favor of a freer and more flexible system, I believe it could become substantially more efficient. This is what the Czechs were trying to do in 1968, but the Soviet military intervention put a rude end to the reforms and to the dreams of many Western liberals and enlightened Communists of a "socialism with a human face."

And so the Soviet economy struggles on, spending heavily—and effectively—on arms, both for Soviet use and for the pursuit of Soviet political objectives in the Arab world and in countries like North Vietnam. They tinker with their economy within the framework of ideological orthodoxy; they organized 102 regional economic councils, then abolished them two years later when they produced no visible results; they go all out for the production and use of chemical fertilizers, but fear to make the collective farm system truly voluntary because the *kolkhozes* (collective farms) might disappear within a few months, as they no doubt would, taking the country's agriculture out from under Party control. And year after year, the country that was the world's largest producer and exporter of wheat in 1913 continues to face periodic grain shortages which must be made up by large imports from Canada, the United States, and Australia.

This is the economic framework within which Soviet leaders seek to use the two Germanies. And they are doing it pretty well.

The DDR supplies the Soviet Union with a large assortment and substantial volume of high technology exports for which the Soviet government pays in raw materials deliveries. During 1970 the DDR exported 419 million valuta* marks worth of machinery for the fishing industry to the USSR, over 300 million marks worth of jacks, lifting equipment, conveyors, and similar items, almost 280 million marks worth of tractors and other agricultural machines, over 200 million marks worth of furniture, and about 100 million marks each of optical-mechanical equipment and photochemical products. For its part, the DDR imported great quantities of petroleum (over 9 million tons), steel pipes (over 102,000 tons), electrotechnical and electronic equipment (in value exceeding 155 million valuta marks) and 131,691 hectoliters (about $2\frac{1}{2}$ million gallons) of wine and champagne from the USSR in 1970.

The DDR hosts about 350,000 Soviet troops who live in comfortable quarters and carry out joint maneuvers with the East German, Polish, Czech, and Hungarian forces. The Rumanians have recently refrained from participating in these exercises as a symbol of their independent foreign policy. The DDR maintains a substantial foreign aid program which is coordinated by the

---

*A valuta mark is a unit of bookkeeping, equal to the theoretical value of a mark—about 30 cents in American money.

Skatchkov Committee, officially titled the Committee for Foreign Economic Cooperation, based in Moscow, and equivalent to AID of the United States.

On their side, the Russians in effect maintain the DDR government in power. They lend it support in bidding for participation in international organizations such as the United Nations. They help protect it against menaces such as the Czechoslovak reform movement of 1968. Only in extreme circumstances, such as those which existed in late 1970 and early 1971, when Ulbricht's sectarianism and stubborn chauvinism began to stand in the way of Soviet objectives farther west, did the Russians turn on the aging zealot and force him out in favor of Moscow-trained Erich Honecker, sixty, no liberal, but far more flexible and cooperative than Ulbricht.

In sum, the Soviet government has used the DDR very effectively, and in the process the DDR has become, as previously noted, the world's eighth largest industrial producer, with a standard of living far higher than that in the Soviet Union itself. The Soviet government gives every indication of intending to continue these relations with the DDR. This intention can be perceived by reading carefully the attacks made in the Soviet press against two former Soviet leaders who are now discredited—Lavrenti Beria and Georgi Malenkow. These men are accused of having planned to abandon the DDR in the late 1940s because it taxed Soviet military and economic power too heavily. Beria, particularly, it has been alleged, wanted to remove all German industry and leave the East Germans to grow potatoes. Beria was executed in 1953, only several months after the death of Stalin. I personally doubt that this is an accurate summary of Beria's position on Germany, but the attacks do indicate that the present leaders intend to do the opposite of what they accuse Beria of having planned.

The Soviet government has tried, also with considerable success, to use the Federal Republic. Soviet leaders, perhaps misled by East German Communists, may have thought right after the war that the West German Communists might be able to seize power as Allied military presence was withdrawn. But the misbehavior of the Soviet occupation troops in every area they touched had made the Russians feared and hated by most Germans. On the other hand, the positive assistance given to the West Germans by the Allies had created feelings of respect and gratitude, particularly for the British and the Americans. As early as 1946 I remember Soviet friends in the military government telling me that, "of course West Germany will not go Communist now. Perhaps later, when the contradictions of capitalism again make themselves felt, and when the Americans get tired of paying all the bills . . ."

So, for more than a decade the Soviet government used the West German economy as best it could, demanding that the Western Allies deliver specific West German factories, installations, and merchant vessels to the Russians as reparations, milking the West German economy by the use of occupation marks until the currency reform of 1948, and encouraging the West Germans to carry out a buoyant foreign trade with the DDR which was highly beneficial to the latter, and hence indirectly to the Russians. Meanwhile the Soviet press attacked the West German government with monotonous consistency, making it a scapegoat for everything that went wrong anywhere in Eastern Europe. It tried successfully, for years, to prevent the establishment of diplomatic relations between West Germany and the East European states. It even managed to point its finger at West Germany's "intriguing" as the excuse for the invasion of Czechoslovakia in August 1968.

While carrying out these attacks, the Soviet government quietly increased its trade with West Germany very substantially. In 1966, for example, the total amount of import/export activity between the USSR and the Federal Republic was about 1.5 billion D-marks. Two years later (1968) it had already risen to 2.3 billion D-marks, and since then has been increasing progressively. And Moscow contrived to maintain a solid negative balance of trade with the Federal Republic, which means that it imported more from Germany than it exported there, and got the Bonn government to make up the difference in credits, which amounted to 550 million D-marks for 1971, and at the end of 1971 came to a cumulative 300 million dollars plus.

But no really big deals were made. And during the late 1960s the Russians became more and more interested in engaging in major technological and financial arrangements with the Federal Republic. The Russians were able, of course, to offer the Germans things the Germans needed. The principal item was energy. West German coal mines were getting deeper and deeper and less efficient. Petroleum furnished an increasing share of the economy's energy. Most of the petroleum came from the Middle East. But the Russians offered an alternative, and even built a pipeline, the Druzhba or Friendship line from the Soviet Ural oilfields right into East Germany and Austria. Soviet petroleum exports to West Germany amounted to about 10 percent of the Federal Republic's consumption.

But then the Russians developed a vast new gas field near Serpukhov, southeast of Moscow, and completed a gasline grid running up from the Caucasus, and in 1970 they offered a deal which provided for the construction of a huge 56-inch pipeline from the Soviet Union into Central Europe, which would be able to deliver to West Germany some 7 billion cubic meters of gas a year by 1979, provided that the Italians (who were also to get gas from it) and the Germans rolled the pipe and helped install the line. The Germans and the Italians agreed, and the line is now being built. It will be a major factor in the energy balance of the Federal Republic, and will help tide the country over what was feared would be a major energy shortage in the mid and late 1970s due to the booming growth of Germany's consumption (about 9 percent a year) and the unreliability of deliveries from the crisis-ridden Middle East.

After the signing of the Moscow Treaty the Russians hoped for even bigger deals. They wanted Daimler-Benz of Stuttgart, the manufacturer of the excellent Mercedes motor vehicles, to take a major part in modernizing the Soviet automotive industry. But Hermes, the West German government export credit guarantee corporation, refused to guarantee the credits for a heavy truck plant which were to amount to more than 1 billion dollars. Without the Hermes guarantee, the German banks would not put up the money as the Russians offered no equity or collateral. And the deal fell through. The Russians finally concluded agreements with Fiat of Italy for a large passenger automobile plant, and with Renault of France for the heavy truck plant. Fiat and Renault furnished the technology and helped arrange the credits. The Russians were angry and disappointed with the Germans, and expressed these sentiments publicly.

Soviet hopes for more imports from Germany were no doubt intensifed by the monetary events of 1971 and 1972 – the weakening of the dollar, and the substantial appreciation of the D-mark and particularly of the Japanese yen. Many top functionaries in the various Soviet ministries, in Gosplan, and in the Party and government leadership still view the United States as the world's greatest power in both financial and technological terms. But the more flexible and better-informed leaders realize that in early 1973 the West Germans and Japanese both have more gold and foreign exchange reserves than the United States; that in such activities as shipbuilding the Japanese have now left the Americans far behind in design, quality, price, and volume of production; that the current breakthrough development in the automotive industry — the Wankel rotary engine — is a German invention developed and perfected by the Japanese; that in many industries — steel, machine building, chemicals, and others — the United States is no longer the world's leader. Soviet economists see quantified evidence of these developments in the mounting adverse United States trade balances, and the immense budgetary deficits of fiscal years 1972 and 1973.

In short, while the Russians wanted and hoped to get a *detente* with the United States and increased inputs and technological support, they were increasingly anxious to get more of everything from the Federal Republic.

During the late 1960s, Soviet attitudes and political and economic objectives with regard to the two Germanies and the rest of Europe began to be focused by Moscow in its demands for a Conference of European Security and Cooperation (CESC). First proposed by the Russians in 1968, its general objectives were clear enough. Though the Soviet Union had fallen heir to Eastern Europe after World War II — 100 million people in six allegedly sovereign states — the Soviet Union had garrisoned the area with Soviet troops. The garrison today is about twenty-two divisions in the DDR, about six in Czechoslovakia, three each in Hungary and Poland — about thirty-four divisions or something like half a million troops. They found it necessary to use these forces in the DDR in 1953, in Hungary in 1956, and in Czechoslovakia in 1968.

On each of these occasions, if the Soviet government had been unable or unwilling to use military power, their Eastern European "Commonwealth" and security zone would have fallen apart under their noses. None of these three military operations was at all hazardous for the Soviet Union: expenses were small and losses were negligible. But politically all were most awkward. They blemished the image that the Soviet Union was trying so hard to create for the world, the image of a kindly, peace-loving Soviet Union living in harmony and cooperation with its smaller partners and neighbors.

With some reason Moscow felt that the consolidation of its control of East Europe was inhibited by the very existence of West Berlin, and by assorted activities such as the broadcasts of Radio Free Europe, RIAS, and Deutsche Welle. The fact that the territorial boundaries made by the Russians after the war, and the very existence of the DDR had not been recognized by the Western community also worked to their distinct disadvantage. A European Security Conference would secure precisely this recognition, Soviet leaders hoped and believed. It might even achieve the optimal objective of an international underwriting of East Europe's frontiers so that if the Czechs, for example, rebelled again, they would be subdued or at least discouraged by Western troops.

The Warsaw Pact meeting in Prague in October 1969 formally proclaimed that a Conference of European Security and Cooperation could be convened in Helsinki in the first half of 1970. This and other early proposals ignored such questions as United States and Canadian participation, and the many specific issues involved in Europe's security, such as the Mutual and Balanced Reduction of forces of the East and West (MBRF), SALT (Strategic Arms Limitations Talks), the signing of a peace treaty with the Federal Republic, and a solution of the problem of Berlin, or of West Berlin. No doubt some Kremlin optimists hoped that the Western powers could be persuaded to agree to a conference which would accomplish several specific objectives as well as the general one outlined above: a *de facto* recognition of the DDR by the Western European states, the elimination or at least diminution of United States influence in Europe, and a Europe consisting in the West of a number of loosely associated but fully independent and sovereign states, while the East would be a solid and disciplined bloc firmly controlled by Moscow.

These Soviet aims were transparent enough, and the NATO council, meeting in Brussels in 1969, suggested a study of CESC. It noted the recent Soviet naval buildup in the Mediterranean as something such a conference might discuss, as well as Berlin, a "just and lasting German settlement," the recognition of "the sovereign equality, political independence and territorial integrity (of the European states) on which there is, as yet, no common interpretation . . ." The Council wound up welcoming the bilateral SALT talks, and stated that the North American members of NATO would "of course" participate in any European Security Conference that took place.

This was not at all what the Soviet leadership had had in mind, if only because sovereign equality, political independence, and territorial integrity were not compatible with the Brezhnev doctrine, which held that the interests and actions of individual members of the Socialist bloc must be subordinated to the interests of the whole bloc (as interpreted by Moscow) and of socialism everywhere.

But the Kremlin leaders still thought that CESC could be useful, and in a series of pronouncements during early 1970 they tacitly agreed to United States and Canadian participation and dismissed the suggestion of MBRF as an artificial obstacle created by the NATO powers to obstruct the conference, which, everyone began to realize, would have more than thirty participating states and would therefore be poorly equipped to take up specific problems such as MBRF which essentially involved the

United States and the USSR. Moscow further insisted that a German settlement was an entirely separate problem and should not be tied to the Security Conference. While Moscow made these concrete points the East European press began running articles depicting the rosy future of a Europe of peace and cooperation whose realization was currently obstructed by NATO and the Common Market.

In May 1970 the text of the renewed Soviet-Czechoslovak Friendship Treaty was published, embodying the Brezhnev doctrine as the supreme principle which must underlie relations among Socialist states. The Czechs in 1968, and also the Rumanians, the Poles, and to some degree the Hungarians had violated this principle in varying degrees, and the last three had gotten away with it without invoking Soviet punitive action. The DDR, on the other hand, along with Bulgaria, had been meticulously loyal to Moscow in this and other respects.

Also in May 1970, the NATO Council, meeting in Rome, opposed an "abstract" approach to the CESC and urged discussions of specific issues. In November the Finnish government, perhaps at Moscow's suggestion, invited all concerned to come to Helsinki to start multilateral consultations on CESC.

In August, with the signing of the Moscow Treaty, a big step was made in the direction of the realization of CESC, and the NATO Council meeting in Brussels noted this and approved the Federal Republic's initiative and success in its moves toward *detente* with the East. It also noted substantial increases in Moscow's military expenditures and its naval buildup, particularly in the Mediterranean, and insisted that a freer exchange of ideas and information and freer movement of people should be a prime subject of discussion at any coming conference. Within the next several weeks these positions were reinforced by President Nixon's pledge to "maintain and improve" U.S. military forces in Europe, while the members of NATO agreed to increase their contributions to NATO, and pledged not to cut NATO's overall military capacity except as a part of MBRF.

During 1971 new elements appeared in European affairs as President Nixon initiated contacts with Peking through Dr. Henry Kissinger during the summer and undertook serious economic talks with Moscow through Secretary of Commerce Maurice Stans in December. In early 1972, the President flew to Peking, and it was announced that he would go to Moscow soon afterward. These events put Moscow on the defensive throughout the world, particularly since the Russians foresaw a bad grain crop, and the consequent need to buy substantial quantities of wheat and fodder grains from the United States and Canada.[3]

By the same token, these developments strengthened the position of Willy Brandt, his government and his *Ostpolitik*. His critics were disarmed. For if a life-long American conservative, who had made his political reputation as an anti-Communist, was paying friendly calls on Peking and Moscow, what was so bad about Brandt's *Ostpolitik?*

West Germany's Foreign Minister Walter Scheel redefined his country's position in the light of the new conditions by asserting that Nixon's visits reinforced the basis for the *Ostpolitik*, and increased the likelihood of CESC. The Berlin agreement was finally signed as Willy Brandt was accepting his Nobel Peace Prize in Oslo, and this brought CESC a step closer. The NATO Council communiqué of December 10, 1971, noted that preliminary multilateral consultations would no doubt take place in 1972 and that the actual conference could be expected in early 1973.

But several stumbling blocks remained to be surmounted or removed. One was the ratification of the *Ostverträge* by the Bundestag, which came only in May 1972, after a cliff-hanging political crisis in Bonn. Another was MBRF, on which no progress at all had been made, for the principal reason that the Soviet government did not recognize the "B" for "Balanced." The significance of this word is great. It means that because the Soviet Union is near and the United States far away, if each were to reduce forces in Central Europe by, let us say, one man, this would be unfair because it would take roughly three times as much time and cost that much more for the United States to put a man back in Central Europe as it would the Soviet Union.

Another obstacle is the suggestion for an increase in the freedom of exchange of information, and the freedom of travel of individuals, something the East bloc countries will resist putting on the agenda of any conference. For, as we have seen, the DDR and the Soviet Union consistently deny their citizens the freedom of travel, and use censorship and radio jamming to obstruct the free exchange of information.

The United States position on CESC was stated by

Assistant Secretary of State for European Affairs Martin Hillenbrand (who shortly thereafter became U.S. Ambassador in Bonn) in April of 1972 in testimony to a congressional subcommittee: "The advantages of CESC outweigh the possible dangers . . . We believe the Conference can constitute a modest step forward within the broader and long-range negotiations intended to lead toward more stable East/West relations."

President Nixon, in his foreign policy report to Congress in February had spoken more directly: "The mere atmosphere of *detente* is insufficient . . . If CESC is well prepared and addresses itself to substantive issues, the United States favors it . . ."

The main publicity during President Nixon's visit to Moscow in May 1972 was devoted to the formal signing of tactical agreements previously negotiated, such as a declaration of principles pledging mutual restraint and a nuclear arms accord limiting both the United States and the USSR to two ABM sites, pledges of cooperation, exchanges and combined research in space exploration, science, technology, environmental problems, health and medicine, and defining of rules to avert incidents involving United States and Soviet warships and naval aircraft operating in close proximity. The far more important discussions of other problems has not as yet been fully reported. But it is generally believed that the President was pressed by his hosts for United States support of and participation in CESC as soon as possible, along with urgent suggestions of increases in trade between the two countries facilitated by vast credits at preferentially low interest rates. These Soviet requests no doubt made it possible for the President to urge the Russians to cooperate with the United States in bringing the Vietnam War to a mutually satisfactory conclusion, and perhaps Soviet cooperation in working toward a negotiated settlement of the complex of problems plaguing the Middle East. We shall learn, no doubt, in time, what responses were made by both sides on these important issues.

But it now looks as though the Soviet drive for a CESC will be achieved sometime in 1973, although it is unlikely that its results will give Moscow everything that it had hoped to realize, both with reference to the two Germanies and to the rest of Europe.

10

The New German Democratic Republic

In connection with the world-wide *detente* of 1972 the DDR stands at this writing on the threshold of international acceptance. It is entirely possible that the Conference for European Security and Cooperation in early 1973 will seat the DDR on the same level as the Federal Republic, and that may well be followed or even accompanied by General Assembly action to seat both Germanies, perhaps along with both Vietnams and both Koreas in the United Nations. And that, in turn, will no doubt be followed by the establishment of formal diplomatic relations between the DDR and the community of Western nations which so far have withheld this token of acceptance. In short, it seems likely that the next few months will see a successful end of the twenty-five-year struggle of the German Communists to establish a separate and equal German Socialist State and force its larger sister state, the Federal Republic, and the world to recognize and accept it.

The quest for legitimacy, the attempt of the Pankow government to win true and voluntary allegiance of its 17 million citizens, and the respect of the world will take many years, and probably many changes, including a free election. But the initial stubborn struggle has been won, as no doubt will soon be juridically acknowledged by a modification in the constitution of the Federal Republic whose preamble proclaims that the basic law of the Federal Republic of Germany was also enacted "on behalf of those Germans to whom participation was denied. . . . The entire German people is called upon to achieve in free self-determination the unity and freedom of Germany."

In 1972 I paid a visit to the DDR, and spent some time trying to get a measure of its achievements and its shortcomings, using my own observations, material published by the government of the DDR, and also studies made mostly in West Berlin by official and unofficial organs of the Federal Republic and other NATO governments assigned to study the DDR.

One day in May I boarded an Interflug IL 18 in Prague and flew to Schönefeld airport, just east of the Berlin city limits in the DDR. Interflug is the airline of the DDR, operating scheduled passenger and freight service all over Eastern Europe and the Middle East and as far south as Tanzania and Mogadescu. It flies Soviet-made aircraft, and is not a member of IATA (International Air Transport Association). Thanks to that, and to the substantial government subsidies it no doubt enjoys, Interflug is able to maintain prices well below those of the regular international carriers, including even Aeroflot, which is in IATA and pretends, at least, to live up to its regulations. Thus a traveler wanting to fly from Cairo, let us say, to Paris can save substantially by flying Interflug from Cairo to East Berlin, which includes a bus transfer from Schönefeld through the wall to a West Berlin airport, and then taking Air France for the 105-minute hop to Paris. And so it was on this flight. About half the passengers on the plane were Arabs and Africans bound for Western European cities. They converged noisily on the large and almost empty transit customs hall in the newly equipped Schönefeld airport and were escorted by jackbooted Vopos and two multilingual Interflug girls through the control turnstiles without even the need of getting DDR transit visas, and out into a waiting bus to West Berlin. The DDR and other East bloc passengers were shunted off into another part of the building for their processing, leaving me as the only non-Communist traveler bound for the DDR. After having dealt with the other passengers and those of a Rumanian plane which had landed at about the same time, a Vopo and a girl approached me, examined the prepaid tour of the DDR which I had purchased in New York, and wrote out a DDR tourist visa for me, for which I paid $2. After a cursory examination of my two small bags, I was seated in a Volga, with a surly-tongued but kind hearted East Berlin driver, and taken to my hotel in the city.

On leaving the airport—in which, incidentally, I did not see a single Soviet uniform—we passed through a control point manned by Vopos, and by two young, nattily dressed, severe-looking Soviet Army MPs who paid no attention to me or my Volga. I asked my driver what they were there for. "If you were a guest of the Soviet authorities, they would escort us," he said. "But mostly they just check their own—members of the Soviet armed forces." "Are there many of them?" I asked. "Very many. But mostly they stay out of sight." We chatted about this and that for a few minutes, as he pointed out that although the buildings in the outskirts of the city were almost all old, with patched bomb scars still visible, everything was clean and orderly. He said he had heard that many United States cities were not clean or orderly and he had also heard that there was some dirt and disorder in some West German cities. I asked him whether he expected relations between the two Germanies to get better. He shook his head. "Not soon."

As we neared the center of the city I was astonished at the changes since my last visit only four years earlier. After the point at which Frankfurterallee becomes Karl-Marx-Allee, for the last mile and a half before reaching Alexanderplatz the buildings were entirely new, and spectacular—ten- and fifteen-story apartment buildings with the bottom floor or two devoted to stores, offices, cinemas, restaurants, nightclubs, exhibitions, clinics. The streets were very wide, and most pedestrian crossings were underground, which permitted traffic to move along briskly and safely. The residential parts of the buildings were fringed with balconies, most of which had railings of assorted colors, giving the whole area a cheerful, colorful atmosphere. No streetcars were in evidence in the center of the city, but subways were efficient, as I discovered when I began using them. The only buses visible were tourist buses, some from West

Berlin, others excursion buses operated by Interhotels, the East German government hotel and tourist agency which operates twenty-four hotels in fourteen cities throughout the DDR.

We drove to the Hotel Berolina, which is the middle-priced one of the three new hotels operated by Interhotel in Berlin. It was a new, fifteen-story building, just off Karl-Marx-Allee, with an electronically operated entry door and a lobby with a large bar on one side, and a hard-currency souvenir shop on the other. I went up to the reception desk and presented my Cosmos tour voucher. The girl looked at it, checked it with a reservations book where entries were made in pen and ink, then turned back to me. "Jawohl," she said. "Your reservation is in order," and she turned to another customer. "But my room," I said. "And the key." "Guests may occupy their rooms at 2:30 P.M.," she said over her shoulder. It was then about noon. My protests were of no avail. Rules are rules and must be followed. Departing guests must leave their rooms by noon, or pay for another day; arriving guests could occupy their rooms after 2:30 P.M. unless they wanted to pay an extra day for early occupancy.

Later in my stay I made the acquaintance of a hotel director, and asked him about this procedure. He shrugged: "It simplifies the servicing of the rooms, and when we are lucky, it makes it possible for us sometimes to exceed 100 percent occupancy revenue, and that means a very nice bonus." He did not need to add that since Interhotel had no competition, the guests had no alternative.

I checked my bags in a cloakroom just off the lobby,

and went out for a walk, down to Alexanderplatz about half a mile, and then around the new and very impressive deluxe Hotel Stadt Berlin. Traffic was light, there were not many pedestrians, and the luxury stores in the area were not crowded. In a large, self-service food store I found a good assortment of fresh vegetables — carrots, cabbage, tomatoes, rhubarb, onions, kohlrabi, lettuce. There were some melons from Bulgaria, and a few rather poor lemons. No oranges or other tropical fruits. "They appear occasionally," I was told. In another department I saw baby food in both cans and jars, assorted jellies and jams, soups, vegetables, and fruits, some from Hungary, Yugoslavia, and Bulgaria. In the frozen food department there were various types of meat and fish, as well as vegetables and concentrated fruit juices. Wines, both red and white, from Bulgaria, Hungary, and the Soviet Union were on display, as well as Soviet champagne. The dairy department offered milk in glass bottles, butter, and several cheeses, mostly of German manufacture. The dry foods shelves were stocked with corn flakes, spaghetti, groats, rice, and other cereals. The meat department was modest: while twenty-four different kinds of sausage were on display, costing between three and five marks a pound, the quality seemed poor, and the choice of fresh meats and fish was very limited. New potatoes were on sale for one and a half marks a pound — very expensive. I asked about fresh eggs, and was told: "Should get here earlier. We had them." The store also had a small stationery and dry goods section with rather shoddy displays of these items. In the delicatessen section there was cold beer in bottles, and cold cuts on rolls.

The whole store was clean and well ordered, and the personnel was reasonably polite. I bought a bottle of beer, a bit of cheese and sausage and a roll, and walked across the street to a very nice park where I ate my lunch in the sun, and tried to compare prices on the things I had just seen with those in West Germany. All were substantially higher when figuring the marks at the official rate of exchange; that is, one D-mark equals one Ost-mark. But when calculating on the black market rate in East Berlin, or the free market rate in West Berlin—about three Ost-marks per D-mark—the prices were low.

After eating I continued my walk, going to a large and very fancy watch store on Karl-Marx-Allee right across from Alexanderplatz. A well-designed and handsomely decorated store, it had several hundred watches on display, all made either in the DDR or the USSR. I am sure that Swiss and Japanese visitors are startled by this phenomenon. The watches were of a wide assortment, running in price from about three-hundred marks for the most expensive men's and women's watches, twenty-nine jewel, with date indicator, down to fifty marks for Timex type watches with no jewels and stamped parts. The prices of the Soviet watches ran about 10 percent more than the German watches of the same type and style. There were also assorted chronometers, alarm clocks, wall and mantlepiece time pieces, and pocket and pendulum watches. I saw no electronic watches, however, and only one or two self-winding models. The store was well attended, but most customers I saw were looking rather than buying.

I went next to a radio and TV store just down the street, where they were featuring the Soviet color TV

Raduga, which sold for 3,050 marks. But the store offered a 500-mark reduction for purchasers that day, and one could buy for 10 percent down, the balance to be paid over twelve months. The sets were not selling well, I was told by the salesman. "Too expensive and, of course, there are very few color broadcasting stations in East Europe . . ."

I walked across Alexanderplatz, which is about the size of Moscow's Red Square or Paris's Place de la Concorde, and through a large seven-story department store in a building right next to the Hotel Stadt Berlin. The assortment of household furnishings, clothing, toys, kitchenware, shoes, and souvenirs was wide, the prices stiff, and there was a notable absence of goods imported from Western countries. Whereas far smaller and less ostentatious stores in Prague offer shoes from Italy, tableware from Scandinavia, and some clothing from France, East Berlin offered only Socialist bloc goods.

I walked west from Alex — as it is still called — down toward Marx-Engels-Platz and went into a huge book store on which the sign, "International Books," appeared in half a dozen languages. The store occupied four stories, and offered a large assortment of books and other publications in literally dozens of languages, published in East Europe and several less-developed countries.[1] One entire section was devoted to phonograph records. Prices were low, even at the official rate of exchange, and at the black market rate of three to one they were very low indeed.

By this time it was well on to mid-afternoon, and I walked back up Karl-Marx-Allee to a large restaurant called Moskva which I decided to visit some evening, then dashed illegally across the hundred-yard-wide boulevard to the Berolina. My room, now available, was on the tenth floor, and I was impressed to see that the elevator was self-operated, unlike those in even the newest Moscow hotels where the elevators are equipped for automatic operation, but the management lacks confidence in the technical sophistication of the clientele. My room was nearly at the end of the long hall, about 150 feet from the elevators; it was 7 feet wide, and about 16 feet long, from which space had been carved out a tiny bathroom, with a small basin, a toilet and shower, and a closet with a folding door. There was a modest wooden single bed, a small table, a chair and stool, and that was all. But it was clean, and light, and airy, and at twelve dollars a night with breakfast, it certainly was not expensive.

I unpacked my gear, and went down to the lobby floor, where a tourist service bureau offered excursions, theater tickets, postcards, and a money change booth. I changed a twenty-dollar traveler's check into Ost-marks, and ordered theater tickets for that night and the following night. I made a reservation on two excursion trips in and outside East Berlin, and then set out to test the efficiency of the telephone system by calling several friends and acquaintances. It was certainly more efficient than those I had wrestled with in Czechoslovakia or Hungary and far more efficient than that in Moscow. Although the phone numbers I had turned out in almost every case to have been changed, I got hold of three friends, one in theater, one a journalist, and one a minor Party functionary. At 6 P.M. I was sitting with my actor friend in the restaurant on the top floor of the Hotel Stadt Berlin, surveying a varied menu, and sipping a glass of excellent Hungarian white wine.

It was a very fancy restaurant indeed, with waiters in white ties and tails, elaborate tableware, a wine list several pages long, and imported whisky and liquors available for those who were paying in hard currency as I was. The view westward over the wall into West Berlin's Tiergarten was spectacular, and the food was excellent. Indeed the food and service could be compared favorably with those in the restaurant at the Imperial Hotel in Vienna, for example. With a good Rumanian red wine, our meal cost 65 D-marks, a good deal less than a comparable meal would have cost in the Kempinski on the Kurfürstendamm in West Berlin, or at the Breidenbacherhof in Düsseldorf.

But these comparisons were not important for my guest, who was greatly pleased. "I seldom eat here," he said. "Too expensive. This dinner will cost a week's wages for a middle-level functionary, two weeks' wages for a captain in the Vopo. But the things we buy regularly are not so expensive. Most of us in the theater have cars. I have a fine new aprtment. But—foreign travel. That we really miss . . ."

After dinner we took a taxi, much less expensive than in West Berlin, to the Staatstheater where I had tickets to *Die Aula* by Hermann Kant, a contemporary DDR dramatist. My friend left me, as he had a theatrical engagement of his own. But I was approached at the door by a plain-looking girl who asked whether I had an extra ticket I might sell. I declined the financial part of the transaction, but invited her to accompany me. She frowned, but on learning that I was a Western tourist, agreed, and she proved to be an interesting companion. She was a student at the university, and was able to throw some light on scenes and episodes in the play that I would otherwise have had difficulty in understanding.

The play was very political and stuck close to Marxist orthodoxy. Nearly all the characters were students in a university, probably in Halle, where the play was first produced. They were all depicted in flashbacks as of staunch worker and peasant origin. They won entry into the university by virtue of their political dependability, and all had a hard time making up for poor secondary educational backgrounds. All resisted valiantly the "corruption" of class enemies on the faculty, including one pro-U.S. professor of medicine. The lectures bristled with revolutionary examples and images and the dormitory life and the administration of the institution were run according to the principles of democratic centralism by a student-faculty committee.

I asked my companion whether everything in her university was so clean-cut, so black-and-white, so simple and convincing. She frowned, then grinned. "Of course not. Real life is much more complicted. But essentially, this is the way things are in our universities. As Lenin pointed out, our universities and our theater must both play their parts in building communism." She looked severe, then grinned again.

In the second act the students have graduated, and are out doing practical work. One, a budding journalist, has been sent to Hamburg to write a historical report on the horrendous Allied raid on that city carried out in July 1943, when some forty thousand were killed in a fire storm started by bombs and fanned by a high wind.

While there he looks up a former fellow student who fled to the West. He finds him working as a waiter in a *Bierstube*, depressed, his career shattered, ashamed and withdrawn. My companion turned to me. "Nun, dass ist ein Bisschen übertrieben," she said critically. "That is a bit exaggerated. We are not children. We know that not everyone in Hamburg is a waiter in a *Bierstube*." After the play, as we were walking out, she went further. "Things are going well for us here now. We live well, and there are plenty of opportunities for creative and useful work. But that doesn't mean we are pleased not to be able to leave, ever . . ."

She left me at the theater door. "I am expected at a friend's," she said, "and besides, you are no doubt being observed." She smiled a bit sadly, I thought, and was gone.

I walked back to the Berolina, by a circuitous route, which took a good hour. I circled around past the old Schiffbauerdammtheater, which is still in operation, then down Friedrichstrasse past the Press Club to Unter den Linden. There was a good deal of activity in evidence near the Hotel Unter den Linden, where some East European tourists or delegates were having a reception which spilled over into the street. But by and large, by midnight the streets were nearly empty, quiet, and rather dark. I stopped in for a few minutes at the Moskva, which was in full swing — a Czech orchestra playing what the large room full of young dancers probably considered the latest in decadent Western music. I had a glass of wine, then walked across the deserted Karl-Marx-Allee to the Berolina and went to bed.

For the next several days I looked around in East Berlin and in several parts of the DDR. It was obvious that downtown East Berlin was a showcase, built at enormous expense to impress foreigners. Other parts of the city had changed little since the original clean-up after the war, while cities such as Dresden and Frankfurt an der Oder looked almost as though they had been purposely left by the DDR authorities as monuments of the destruction of World War II.

One phenomenon that I noticed everywhere was the absence of crowds. This may be partly an imaginary impression since I knew the basic conditioning fact; namely, that the DDR had had for a generation a zero population growth. Emigration just about balanced natural increase until the wall in 1961, and since then the East German birth rate has fallen to about the same level as the death rate, though no official figures have been published. Whereas West Germany, France, Switzerland, and Scandinavia have invited millions of foreign workers into their countries, many of whom are in the process of being assimilated and incorporated into those nations, the DDR has only a negligible number of foreign workers, perhaps twenty-five thousand, mostly daily commuters across the frontier from Poland.

In talking with a number of DDR citizens in different walks of life, I found a distinct cleavage between those citizens who identified themselves with the DDR government, and those citizens who were making the best of current reality without any personal commitment. Among the latter I was constantly aware of the unspoken feeling: "We go along now, because there is no alternative. But if sometime in the future there should be an alternative—a free election, an opportunity to emigrate, freedom to express desires for these things — you watch. There will be sudden and spectacular changes in the DDR." Among the former (and more than half the people I talked with were working in or for the government, and were committed) I felt a stubborn, defensive, and almost pathological insistence on legitimacy, on the moral and historic righteousness of the government and its positions.

In their conversation they unfailingly attached the phrase "capital of the DDR" to the word Berlin, as indeed do all DDR maps, books, and publications. They insist on repeating on all occasions the assertion that the DDR is the first German Socialist state, and therefore the historic vanguard of the German people. As the vanguard, they insist in effect, "We are right even when we may be wrong . . ." The interpretation of this dialectic thought goes something like this: "The DDR does indeed limit human freedom by its prohibitions on foreign travel, which in a sense is wrong; but because thereby it defends and secures the independence and viability of the first German Socialist state, it is right. Any other policy on the part of the DDR would be a reflection of bourgeois sentimentalism, or of weakness . . ."

In arguing with several DDR government-employed friends, I found it most interesting to get them started on the issue of nationality. The DDR constitution, promulgated in 1949, stated clearly in the concluding sentence of Article 1, "There is only one German nationality." On the other hand, recent statements by top DDR officials have seemed to contradict this position. For example, Erich Honecker, speaking at Rostock on January 5,

1972, said: "Our DDR and the Federal Republic relate to each other in the same way that either relates to a third state. The Federal Republic is a foreign state: even more, it is an imperialist foreign state . . ." In connection with this new position, the DDR officials have stopped using the adjective German in any political sense. In filling out questionnaires for any DDR purpose, the word nationality has been replaced by *Staatsangehörigkeit* or citizenship. This is incidentally in contradistinction to similar documents in the USSR where nationality—Russian, Ukrainian, Tatar, Uzbek, and so forth—is included in census statistics, as well as applications for passports and visas, marriage and birth certificates, and so on.

The DDR is also finding great difficulty in establishing its legitimacy. It cannot, of course, use the arguments of the hereditary monarchy, nor can it base itself on a popular revolutionary movement (as did Jefferson in the Declaration of Independence), since the DDR government was installed by a foreign military force without any pretence of a popular referendum or plebiscite. Lamely, it must use analogies with the Soviet Union, and claim legitimacy as an expression of a historical evolution. Needless to say, this argument lacks conviction, even to the most orthodox-minded citizens of the DDR, most of whom ignore the issue and live their lives as best they can on the basis of an existentialist and pragmatic materialism.

In my talks with East German friends and acquaintances, and in my visits to bookstores, museums, expositions and libraries, I got as much factual and statistical information as I could, which I later subjected to checking and comment from scholars and analysts of the DDR in West Berlin and farther west. Using this material, let me lay out a brief survey of the economy and social structure of the DDR.

The population of the DDR is 17 million, its growth is zero, and it is almost entirely ethnic German. Minorities are negligible, and foreigners are limited to a few thousand students and tourists and some day workers along the Polish frontier.

The gross national product (GNP) in 1971 was about 37 billion dollars. This works out to a per capita GNP of about $1,850, slightly more than in Czechoslovakia, where the figure stood at $1,830. These figures are inexact when expressed in U.S. dollars, because of the absence of any direct convertibility between the Ost-mark and the dollar, and indeed between any of the Socialist countries' currencies and the dollar.

East Germany's foreign trade can be more exactly measured: in 1970 it was just under $10 billion. Exports were $4.5 billion, imports $4.85 billion. Thus the DDR's exports make up about 12 percent of the GNP, about halfway between the high level of West Germany, and the very low—roughly 4 percent—level of the Soviet Union.

The DDR has maintained a surplus of imports over exports thanks to the financial support of the Federal Republic, to whom the DDR currently owes more than one billion marks. If one adds to this the fact that East/West German trade is carried out at the official rate of exchange of one Ost-mark for one D-mark, it can be seen that the Federal Republic has been subsidizing the DDR heavily for years by paying for their imports.

The breakdown of the DDR's foreign trade, when expressed in valuta marks for the period 1966-1970, indicates that the Soviet Union was far and away the DDR's largest trading partner, with 65.6 billion marks both ways (imports plus exports); Czechoslovakia was next with 15.3 billion marks; then Poland with 11.2 billion, followed by Hungary, Bulgaria, and Rumania. The DDR's trade with the entire Comecon was 110 billion marks in that period. With Yugoslavia, which is not a true Socialist state, it was 2.8 billion marks.

The DDR's trade with the capitalist states was: 15.4 billion marks with the Federal Republic, just under 1 billion with West Berlin, and between 1 and 2 billion each with France, Italy, and Benelux.

To take the 1970 figures alone: The DDR's trade with the USSR was 15 billion marks; with the Federal Republic and West Berlin, 4.2 billion marks; with Czechoslovakia, 3.7 billion marks. With the United States it was a comparatively paltry 207 million marks; with Japan, 148 million marks; with Peru, Iraq, and the Sudan, about 50 million marks each. Thus the DDR does some 40 percent of its foreign trade with the USSR, and more than 70 percent with the Socialist bloc. This compares strikingly with Rumania, for example, which did less than half its total foreign trade with the entire Socialist bloc in 1970. The DDR is the Soviet Union's most loyal associate.

The DDR is an efficient economy when compared to the Soviet Union, Czechoslovakia, or Hungary. It has the world's highest index of people gainfully employed, and the world's highest percent of women working in industry and trade. One reason, of course, is that with a zero population growth, there are relatively fewer children in the DDR. A more important reason is the proverbial inclination of the Germans to work. And although the DDR bureaucracy is top-heavy and oppressively political, the efficiency of administration is probably the highest in the Soviet bloc.

But when comparisons are made with Western nations, and most specifically with the Federal Republic, one finds striking differences. A comparison of average monthly wages in 1970 (in marks) shows:

Area	DDR (Ost-marks)	Federal Republic (D-marks)
Industry	770	1,160
Building construction	833	1,320
Agriculture	710	870
Transportation	806	1,300
Trade	668	1,030

A citizen of the DDR pays 19.5 percent of a 4,000-mark annual income in taxes, while a citizen of the Federal Republic has to pay 22 percent.

On the other hand, rents in the DDR are heavily subsidized, and much lower than in the West, and books, educational material, local travel expenses, medicines and medical care, theater and cinema tickets are all substantially cheaper in the DDR than in the Federal Republic.

When all this is added up and evaluated, people whose judgment in such matters I respect believe that in material living standards the people of the DDR in

1971 were about 85 percent as well off as those in the Federal Republic.

But other things must be taken into consideration. West Germans can and do travel all over the world. Citizens of the DDR are severely restricted. The Pankow government has made much of the recent agreement among the governments of the DDR, Czechoslovakia, and Poland, according to which the citizens of each may visit the other countries without visas. And indeed many people have made use of this new ruling. When I was in Prague in May I was told the country was flooded with East Germans and Poles who came in, often in their own vehicles, and bought up luxury food items such as oranges, and durable consumer goods, which were unavailable at home. Often, I was told, they paid for these purchases in staple food products which are more expensive in Czechoslovakia. These Comecon tourists usually cannot pay for purchases in money because the Soviet bloc countries' currencies are not freely interconvertible, and travelers are allowed only small amounts of the currency of the country they are to visit, usually about twelve dollars a day, for living expenses. But adaptable men and women who learned to survive in the severely restricted economy of Fortress Europe as operated by the Nazis during the war, have no difficulty in making adjustments, and a thriving black market in money and many commodities now is to be found all over Eastern Europe.

Another basis of comparison is in high-quality goods. In most cases these are simply unavailable in the DDR and indeed in East Europe in general, whereas in West Germany, Switzerland, or France one can buy literally anything. Of course, it can be argued that this affects only a small minority in both societies — the concert artists, professors, industrial and political leaders — and that the average person is better off without luxury goods. But the fact remains that even ordinary people often like to acquire something of high quality, and in the DDR this is far more difficult than in the West. Indeed, there are many items a Westerner would consider necessities that are not easily available in the DDR — paint, tires, batteries, citrus fruits. Often there are power shortages caused by the imbalance between the needs of the DDR's export industries and the needs of the consumer, both of which must get their power from limited coal and gas resources.

Agriculture, industry, construction, and trade are all in the hands of cooperatives or state organizations in the DDR, except for an occasional shoemaker or tailor working alone on a state or city license. In agriculture 6.3 million hectares of land are under cultivation, and supply the domestic consumers with the grain, potatoes, sugar, vegetables, and dairy products they need. This is done with the aid of 140,000 tractors and other mechanized equipment. Small aircraft are used extensively in agriculture, and in 1969, the DDR authorities claim nearly one million hectares were planted from the air.

The DDR is justly proud of its educational system. A ten-year primary and secondary program is compulsory and free. Having finished this the student may go to work or to a trade school, and perhaps half of all the students do this. The rest go on for two more years in secondary school to complete the twelve-year college preparatory program which gives its graduates their *Abi-*

tur, or college preparatory certificate, corresponding to the *Baccalauréat* in France, or the Matriculation in Britain. The students then may go on to one of the country's fifty-four universities and technical higher schools.[2] Nearly a quarter of a million young citizens of the DDR are currently studying in higher educational institutions. The entire educational system of the DDR is financed and controlled by the Ministry of Education. There are no private or church schools.

The DDR's health services are likewise entirely under state control and maintain high standards. There are no private doctors or dentists.

Sports activities in the DDR are highly developed, and under centralized state control. Great effort and generous financial support have gone into this aspect of the country's Socialist cultural development. The results are excellent. At the 1972 Olympics in Munich the DDR appeared with a highly competent team, especially in swimming and field and track events. Highly trained, and encouraged to concentrate every effort on defeating the athletes of the Federal Republic, the DDR took twenty gold medals, twenty-three silver medals, and twenty-three bronze medals, far ahead of West Germany, which won thirteen, eleven, and sixteen respectively. Especially in women's gymnastics, the DDR teams swept the field, sharing the honors only with the Soviet Union. Between them, the two countries took all the gold, silver, and bronze medals in this particular competition.

There have been significant changes in the operation of the DDR's economy since Walter Ulbricht was removed from power in 1970 and Erich Honecker was promoted to top position. Ulbricht was a "seat of the pants" manager, who made his own decisions often on political instinct. It is noteworthy that his principle economic theorist and Minister of Economics, Erich Apel, shot himself on December 3, 1965, partly because he objected to the continued milking of the DDR economy by the Russians, but also out of frustration caused by Ulbricht's unscientific and, in a sense, un-German methods of leadership. Honecker has begun to use market research and computer techniques in order to allocate resources more effectively. Since Ulbricht was deposed, the Comecon has become more integrated. For example, the Trabant automobile is no longer being made in the DDR, but by Skoda in Czechoslovakia, and the DDR will concentrate more on the chemical industry. I was interested to find out whether the new DDR leaders would push for more flexible procedures in the Comecon; for example for currency interconvertibility, which the Czechs suggested in 1968, but which Ulbricht vigorously opposed. One DDR economist responded with a shrug: "It doesn't make any difference what we think or want. The Russians oppose convertibility, and insist on trade being carried out essentially through bilateral trade agreements, which will permit them to retain control, and to benefit from pricing arrangements." He then made a remark which sticks in my mind as provocative and perceptive. "What the Russians want eventually is for the ruble to become the SDRs[3] of the Socialist bloc financial system."

On careful reading, I found that the East German press is not as stodgy and regimented as it first appears. The local press particularly features numerous bits of information which throw light on the operation of the whole economy. For example, an item in a Leipzig paper stated that during the previous month more than one-fourth of the shoes produced in Halle (which is the center of the DDR's shoe industry) were rejected because they could not pass quality control. When I asked what happened to the shoes, one friend said cynically: "They go into our foreign aid program in Africa."

I asked many people both inside and outside the DDR whether any signs of convergence could be seen. The answer was in every case negative. The two Germanies are not growing together on the basis of their common language and culture. On the contrary, the DDR government is making every effort to nip any such tendencies in the bud, and to keep the DDR Eastern-oriented and Socialist. Those aspects of German tradition that the DDR leadership tries to use and implant—discipline, regimentation, and order—are precisely those which the Federal Republic is trying to relax.

I left the DDR on this trip feeling that the changes there during the past several years have been striking and very positive, and that perhaps the economic basis had been laid on which the DDR political leadership could soon relax its severe restrictions on travel and civil liberties without fear of suffering a disastrous loss of skilled manpower or of political control. I still feel this proposition is essentially correct, but the key factor is the willingness of the political leaders to become more liberal. There are now millions of East Germans who have interesting, well-paid and secure jobs, decent living conditions, and prospects for further improvement. Many of these would like to travel to the West, and then return, *if* they felt sure that freedom of travel would not again be restricted. But the DDR authorities cannot be expected to make such assurances. In the words of a middle-level DDR functionary with whom I discussed this issue: "Why should we? The Soviet Union has gotten on very well now these fifty-five years without giving its people freedom of foreign travel or an opposition press or a convertible currency. We in the DDR are militarily secured by the might of the Soviet army. We are ideologically secure in our confidence of the correctness of Marxist-Leninist theory, in our belief in the inevitability of the collapse of capitalist-imperialism under the weight of its own injustice and inefficiency. Any liberalization on our part would encourage our enemies, and lead to capitalist restorationism, as it did in Czechoslovakia in 1968. If many of our people are not yet convinced of the correctness of our line, we will continue to teach them, patiently and firmly. History is moving forward, and we German Communists are not about to betray communism . . ."

11

The Federal Republic Moves Toward Leadership of Europe

During the spring and summer of 1972 I made an extensive trip around the Federal Republic, working on various related assignments.

I began at the end of April where I had first started in Germany—with a visit to my old friend Ernst, with whom I had bicycled around Germany in 1927, and his family in Koblenz, with whom I had lived during part of that year. Now the aging but still vigorous director of a small construction materials company, Ernst and his wife met me at the Koblenz railroad station one Sunday morning and drove me in their old, well-kept Mercedes to the house in suburban Horchheim which I remembered so vividly. The house was little changed, but the city and the neighborhood had been altered almost beyond recognition. A new four-lane highway bridge was being built across the Rhine about three miles upstream from Koblenz, and in the process of construction half of Horchheim had been displaced.

Downtown Koblenz also had grown and changed, though the layer-after-layer structure of the city was still visible to the perceptive eye, from the remains of the Roman fortress at the strategic confluence of the Rhine and Mosel rivers, through the crumbling castles of the Middle Ages, the Baroque cathedrals, to the somber, rural houses which survived World War II but were giving way to the construction jobs of the *Wirtschaftswunder*.

Ernst's house had been improved, too — a new wing, a modern kitchen, a large color TV, and a garage. The chicken house and kitchen garden, which had been an important part of the household in the 1920s and absolutely vital during the hungry days right after World War II, were now in disarray. "Why bother with chickens and lettuce? They are so easy to buy."

Over a glass of local wine Ernst told me things were hard for a small businessman under the *Wirtschaftswunder*. "The big companies handle cement and lumber in such large quantities that we can't compete and it is hard to keep thirty employees busy at increasing wages by selling door hinges . . . Our main asset now is our downtown real estate. If we can get a zoning break we may liquidate. I want to retire anyhow, and the boys will have no trouble finding other jobs . . ."

Daughter Ingrid with her bank-executive husband came by for lunch as did son Frank with his wife and new baby. Son Wolfgang was having marital difficulties and did not appear, but several cousins and neighbors dropped in to say hello to the Johnny they had first met in 1927, or more immediately remembered from visits right after the war. Everyone seemed to be doing well, all had cars, most were talking about plans for a vacation abroad during the coming summer. All were very much for Brandt and his *Ostverträge* and angry with the Christian Democrats. "They are for the new *Ostpolitik,* too, but they want to negotiate it themselves and get the political credit. They should have acted earlier under Kiesinger or Erhard," Ernst remarked.

They questioned me about the Vietnam War. There was no hostility, but concern and pain. "Is it really necessary?" They are concerned, too, about the German army. "Do we really need it?" No questions about the United States, which seemed very far away, but many about the Soviet Union which now seems much nearer. I asked about the recession. They shrugged."*Naja,*" said the bank executive. "It's not really a recession. We still have full employment, and more than two million foreign workers. But growth has slacked off, and high time . . ." No one argued. All were completely comfortable in material terms. All day no one mentioned the Nazis or the war. No one mentioned reunification either, though in other families with close relatives in the East the issue would have been discussed.

More talk. A long walk. Then we had a modest but good dinner, and more excellent wine. The time had come to leave, and Ernst drove me to the station. "Johnny, komm doch wieder. Vergiss uns nicht. . . ." ("Johnny, come again. Don't forget us.")

I had two meetings the next day in Düsseldorf, the Rhine-Ruhr industrial capital, Germany's sixth largest city after Berlin, Hamburg, Frankfurt, Munich, and

Essen. The ride from Koblenz to Düsseldorf took less than two hours. The train was comfortable, clean, on time. I took a taxi to the Breidenbacherhof—solid, bourgeois, with excellent food and service. There two friends in the steel industry joined me for drinks. Both are conservative Rhineland Catholics who would probably have voted for Hitler in 1937. Now they were angry with CDU leader Barzel. "What does he think he's accomplishing, opposing the *Ostpolitik*? We need orders for steel. Does he think he is going to get them from France and Italy? We need the East."

My meetings with business executive groups the next day went well. There was a great deal of interest in Japan (where I had been a few weeks before), which is beginning a very active sales and investment effort in Germany. Questions involved key issues such as the ratio of productivity growth to wage increases in Japan's export industries, and how the Japanese have managed without importing foreign labor. There was almost no mention of the United States. From here, too, it seems far away.

That evening I went to the middle-class suburb of Grafenberg for dinner with friends. There was much discussion of the up-coming Olympics, some critical comments on the production of *Don Carlos* in the excellent local opera, uncertainty as to whether the expansion of the Common Market from six to nine will be good for Germany; most thought it will be. Some evidenced anger at student radical terrorists. Again, there were almost no questions about America.

Next morning I went for a walk in the Grafenbergerwald, a lovely wooded city park. The residents of this suburb can walk from their homes—mostly apartments in large, rebuilt houses—to the Grafenbergerwald in a few minutes, and most of them can get to their offices or other places of work by streetcar, though many drive in their own cars.

A bit farther out of Düsseldorf many workers and technicians who man the Rhine and Ruhr valley heavy industries and mines live on small farms where they keep fowls and animals, and ride to work on bicycles, though most of them now also have cars.

On the following day, May 1 (the internationally observed workers' holiday), I went to the Düsseldorf station to take the justly famed Trans-Europe-Express to Stuttgart, where I had a meeting scheduled for the following day. It was a beautiful sunny morning, and a holiday for most German blue- and white-collar workers. Theoretically there should have been giant workers' demonstrations, but during recent years West German workers have been less class-conscious and more preoccupied with sports and hobbies and taking their families on trips in their cars. Demonstrations are not well attended. (In the DDR, on the other hand, attendance at demonstrations and other political activities is mandatory.) But on this May 1, the large square in front of the railroad station was teeming with foreign workers. Most of them were not going anywhere. The station was a place all of them knew, and they gather there on holidays to talk, and perhaps drink a beer. Mostly men, they were standing in groups, smoking, waving their arms, talking to each other in Italian, Turkish, Portuguese, Farsi, and Swahili. Many were borrowing and reading newspapers and magazines in their own languages, and I was told that some of these foreign workers in Germany were experiencing a free press for the first time, and open discussion of burning political problems back in their own countries.

The TEE pulled in from the north right on time and I climbed aboard. Within seconds we were buzzing along toward Leverkusen and Cologne. The car was half full, comfortable, clean. Stewardesses brought around coffee and tea, but there was also an excellent dining car. Between Cologne and Koblenz fruit-tree blossoms were blowing like snow across the well-kept green fields lying between the factories and towns. After Koblenz the railroad winds along the left bank of the Rhine, through quaint riverside villages, past some of the world's best white-wine vineyards, under the stark ruins of medieval castles, many now rebuilt and modernized and inhabited, past the famed Lorelei rock where the current is swift, and the channel narrow. This May 1, no barges were navigating dizzily up and down one of the world's busiest inland waterways. They were at anchor along the banks, laundry fluttering along the decks under German, French, Dutch, and Swiss flags.

But other boats swarmed along the silver river: rowboats, sloops, assorted family motor launches, small boys in homemade canoes, enjoying the lovely weather and the priceless Rhine. Picnickers strolled along the banks.

At Remagen I automatically looked for the famous bridge, although I knew it had been destroyed early in 1945 by German fire, after it had served the invaluable purpose of getting more than a division of Patton's troops across the river in one of the war's most decisive operations. Farther south, from Mainz to Mannheim, both mountains and big factories were less in evidence, and the season more advanced.

What a contrast this was to the Rhine I had seen in mid-1945, obstructed by the twisted girders of bombed-out bridges, studded with the burnt-out wreckage of war, the towns and villages rubble-strewn and populated only with a few furtive, pale civilians queuing up for something to eat. I would not have believed then, in 1945, that in twenty-seven years Germany would be prosperous and living in cooperation with most of its neighbors without any trace of the martial spirit and military institutions which had been so much a characteristic of German life since Frederick the Great.

Stuttgart, which I used to visit monthly in 1946 to report on meetings of the Länderrat, a precursor of the West German government, has now been completely rebuilt. It is the home of one of Germany's most famous companies, Daimler-Benz, and of several smaller allied industries, among them Porsche and Bosch. Also, like most German cities, it has an opera, several theaters, a world-famous ballet, and a number of educational institutions. My meeting was with a Daimler-Benz executive group, and they were most interested in Japan—with reason. "Do you realize that during the past twelve months the Japanese have increased their share of the Swiss automotive market from 2 percent to 10 percent?" one Mercedes executive asked me. Others pointed out that the Japanese had perfected Dr. Wankel's rotary engine, and were marketing it most successfully in the Mazda cars and trucks. Happily for me, I had visited both the Mazda plant in Hiroshima, and several Toyota plants in Nagoya while I was in Japan, and had no trouble holding their interest. I also learned a great deal. My only regret was that the company's chairman, Dr. Hermann Abs, was not there. Abs, although reaching retirement age, is still chief executive officer of a score of Germany's most important companies, including the Deutsche Bank, Lufthansa, and the Bundesbahn (Federal Railway). On many previous occasions as far back as 1950 I had found him to be one of the wisest and best-informed businessmen in the world.

After the meeting I was taken through a new division of the plant, and given rides in some new experimental automotive vehicles. Then I went on to Munich where I spent several days holding meetings with groups in Siemens and BMW, looking at the preparations for the Olympics in August, and visiting friends working in Radio Free Europe and Radio Liberty.

These radio operations, along with RIAS in Berlin, fulfill a most important function by maintaining an East/West dialogue, in spite of major efforts by the Soviet bloc countries to jam their broadcasts and discredit them as political bandits and intellectual prostitutes. In addition to programming executives, editors, and technicians preparing the broadcasts in various languages, these organizations maintain audience research divisions whose analysts are among the best-informed people in the world on the Communist bloc. Even without the reports of these researchers, I know from my own extensive travels in the Communist countries that the broadcasts are widely listened to in spite of jamming and produce important secondary benefits by forcing the Communist media to tell their citizens things they would prefer to conceal for fear of losing credibility among their own people. In the case of Radio Liberty, an even more important function is served in re-broadcasting to a large Soviet audience articles and novels and other material from *samizdat*, the vigorous but tiny Soviet underground press, thus considerably increasing the audience of these works. I always learn a great deal from these visits in Munich, and try to stop by at least once every year.

If this trip had been two months later I would certainly have gone to the Dokumenta exposition in Kassel, the Bach festival in Ansbach, and to Bayreuth to hear some Wagner produced and sung at its best. Had the time been right I might also have gone to the Hannover Fair, one of Europe's largest, and a good place to follow new developments in science and technology. Instead I flew to West Berlin.

I lived and worked in Berlin for three years right after the war, and still consider it the world's most interesting city, unique in many respects. For here, 110 miles behind the Soviet bloc's powerful front-line troops with their airfields, their heavy ordnance, and offensive and defensive nuclear installations, more than two million Germans and small garrisons of British, French, and U.S. troops[1] live under laws almost identical to those in the Federal Republic, use West German money, postal and telegraph service, enjoy the same freedoms of speech, press, and assorted political activity. West Berliners also have several special privileges and prohibitions. As was mentioned earlier, they may not vote in the national elections of the Federal Republic and are not liable for military service. They enjoy certain tax privileges and their air travel to and from the Federal

Republic proper is subsidized. They are under constant threat of siege, although since the conclusion of the Four-Power agreement of September 3, 1971, there has been no harassment against access to the city by road, water, railroad, or air.

West Berlin's fashion salons, its cinema studios, electrical industries, its theater, and publications are among the most prestigious in Europe. Its educational institutions are justly famous, but at the same time notorious for the way in which small, well-organized groups of extremist Communist and Maoist students misuse the law and the permissive rules on academic freedom in such a way as to make life intolerable for other students and professors with whom they disagree.

I spent three days in Berlin on this trip, talking with both German and Allied friends, and wandering around the city I knew so well twenty-five years ago. Kurfürstendamm remains the Champs-Elysees of the city — expensive stores and restaurants, the broad sidewalk dotted with cafés. All day long, but particularly in the late afternoon, crowds of people of every age and calling promenade. Now the last four blocks of the "Ku-damm" are crowded with a vast variety of hippies, or "street" people. Dressed in anything, or in some cases almost nothing, they sell beads, leather articles, costume jewelry, paintings, ceramics, sculpture, some made on the spot on the sidewalk. Business was good on that afternoon in early May. People seemed to be buying anything and everything.

I walked eastward to the end of the Ku-damm where the stark ruins of the Kaiser Wilhelms Gedächtniskirche (the Kaiser Wilhelm Memorial Church) still stand as they were when the city fell to the Russians on April 30, 1945—gaping shell holes, shrapnel-scarred facades. Next to it the new wing featured modern stained glass and a large auditorium where concerts—mostly Bach's choral music—are held nearly every evening, admission free. But the square around the two churches had been taken over by the street people. Several hundred of them were sitting on the steps as I walked by, talking, arguing, singing, drinking beer and wine, smoking, some sleeping on newspapers, some necking on newspapers under leftist political signs and slogans. By no means all were German; there were Americans, Italians, Scandinavians, Africans. Solid, well-dressed West Berliners promenading with their wives looked at the scene with disapproval and even disgust. A bored policeman walked by from time to time.

Then, as I waded through the sprawl on the steps to see what the program for that evening's concert was, a demonstration hove in sight, marching eastward from the direction of Kantstrasse. Perhaps two hundred, mostly young marchers, waved red flags, and chanted slogans: "Mao—Tse-tung, Mao—Tse-tung." Two police vans drove before and two behind the demonstrations, indicating that they had a permit. As they reached the Gedächtniskirche, the marchers began shouting to the motley and largely supine crowd on the steps to join them. But most waved in irritation. Then a leader of the marchers shouted to his followers: "Let's go get them." And with that the marchers broke ranks and stormed up the steps, trying to force the hippies to join them. But many were too lazy, some perhaps too drunk, others indifferent, a few hostile. Several fights broke out.

At this point the police intervened, for—as a riot squad captain explained to me later—this was not in the marchers' permit. Truncheon-wielding uniformed police leaped from the vans and tried to herd the marchers back on the street. Sirens wailed. More police arrived. Several demonstration leaders and as many hippies were arrested. Gradually the marchers resumed their march, and the others their assorted activities. One middle-aged Berliner in business clothes who had been roughed-up by mistake protested indignantly to a police official who had just arrived. "Can't you get all this riff-raff off our streets?" The official shook his head. "That's the way the Nazis did things. We have to live by the law. The marchers had a permit for a political demonstration. These—" and he indicated the hippies, "have a right to be here. They are relaxing in a city park. None of their eccentricities of dress or behavior are illegal. We arrested several just now for rioting, which is illegal. But it will be difficult to prove. They'll be out by evening . . ." The middle-aged man was not satisfied. "There should be order . . ." he growled, as he walked away.

He had a point. West Berlin and, indeed, all of West Germany is permissive. The authorities lean over backward to avoid coercion. Even in the armed forces people say and do pretty much as they like. Many Germans disapprove and it is to these West Germans that the leadership of the DDR appeals with their discipline, their goose-stepping soldiers, their suppression of eccentricities of dress and behavior. It is fortunate that the Communist leaders in the East have made themselves hated and distrusted in other ways, because millions of West Germans instinctively want "order," and disapprove of the permissiveness of the authorities of the Federal Republic.

After a lovely day sailing on the Wannsee with journalist friends, I decided to go to Bonn where the debate on the *Ostverträge* was becoming exciting, Brandt having lost his slim majority so that on one vote the count was 248 to 248. The PanAm flight to Bonn-Cologne was fully booked, but I made it as a standby, and found myself in less than two hours in the modest but efficient editorial office *Time* maintains in a new and modern office building a short walk from the complex of buildings that house the legislative and executive branches of the government of the Federal Republic.

While trying to arrange a pass for myself to the Bundestag, or Lower House, where the debate on the *Ostverträge* was going on, I called Chancellor Brandt's personal secretary to see whether I might get to see the embattled leader. It was a bad day, of course, and it was thanks only to good luck and the help of my colleagues that I got into the Parliament building, and was able to catch a brief glimpse of the Chancellor.

The Social Democrats, led by Willy Brandt, with 224 seats in the Bundestag, governed by the Federal Republic in coalition with the FDP (Free Democratic Party) with 30 seats. The FDP leader, Walter Scheel, was Foreign Minister and Deputy Chancellor. When formed, this coalition government enjoyed a parliamentary majority of 12 — a reasonably safe position. The Christian Democratic Union, or CDU, led by Rainer Barzel, an East Prussian lawyer, and the Bavarian wing of the party, known as the Christian Social Union, or CSU, constituted the parliamentary opposition. But bull-necked Franz Josef Strauss, the CSU leader and one-time Minister of Defense, tried to avoid any actions or statements that might antagonize any political group and thus jeopardize his ambitions of one day becoming Chancellor. The personal friction between Strauss and Barzel often disrupted harmony in the opposition, which was solidly based on the support of most of the rural population, particularly in the predominantly Catholic South, as well as the conservatives throughout the country, although as we have seen, part of the export-oriented business community had swung over to support Brandt.

According to law, general elections must be held at least every four years. In case a government loses a vote of confidence, it must resign, whereupon the President asks the opposition to form another. But the Chancellor may request new elections, in which case the Bundestag is dissolved and the country is run by civil servants until a new Bundestag is elected and convened and a new government formed. In May 1972, Brandt's coalition had almost no parliamentary majority, but it had never lost a vote of confidence (several were tied) and most observers thought that if a new election were called, Brandt would come out a winner. However, this would have deprived the Federal Republic of a government during several weeks while vital issues of foreign policy—the *Ostverträge* and the expansion of the Common Market—were being settled. Brandt therefore resisted the temptation to call for new elections, and decided to fight it out in the Bundestag with the opposition.

The opposition, as we have seen, suffered from the conflict of ambitions at the top between Barzel and

Strauss, and from the fact that most of the country approved the *Ostverträge* and the enlargement of the Common Market. Barzel's position boiled down to the claim that if he became Chancellor he could renegotiate both more advantageously.

For three days the issue hung in the balance, Barzel obstructing the ratification of the treaties, Brandt maneuvering to get it done. On several occasions the suspense became intense. Millions watched all three TV networks' live programs from the Bundestag as this was going on. If the government did fall, would the Russians — who were impatient and suspicious of parliamentary democracy in any case — wait out the delays, or might they give up on *detente* with the Federal Republic and go back to unqualified support of the DDR and vilification and hostility for the Federal Republic?

During the three days before the final ratification of the treaties on May 17, I circulated around the German capital, following the ebb and flow of the debate in the Bundestag. I also followed the reports of Egon Bahr's continued talks in East Berlin with DDR State Secretary Michael Kohl, leading up to a transportation treaty, which was to be the first of several concrete undertakings that in sum were to constitute the establishment of normal relations between the two Germanies.

Shortly after the ratification and the conclusion of the transport agreement with the DDR, Chancellor Brandt made an audacious decision: rather than staggering on with a paper-thin parliamentary majority until some time in mid-1973 when general elections would be called for by law, he would force elections earlier. This he did by perpetrating a vote of confidence on Friday,

September 22 in which he and his cabinet deliberately abstained, thus ensuring defeat, which his SPD/FDP coalition suffered by 233 to 248 votes. As provided by the Federal Republic's 1949 constitution, the Bundestag was forthwith dissolved, and new general elections called for November 19, 1972. Brandt explained that this unusual procedure was necessary because "the majority relationships created by the voters in 1969 have changed in such a way that neither the government nor the opposition has a majority capable of action. . . ." Beyond that, Brandt hoped and believed that the November elections would return him to office with a larger majority.

Brandt's gambit paid off. When the votes were counted, the SPD had won 45.9 percent of the total and its FDP coalition partners 8.4 percent, while the CDU/CSU had only 44.8 percent. Thus Brandt assumed the leadership of his second four-year administration at almost the same time as President Nixon did, and with a solid, 54-percent majority.

But his problems were not thereby all solved. The *Wirtschaftswunder* had slowed down markedly during the last half of 1971. Consumer demand decreased, as did the demand for investment goods and exports. For the year as a whole the GNP rose by only 2.8 percent in real terms, far below the previous decade's average of 7 percent. Industry cut back on overtime but unemployment remained virtually zero. The cost of living index for June 1972 was 5.4 percent above the level of June 1971, which disgruntled consumers, but wholesale and industrial prices fell somewhat in the fall of 1971. The cumulative appreciation of the D-mark by 20 percent since 1969 certainly was one important factor in causing the slowdown in the West German economy. It made Germany's exports more expensive, and less competitive in third markets with exports from Japan and particularly from the United States whose currency was depreciated during the same period. Also the dollar devaluation made imports from the United States into Germany cheaper, and more competitive.

Toward the end of the summer of 1972 things began to improve in every respect in West Germany. Consumer spending picked up, as did construction and exports. While it had been widely expected that 1972 would be a recession year for the economy of the Federal Republic, by late August German economists were predicting that the GNP would grow from 1.5 percent to 3 percent for the year compared to 1971. Foreign economists (*Fortune's* editors, for example) were even more optimistic, and predicted that by early 1973 the West German GNP would be growing at the rate of 4 percent a year. The upturn was broadening, *Fortune* reported, home building was strong, and businessmen were optimistic. Exports and export orders were growing, in spite of the revaluations of the mark and increases in labor costs in manufacturing in the Federal Republic.

A major problem for the West German economy during the second half of 1972 remained inflation, as indeed it was in many other countries. The government was rumored to be contemplating cuts in government spending and tax increases as inflation controls, but such measures would also tend to dampen the recovery boom even before it really got started.

A second serious problem for the West Germans was industrial investment, which declined as much as 9 percent during the first half of 1972. But with the resumption of growth in export orders it was expected that the investments would again rise vigorously toward year's end as German industry tooled up to compete for export orders.

German agriculture did well in 1971: grain production grew 21 percent above the level of 1970. Prices rose slightly and a continued urbanization pushed farm family income up by better than 10 percent. In 1972 production of meat and poultry slackened off somewhat, but grains and vegetables continued strong so that Germany's rural population felt no pain. The West German economy in general of course remained in part dependent on imported agricultural products. Indeed, in 1971 U.S. agricultural sales to the Federal Republic totaled 770 million dollars, up 10 percent over the record year of 1970.

The Bonn government, of course, tried to use its powers and periodic guidelines to solve economic problems and lighten the burden on the people caused by the economic slowdown in the early months of the year. For example, in 1972 it repaid some 5.9 billion D-marks of income tax surcharges and also paid another billion D-marks to social security beneficiaries. These and other measures were instrumental in preventing serious hardship among lower-income citizens in the cities and in the rural farming areas.

Germany's overall financial position remained very strong. In mid-1972 its gold and foreign exchange reserves were greater by far than those of the United

States, its balance of payments and balance of trade were in heavy surplus, its external debt a mere 1.2 billion D-marks—less than 0.5 percent of GNP. These figures bear out my visual impressions during my May trip around the country of an economy in a state of expanding prosperity.

Three factors are important in attempting longer range forecasts for the German economy.

The first are the effects of the expansion of the Common Market which were juridically consummated on January 1, 1973. The best opinions I could get on this subject both in Germany and in other parts of Europe indicated that the expansion of the six members to nine would be beneficial to German manufacturers as British and other markets, which are now protected, open up to unrestrained exports from the continent. On the other hand, there was some apprehension that London would gradually become the financial capital of the New Europe, thanks to the experience and prestige of British financial institutions, to the possible detriment of the banks in Frankfurt and Hamburg.

The second consideration is whether Willy Brandt's *Ostpolitik* really will produce the orders and investment opportunities in East Europe of which many German industrialists dream. I myself am rather skeptical on this point. Not that the Russian and Poles and others in the Soviet bloc do not desperately want modern technology and entire manufacturing establishments in a dozen fields of industry from huge automotive plants to petrochemical enterprises to precision machine tool and optical manufacture. The desire and the need are undoubtedly there. The question is how the Communists propose to pay for the many things they would like to buy. The Communist states are already heavily in debt to the Federal Republic.

When Willy Brandt, during his several lengthy talks with Soviet leaders, posed this question, he was told: "The Soviet Union is a veritable storehouse of natural resources. We are now willing to share these with others. We will pay in fossil fuels, minerals, forest products, and the labor power required to develop them." This sounds fine. But the Soviet constitution and the laws of the other Socialist states prohibit the sale of equity, or the granting of concessions, or the exploitation of their labor by any capitalists, at home or abroad.[2] What I fear the German business community will be invited to do is to invest billions to develop Siberia's immense but distant and fairly inaccessible resources, building plants and other installations that will belong to the Soviet government and be operated by them, without any equity or collateral, against contracts for future delivery of materials produced. Suppose some future Soviet government fails to deliver the ores or timber or petroleum? In what court does a West German company sue the Soviet government?

An indication of what may await the hopeful Germans is suggested by the proposals made to United States officials and United States businessmen during President Nixon's Moscow visit of May 1972. A consortium of United States gas and oil companies was invited to build thousands of miles of gas pipelines, a huge natural gas liquification plant in Murmansk, and several special tankers to move the fuel to the gas-hungry United States — a total investment of several billion dollars for installations which, except for the tankers, the Russians would own. In return, the Soviet government was prepared to sell the United States consortium 8 percent of the gas produced.

In other negotiations the Russians suggested interest rates of 2 percent to 3 percent over ten years for the purchase of American grain. And an indication of the way in which the Soviet Union pays its debts was suggested by the Soviet agreement on the settlement of the World War II lend-lease account. During the war the United States sent the Soviet Union 10.8 billion dollars worth of assorted arms and other items. The military goods were considered by both sides to have been gifts. The indebtedness involved only 25 percent of the total; that is, the civilian goods which both sides agreed should be paid for. In twenty-seven years, not one kopeck had been paid. Several times negotiations had been broken off because of the large gap between what the Russians offered and what the United States government considered acceptable. During the Nixon visit the United States scaled down its earlier demands for the settlement of the 2.7 billion dollar debt to 800 million dollars. The Soviet government raised its earlier offers to 300 million dollars. In other words, the United States demanded thirty cents on the dollar and the Russians offered ten cents on the dollar. In mid-October a settlement was signed under which the Soviet Union is to pay 500 million dollars in twenty-eight annual installments, the last of which will be due in the year 2001. No interest is provided for, either for the period between 1945 and 1972 or the payment period. Thus the debt is to be paid at about twelve cents on the dollar, slightly more than the British undertook to pay in their lend-lease settlement.

A final vital factor in forecasting the economic future of the Federal Republic is manpower. As the Central Bank pointed out in its last annual report, West Germany's domestic labor force is shrinking because of earlier retirement and longer education, while it is becoming increasingly clear that the shortage cannot be made up indefinitely by the recruitment of foreign workers who already numbered 2.25 million in mid-1972, and whose presence in Germany is creating problems. Here I am more optimistic than the Central Bank. Labor-saving devices can continue to replace human hands, as they have done so spectacularly in Japan, whose economy has grown more rapidly than Germany's during the past decade, and without any importation of labor. Also, in the future, Germany can do more than it has done in moving its industries abroad in joint ventures, as the Japanese again have done so successfully. Nevertheless, the manpower problem is considered serious by many Germans, and therefore it is, whether it need be or not.

In winding up this survey of the state of the Federal Republic, I want to write a few lines about leadership, and about Willy Brandt.

I was present in early 1972 at a Council on Foreign Relations dinner in New York at which Willy Brandt was guest of honor. During a long question-and-answer session Brandt was asked his feelings on his recent award of the Nobel Peace Prize. "I am happy about it, clearly," he said with a smile. Then he turned deadly serious. "I am particularly happy that this world-famous prize for peace has been awarded to a German. The world has long recognized and appreciated German achievements in art, music, literature, in science and technology. We are known for our diligence, for the quality of our machines, and the efficiency of our organizations. But we have not been renowned as creators or maintainers or guarantors of peace. In this context, I am happy and proud that this time a German was awarded the Nobel Peace Prize."

Another episode: Americans far younger than I remember with pride George Marshall's speech at Harvard in June 1947, launching the Marshall Plan. In it he extended the hand of the United States to others, not to win a war, an operation with which Marshall as U.S. Chief of Staff had been intimately associated, but to win the peace—to conquer hunger and need and injustice. He said that the problems of Europe were so serious that a new approach was needed to replace the piecemeal aid then being given, and called on the European countries to draft their own rehabilitation program which would be financed by American aid. The Marshall Plan resulted in aid in the amount of about 13 billion dollars over a three-and-a-half-year period, 1.5 billion dollars of which went to Germany. On June 5, 1972, just after having secured the ratification of the *Ostverträge*, Willy Brandt went to Harvard, where he delivered a simple speech, thanking the United States for the Marshall Plan, which he called ". . . one of the strokes of Providence of this century . . . ," and announced that his government would donate nearly 50 million dollars to the United States during the next fifteen years for the establishment and operation of an independent, American-run educational foundation specializing in European problems in the

United States, and called "The German Marshall Fund of the United States."

In the first of these two episodes Germany appears in the new and unaccustomed role of a nation of peace, and Willy Brandt as a gifted leader in this new direction of Germany's national efforts and energies.

In the second, Germany assumes European leadership as it symbolically reciprocates the United States largesse which was extended to all of Europe and so vitally assisted it. And in the process, Brandt steps forward modestly but unmistakably as a spokesman not only of Germany, or of the two Germanies, but of Europe.

12

The Future of the Two Germanies

The most important single factor bearing on the future of the Federal Republic and the DDR is that both are part of Europe, and both have assumed positions of leadership in the Western and Eastern European communities respectively. So the future of the two Germanies is a facet of the future of Europe.

Over many centuries several attempts have been made to unify Europe under the control of one nation or leader. The Romans, Charlemagne, the English in the fifteenth century, and the Spaniards in the sixteenth century, the French under Louis XIV and again in the nineteenth century under Napoleon, the Germans under Hitler — all succeeded in conquering large parts of Europe, but, except for the Romans, their dominance was brief, bloody, and destructive, rather than creative.

Now, toward the end of the twentieth century, it

seems unlikely that any European power or leader will make this attempt again, if only because two non-European nations—the United States and the Soviet Union—heavily outweigh any of the European powers, and tend to balance each other as both attempt to maintain at least some control over their respective spheres of interest in Europe. Even more important, perhaps, is the fact that the Western Europeans have become internationally rather than nationally oriented and are in the process of creating a new supranational community. I refer, of course, to the European Economic Community and its enlargement from six members to nine.

It has been my good fortune to watch this important process of voluntary cooperation and association of European nations, many of whom had been traditional enemies for centuries. The vision and courage of the founding fathers of the Common Market, Robert Schumman, Paul Henri Spaak, and, perhaps most important, Jean Monnet, deserve the highest praise for the way in which they gradually overcame the resistance of great but nationalistic minded leaders, such as Charles de Gaulle, whose eighteenth- or nineteenth-century orientation led them to believe that Europe was and should remain a community of completely sovereign states.

Powerful historic influences assisted the advocates of European union. During the decade of the 1960s the Common Market's basic indices—GNP growth, increase in foreign trade, and so forth—ran consistently ahead of those of the less integrationist European Free Trade Association. From 1958 to 1970 trade among the members of the EEC rose by 530 percent, and with the rest of the world by 183 percent. Mergers and consolidations made possible by the enlarged market increased the volume of production and lowered unit costs, giving more people more consumer goods at lower prices. Customs and other frontier formalities practically disappeared as people, ideas, goods, and capital moved freely. Serious progress was made toward the harmonization of tax laws, the coordination of immigration and emigration procedures, the modification of corporate and antitrust and labor legislation toward common concepts.

Perhaps even more important was the human integration that took place as bankers and bartenders and their children swarmed over each other's countries in their newly acquired cars and motorscooters, learned each other's languages, admired each other's folk dances, sampled each other's wines and cheeses. I vividly remember my many visits to Venice, that lovely city now gradually sinking into the swampy waters of the northern Adriatic where refugees from the smoking ruins of Rome originally settled. In the late 1940s few visitors came to Venice; Europeans had other things to do, lacked money and mobility. Tourists then left their cars in a small parking lot at the foot of the peninsula and proceeded into the city by canal boat or gondola.

By the early 1960s, millions of Europeans were on wheels, and so many of them wanted to visit Venice that the parking lot had to be much expanded. One could watch as the recognizably French bourgeois stepped from his Citroën and shouldered his way along with the stolid Swiss, the long-haired Frankfurt student, and the tweedy British academic into the city. Then, during the next several years, a remarkable change took place. The vehicles arriving at the parking lots retained their national registration plates (except for a few from Brussels or Strasbourg with European (EU) plates), but the men and women, boys and girls who emerged from the vehicles began to lose their national traits, those characteristics referred to with such persistence by Charles deGaulle as their "*personalité nationale.*" The thousands of Europeans who stepped from increasingly attractive vehicles were, of course, different. Some had long hair, some short; blue jeans vied with lederhosen, bell-bottomed slacks, and conservative grays. The differences, however, were no longer those of nationality but rather of taste, of income level, or professional status. The citizen of a sovereign state was emerging as a *homo Europeicus* — a European man. When I last visited Venice in 1972, it was no longer possible to tell what country most of the visitors in Venice came from, by appearance or, in many cases, by language or gesture.

During the past several years this human growing-together of Europe has begun to find organizational expression. The institutional framework for European economic and political union has developed in Brussels and Strasbourg, along with thousands of men and women "Eurocrats" who had nearly submerged their national identities, who drove EU cars, and sent their children to trans-national schools. True, the EEC commissioners were still responsible to their national governments, which retained veto powers. But the movement was strong to work toward the direct election of European legislators and the naming or election of an executive authority that could act by majority vote. Bankers and finance ministries were hard at work drafting plans for a European currency.

All these developments left the Russians and their associates in Eastern Europe unhappy. As good Marxists, the Communists had believed that the Common Market would not work. By definition, capitalist imperalist states were incapable of cooperation. And yet, here it was working, and rather better than many of its advocates had believed possible. On the other hand, the Communist equivalent, the Comecon, worked very badly. When the Russians tried to organize a Comecon investment bank, the Rumanians stubbornly refused to have anything to do with it. A Rumanian economist friend explained: "Its purpose is the channeling of Rumanian investments into the Soviet Union. We prefer to invest in our own economy." The East European states strictly controlled the movement of goods and people and money across their national frontiers, and so secretive and controlled were their financial operations that they could not, even if they wished to apply,[1] qualify for membership even in the General Agreement on Trade and Tariffs (GATT) or the International Monetary Fund.

While Eastern Europe was thus still wrestling with residual economic feudalism, Western Europe, with the enlargement of the Common Market to include Britain, Denmark, Ireland, and perhaps Norway, in the future, was emerging as a new supranational state with a population of 260 million, a GNP of some 625 billion dollars, and nearly 40 percent of world trade. This new state would have a population and a share of world trade larger than either the United States or the USSR, and a GNP second to the United States but well above the level of the Soviet Union.

It seems to me likely that the point of no return has been passed for Western Europe. In spite of temporary setbacks like the Norwegian referendum of September 1972, the emergence of the enlarged Common Market is now irreversible. It will almost certainly enjoy continued vigorous growth, shared by other non-associated West European nations such as Switzerland, Sweden, and the Iberian countries at the same time as all these countries improve their relations with the Soviet bloc.

Japanese influence will almost certainly increase in Western Europe and United States influence decrease as the European nations try to use United States experience in continent-wide economic development to their own advantage while avoiding social failures which have blemished United States prosperity—urban blight, racial conflict, drug abuse, and crime.

By the end of the decade of the 1970s, the Common Market will probably have created a new currency, issued by a European Economic Community International Monetary Fund backed by SDRs—Special Drawing Rights—or some variation of this ingenious device. The creation of a West European Federal Reserve Bank will come only later, in the 1980s, for it must be preceded by complete harmonization of taxation procedures, and a sacrifice by all of a major element of sovereignty, which will probably not be acceptable in this decade.

A Common Market executive, responsible to a directly elected West European Parliament will probably come in the 1980s, along with the integration of the armed forces and the educational systems.

As this new Western Europe gets organized, I expect that London will become its financial capital, thanks to the experience and prestige of British financial institutions. On the other hand, I expect that British industry will have difficulty competing directly with continental industry, and large numbers of British technicians and workers may cross the Channel to seek jobs in more efficient plants where they will be motivated to work more productively than they previously worked in British plants.

These developments will almost certainly be accompanied by continued *detente* with the East bloc. Very likely agreements will be reached on mutual and balanced forces reduction which will save both sides effort and expense, and reduce the danger of war.

That this new Western European superstate, with its already high levels of consumption and security, its freedoms and opportunities for travel, education, culture, and creative activity is bound to exercise great influence on the East European states is as clear to the Soviet leaders as it is to everyone else. But Soviet leadership shows every indication of a determination to prevent defections from the Socialist camp, as Czechoslovakia would undoubtedly have done if the Soviet government had not organized a military invasion in August 1968. Soviet troops are now building permanent, masonry barracks and officers' quarters for their troops in both Czechoslovakia and Hungary.

On another level, the Soviet government has gone to great lengths to organize a Conference on European Security and Cooperation which will probably take place in early 1973 with the participation of both Germanies and the United States. The main purpose of this conference — from Moscow's viewpoint — is to freeze

THE FUTURE OF THE TWO GERMANIES 249

present frontiers between East and West Europe, and get general recognition of permanent Soviet control over East Europe. Moscow's motives are very clear. A Soviet journalist friend who enjoys high regard in Moscow put it this way:

> "Let's face it. Right after World War II Western Europe seemed on the verge of revolution. We believed that the coalition governments in France and Italy would be able to put Communists in power in those countries, while we hoped that the greater discipline and dedication of the East German Communists would make it possible for them to take over in West Germany. Well, it didn't work out that way. During the past twenty-five years West European capitalism has made a remarkable economic and social recovery. There have been no revolutions, or even any of the serious disorders many of us expected. On the other hand, we have had three serious crises in Eastern Europe: in East Germany in 1953, in Hungary in 1956, and in Czechoslovakia in 1968. In all three cases only vigorous Soviet military intervention prevented a capitalist counterrevolution. So we *must* face it. Millions of Eastern Europeans do not know yet what is good for them, and for the world. It seems that a United Europe with free elections today would be not only a non-Communist Europe, but probably an anti-Communist Europe. This we cannot tolerate. We therefore must perpetuate for some time a divided Europe, and try to get the United States to recognize it and underwrite its frontiers and the status quo of its social systems. We have given up on Communist revolution in Western Europe for this period, except possibly in Greece or Spain. We ask you to renounce support of counterrevolution in Eastern Europe, except possibly in Yugoslavia. The details of this deal should be worked out at the European Security Conference . . . ."

My friend's logic was good, and most of his facts solid. Particularly if the ECSC meets in early 1973 and all its participants — including the United States and Canada — underwrite European security as the status quo in a divided Europe, Europe will remain divided in the foreseeable future.

I am confident that eventually the Soviet Union will be forced out of Eastern Europe by the same combination of budgetary and liberal idealist pressures at home which forced the British to give up India. But I doubt that it will be in my lifetime. Eventually the Soviet Union may produce liberal leaders, but so far they have not put in an appearance. The Soviet government is dealing effectively and fairly bloodlessly with its few dissidents. The Communist Party completely dominates every aspect of Soviet life, and of the lives of the East European states, most of all in the DDR. The Soviet military is in complete control of Eastern and most of Central Europe with the awkward exception of West Berlin, with which they have learned to live.

And as long as this situation obtains, Germany will remain divided. Any reunification will be effectively opposed by the Soviet bloc, supported by many of the West European states. The two Germanies are permanent — or at least as permanent as anything is in our rapidly changing world.

Sometime in the distant future historic evolution may erode the differences between the Communist and the non-Communist world, making possible a real United States of Europe — all Europe. And in such a Europe the two Germanies might unite. And indeed, in a really free United States of Europe, it would not make much difference, since free elections would determine governments, and individuals, property, ideas, and money could move freely across the old national frontiers as they do today in Western Europe.

But unless some catastrophe should overtake the Soviet Union—such as a lost or stalemated war with China—it will not come in this century.

In this context—a divided Europe—the two Germanies will, in my opinion, continue to do well. In the meantime, gradual improvement in the relations between the two Germanies has begun to take place. During recent months both German and Allied traffic between West Germany and West Berlin has not been harassed or obstructed by either the Vopos of the DDR or the Russians. In mid-October 1972, the East German government granted an amnesty for all citizens of the DDR who left the country illegally before January 1, 1972, although their citizenship and that of their children remains revoked. At the same time, the DDR began to release a considerable number of political prisoners from its jails, many of them citizens of the Federal Republic, and allowed them to leave East German territory. Most recently, on November 8, 1972, a treaty was signed by the two German governments, Article I of which states: "The Federal Republic of Germany and the German Democratic Republic shall develop normal, good-neighborly relations with each other on the basis of equal rights." Article III affirms the recognition of the inviolability now and in the future of the frontier beween the two German states, and in Article IV both governments affirm that neither has the right to represent the other or act in its behalf. Article VIII provides for the exchange of permanent diplomatic missions in the two capitals.

The Germans work diligently and efficiently. This virtue will no doubt continue to assure them relatively high standards of living in both East and West. Since neither Germany is now or is likely to be in this century capable of initiating offensive military policies or operations, the rest of Europe is safe from any new German aggression.

These developments will leave thoughtful Germans and others, East and West, to reflect on the conflicting tendencies of unification and fragmentation in recent history. Since antiquity, human societies have tended to unify, as families united to form tribes, as tribes associated themselves in city-states, and as these in turn consolidated themselves into nations. This process went on as feudal England was united into one nation in the late Middle Ages, as Richelieu unified France in the seventeenth century and the Takagawa Shoginate unified Japan at about the same time that Ivan the Terrible did the same in Russia. In the nineteenth century, Italy and Germany were unified into nationalist states in what seemed to be a continuation of a natural and progressive historic development.

But at the same time a countervailing tendency became apparent — a tendency toward fragmentation. In the 1770s, thirteen English colonies in North America, led by English-speaking and English-educated intellectuals headed by a conservative and respected English colonel who had sworn allegiance to His Majesty George III and served him faithfully, rebelled and established a separate state which has since prospered. A generation later a dozen Spanish and Portuguese colonies in Latin America did the same thing and got away with it, creating some nineteen nations which continue to this day to speak Spanish and Portuguese, and to cherish Iberian cultural ties, but have become legitimate states.

Both the North American and Latin American fragmentations were carried out with military operations in which people were killed, and animosities engendered and perpetuated. But at the turn of the present century a fragmentation occurred bloodlessly and even amicably, as Norway and Sweden decided to leave the previously unified monarchy and become separate states. Since then they have maintained friendly, even fraternal, relations.

On the other hand, other attempts were made at secession which failed. One of the most bloody was that made by the Confederation of Southern States in 1861–65. A million men were killed before this attempt was put down, and an exhausted but wiser union re-established. More recently serious separatist secession movements have been attempted by Biafra, ending in failure, again with the loss of perhaps a million human lives. Bangla Desh, on the other hand, succeeded, as did Algeria earlier, in both cases with enormous losses, both economic and human. Taiwan's attempt to become an independent state has been frustrated in the first place by a minority government of mainland origin whose ambitions exceeded its capacities, and by the intercession of outside powers such as the United States—and the outcome of the attempt is still not clear. There is indisputable evidence that several of the Soviet Union's national minorities would like to separate and form independent states, or—in the case of the Baltic Republics, Georgia and Armenia, and perhaps the Ukraine—reform themselves as independent national states. So far the Moscow government has been able to prevent these separatist movements from becoming serious, just as the Canadian government has been able to contain the sometimes violent outbursts of a number of French Canadians who want to form an independent Quebec.

These examples of historic and contemporary attempts at fragmenting nation states into separate nations should be borne in mind when considering the division of Germany into the Federal Republic and the DDR. Those who shrug off the analogy by saying that, after all, the DDR was the creation of the Russians, should perhaps remember Lafayette and Kosciusko who had something to do with the success of the American Revolution, and recall that India certainly had a great deal to do with the successful formation of the state of Bangla Desh.

Though the general problem of consolidation and fragmentation of national states is certainly germane to any thoughtful consideration of the position of the two Germanies today, it must be recognized, I believe, that the DDR has by now established itself as a state. It exists and functions as one of a community of nations (embodying nearly half the human race), which does not pretend or aspire to base state power on the will of the governed. It contends, with Mao Tse-tung, that power comes from the barrel of a gun, and that legitimacy comes from the effective control of power.

In the immediate or near future it is unlikely that any domestic circumstances would trigger another uprising in the DDR like the one that occurred in 1953. And if this did happen, the Soviet occupation troops could easily deal with the rebellion. Only the intervention of a major outside power could make possible a forceful overthrow of the Communist regime in the DDR and the exercise of the right of self-determination by the people of the country.

There are, of course, many Germans and non-Germans who feel that it is both unnatural and unjust that the German people, with a common language and culture and tradition, should be divided permanently into two states. This does not disturb me. After all, for some time now five separate and viable states—the United States, the United Kingdom, Canada, Australia, and New Zealand—have shared the English language (albeit with some differences in accent). A number of states currently share the Arabic language and culture, though some of them are not particularly stable or viable. In history several examples of the same thing have appeared, the most outstanding being the existence for many generations of four major states—Athens, Sparta, Troy, and Macedon, and a number of smaller ones—all sharing the Greek language and cultural heritage, with a long record of bitter wars among themselves and equally bitter common struggle against an invading Asian enemy, the Persians.

What does disturb me is the deprivation of the right of self-determination for the East Germans, although I hastily add that I am equally unhappy that the Russians, the Poles, and the residents of Rhodesia have not been able freely to determine the form of government or the social system under which they live.

What also disturbs me is the fact that the two Germanies constitute a danger of war should some future, irresponsible government in either the Federal Republic or the DDR attempt to take over the other either alone, or with the aid of an outside power or coalition.

In immediate economic and political terms, the United States is already having to take account of the two Germanies. Both will probably be members of the United Nations before this book is published, as both were represented at the Olympics in Munich. Quite possibly they will begin to help each other in various ways, as indeed, toward the end of the 1972 Olympics the impressive DDR athletic teams went out of their way to applaud victories by West German athletes. United States tourists and businessmen are going to want to visit Leipzig and Weimar and Jena, and United States trade with both Germanies is likely to increase, although the unrealism of the nominal value of the Ost-mark is likely to complicate trade with the DDR. The revaluation of the D-mark, on the other hand, has made United States exports into the Federal Republic more competitive than they previously were, especially pumps, valves, compressors, chemical and plastic products, paper and paper products, and certain categories of building materials. The Federal Republic, of course, is already a major buyer of United States exports. In 1971 the agricultural products alone amounted to 770 million dollars, up 10 percent from the previous year's record. And United States management techniques and the computers required for their proper utilization are certain to be in major demand in both Germanies.

Perhaps the United States can learn something from the bitter experiences suffered by the German people.

THE FUTURE OF THE TWO GERMANIES

After less than a century as a unified state, Germany suffered invasion and defeat and fragmentation along with national humiliation and heavy losses of life. Why? To say that they were misled by a mad demagogue is to beg the real issue. The real issue is that the Germans, in spite of being technically one of the best educated peoples in the world, allowed their ambitions to outrun their resources, and their knowledge and technology to overshadow their wisdom. They lost touch with reality and justice and allowed themselves to become beguiled with the image of themselves as a "master race," using the mineral and human resources of others for their own enrichment.

The United States split off from its European parents and unified itself nearly a century earlier than the Germans. After several generations of developmental effort, the United States emerged as *the* world power in 1945, with most of the world's monetary gold in Fort Knox, with a monopoly of the atomic weapon, with a superiority in technology and industry so great that we were able to promise and deliver some 80 billion dollars worth of assorted aid to a score of nations in Europe and Asia, both former enemies and allies, without which many of them would have been unable to get back on their feet. During those heady days we became accustomed to being respected and obeyed around the world, particularly in those areas where we believed our positions were of sufficient importance for us to insist on their realization.

But during the next twenty-five years conditions changed radically. Currently both West Germany and Japan have more gold and foreign exchange reserves than we have. In 1971 the Soviet Union made 134 million tons of steel to our 120 million tons — the first time in my lifetime that the United States has not been first in the world in the production of steel. In 1971, also, the Japanese built half the total tons of merchant vessels built in the world, and the United States shipbuilding industry is dying from high costs and public neglect. The new Soviet navy today challenges ours in many areas. German, Japanese, and other foreign producers today challenge our automotive, electronic, optical, and other exports around the world and even in the United States market itself. Our military over-commitments in Southeast Asia have led us to embarrassment and humiliation if not to defeat.

Happily we never fell under the spell of official racism, as did the Germans under Hitler, nor did we abandon our belief in democratic procedures, as did the Germans. But we did fall into a complacent arrogance, assuming that our institutions and beliefs, our "American way of life" was superior to others, and would work for others as well as we believed it had worked for us. Thereby we tasted the poisoned fruit that so misled the Germans under the Third Reich.

The price we have paid so far for our lack of vision and wisdom has been far smaller than that paid by the Germans: — a military conflict in Vietnam which has cost some 140 billion dollars and 47,000 American lives without producing any visible results, a heavy budgetary deficit, adverse balances of trade and payments, and perhaps most serious, a pronounced deterioration in the fabric of our society at home, expressed in racial conflict, urban strife, and serious problems of drug misuse and crime.

The Germans suffered far more. But since World War II, despite foreign occupation, fragmentation, and destruction, the Federal Republic particularly has re-established normal conditions and opportunities for its citizens and has projected a positive image in the world. One of the reasons is that West Germany has sought to identify itself and its endeavors with international, rather than national goals. Another reason is that West Germany has kept its expenditures and programs and ambitions realistically in balance with its resources and capacities.

The record of the United States in working toward peace and security for all nations rather than for narrower nationalist objectives has been good during the past two generations. But the level of our realism in maintaining a sound relationship between our expenditures and programs, our ambitions and our resources has been wanting.

Perhaps it is in this area that the United States may have something useful to learn from the two Germanies.

NOTES

Chapter 1

1. Bithell, Jethro, ed., *Germany: A Companion to German Studies*, Methuen & Co., Ltd., London (5th edition), 1955.
2. Taylor, A. J. P., *The Course of German History: A Survey of the Development of Germany Since 1815*, Hamish Hamilton Ltd., London, 1945.
3. Marx, Karl, *The Communist Manifesto*, Henry Regnery Co., Chicago, 1960.
4. Taylor, A. J. P., *The Course of German History*, G. P. Putnam, New York, 1962.

Chapter 2

1. The French had been allies of the "Big Three" (U.S., UK, and USSR) all along, but were not in the European Advisory Commission and did not have an

occupation zone in Germany or a sector in Berlin until these were carved out for them from the U.S. and British areas in late 1945.
2. This ruling is generally recognized in mundane circumstances. For example, a man accused of driving 40 mph in a 20-mile speed zone cannot vindicate himself by proving that at the time he was passed by another motorist doing 50 mph.

Chapter 3
1. Laqueur, Walter, *Europe Since Hitler*, Penguin Books Ltd., Middlesex, England. First issue 1970; this issue, Pelican Books, 1972, p. 96.
2. *Ibid.*
3. *Statesman's Yearbook (1966-67)*, S. H. Steinberg, ed.; London, Macmillan & Co., Ltd.; New York, St. Martin's Press, 1966, p. 1047.
4. Manchester, William, *The Arms of Krupp*, Bantam Books, New York, 1970, p. 883.

Chapter 4
1. These parties were nominally bourgeois non-Communist parties, though many of their leaders were known to be secret Communists.
2. These "private" companies have been consistently cut back, until in the summer of 1972 the East German government could proudly announce that "the socialization of the private sector" has been completed. Now only inns, small retail operations, and one-man repair shops will be outside state ownership and control. See *Time* magazine, July 10, 1972, "Tightening Up the Communist Bloc."

3. The DDR set the figure at 25, 19 of whom were demonstrators and 3 Vopos; probably closer to reality is the unofficial figure of 267 demonstrators killed and 1,067 wounded.
4. *Statesman's Yearbook,* op. cit., p. 1046.

Chapter 5
1. *International Herald Tribune,* Paris, June 6, 1972.
2. Radio Liberty Research Paper #124/72, Munich, May 29, 1972.
3. *Annual Register of World Events,* 1959, Longmans, London.
4. As happened to General Vlasov and his staff. They were forcibly repatriated to Russia by the U.S. Seventh Army—to the shame of the United States—and all were executed.

Chapter 6
1. Quigley, Carroll, *The World Since 1939: A History,* Collier Books, New York, 1968, p. 441.
2. *Ibid.*
3. The Federal Republic's regular forces currently total 467,000 men: a 327,000-man army; a 36,000-man navy; and a 104,000-man air force. All these forces are part of NATO's shield against a possible invasion from the East.
4. Manchester, *op. cit.,* p. 659.
5. By 1971, this figure had dropped to 40 percent.
6. It is worth noting in this connection that the Japanese economy in the second half of the decade of the sixties developed even more rapidly than the *Wirtschaftswunder.* Japan overtook West Germany as the

world's third largest economy in 1970, having overtaken it in steel production only two years earlier. And the Japanese did this almost without iron, coal, or oil, the three most important material ingredients for a modern industrial economy. Both France and Italy have now built large and very modern steel plants on tidewater—the French at Dunkerque and the Italians at Taranto, on the heel of the Italian boot. It seems likely that during the next decade Germany's steel industry will tend to lag behind its two neighbors and partners in the Common Market, although the German steel industry is today still Europe's largest.
7. At this writing, the mark is still floating, but there are indications that the *de facto* revaluation will soon be officially recognized.
8. In the mid-sixties the total number of convictions in all of West Germany was about 600,000 per year; during 1970, 5.5 million serious crimes were reported in the United States.
9. In 1960, 133 million tons of goods were shipped along the Rhine, and the figure grew to 271 million tons in 1970, accounting for about 80 percent of the internal water transport in West Germany. In 1970, there were 14,387 ships with a carrying capacity of 9.7 million tons operating on the Rhine.

Chapter 7
1. Quigley, *op. cit.*, page 442
2. This agreement, concluded in November 1959, ensured that 46 percent of the trade of the DDR would be with the USSR, and over 76 percent with the So-

cialist countries as a whole. See *Statesman's Yearbook, op. cit.*, page 1082.
3. *Statesman's Yearbook, op. cit.*, page 1082.
4. Unfortunately, such facilities are not always available to the East German students themselves, many of whom consequently resent the relatively luxurious life afforded the foreigners.
5. *Statesman's Yearbook, op. cit.*, pp. 1080–1081.
6. *Ibid.*
7. The Soviet Union's response to the Common Market. The Committee for Economic Cooperation's members include the Soviet Union, Poland, Rumania, Hungary, Bulgaria, Czechoslovakia, the DDR, and the Mongolian People's Republic.

Chapter 8

1. Unless otherwise indicated all the Brandt quotations on pages 149 through 153 come from *A Peace Policy for Europe*, by Willy Brandt, Holt, Rinehart and Winston, Inc., New York, 1969, pp. 12, 20, 39, 60, 63, and 75.
2. Charlemagne was founder and emperor of the Holy Roman Empire in close association with the Roman Catholic Church in 800 A.D. The territory of this loose-knit group was similar to that of the Common Market in 1970.
3. *Der Spiegel* (a West German weekly magazine), #13, March 23, 1970.
4. This geographic phrase is deceptive, or even dishonest, however, as it overlooks the fact that the Poles received Szczecin, which lies on the west bank of the Oder.

5. The Berlin Settlement was signed and went into effect on September 3, 1971.

Chapter 9
1. It is interesting that Hitler repeated the blunders of Napoleon. Many historians believe that had Napoleon freed the Russian serfs, he would have won the support of both the rural population and the liberal intelligentsia and aristocracy. He did not take this course because he feared it would disorganize the country's agriculture and complicate food supplies for his army.
2. Passenger vehicles per 1,000 population:

U.S.	440	Italy	160
East Germany	60	France	240
USSR	5	Japan	70
Czechoslovakia	50	United Kingdom	210
		West Germany	190

Some further interesting comparisons: While Moscow has a total of 150,000 passenger automobiles, Paris, with about the same population, has nearly 2 million. Moscow has only thirteen automobile repair shops; Paris or Berlin thousands. An index of the availability of automobiles to ordinary citizens in the USSR and in the West is indicated by the fact that a Soviet industrial worker must work forty-six months, full time, to earn the money to buy a small car; in the United States it is six months.
3. The Soviet grain crop was indeed bad in 1972, and by the end of the year Moscow had purchased nearly

a billion dollars worth of wheat and fodder grains, mostly from the United States.

Chapter 10
1. Although there was a wide selection of books, it should be understood that certain types of literature are simply not available in East Germany (or the Soviet Union), such as capitalist literature and philosophy; for example, works by post-war German writers such as Frisch and Grass, or Americans such as Steinbeck and Henry Miller.
2. Admission to a university is not, however, necessarily automatic for students who have completed their *Abitur*. If the parents of the student are suspect, i.e., belong to the intelligentsia, or have made politically deviate statements or actions, the student is often refused admission to the university. In this case, he or she is generally sent to work in a factory for a year or so. If, at the end of that time, the workers in the factory decide that the student is politically dependable, he or she may — or may not — be admitted to the university to pursue his or her studies.
3. SDRs — special drawing rights, or "paper gold" were invented by a group of Western financial leaders in Stockholm in 1970 to replace gold as the backing for the dollar and other currencies.

Chapter 11
1. United States, 6,000; United Kingdom, 3,000; France, 2,000.
2. During 1972 Rumania modified its constitution and now claims to be able to offer equity up to 49 percent

in industrial enterprises to foreign investors. Rumania has also applied for membership in both the International Monetary Fund and the World Bank. Equity is ownership. If a man buys half his brother's furniture repair business, he has a 50 percent equity in it. A concession is a business arrangement in which a country or state empowers an outside company or organization to explore for oil, or mine coal, or manufacture pencils, sharing the profits and the products in some agreed-upon manner.

Chapter 12
1. The Rumanians did apply in early 1972 but no action has been taken at this writing.

SELECTED READING LIST

Bithell, Jethro (ed.), *Germany: A Companion to German Studies*, Methuen & Co., Ltd. (London), 1932.

Brandt, Willy, *A Peace Policy for Europe*, Holt, Rinehart & Winston, Inc. (New York), 1969.

Clay, Lucius D., *Decision in Germany*, Greenwood Press (Westport, Ct.), 1950.

Crowley, D.W., *The Background to Current Affairs*, St. Martin's Press (New York), 1966.

Jaspers, Karl, *The Future of Germany*, U. of Chicago Press (Chicago), 1967.

Kohn, Hans, *The Mind of Germany: The Education of a Nation*, Macmillan (London), 1965.

Laqueur, Walter, *Europe Since Hitler*, Penguin Books (England), 1972.

Leonhardt, Rudolf Walter, *This Germany: The Story Since the Third Reich*, New York Graphic Society (New York), 1964.

Ludz, Peter C., *The German Democratic Republic from the Sixties to the Seventies: A Socio-Political Analysis*, AMS Press, Inc. (New York), 1970.

Manchester, William, *The Arms of Krupp: 1587–1968*, Bantam Books (New York), 1970.

Murphy, Robert D., *Diplomat Among Warriors*, Doubleday (Garden City, NY), 1964.

Nelson, Walter H., *The Berliners*, McKay (New York), 1969.

Nelson, Walter H., *Germany Rearmed*, Simon & Schuster, Inc. (New York), 1972.

Passant, E.J., *A Short History of Germany, 1815–1945*, University Press (Cambridge, England), 1960.

Quigley, Carroll, *The World Since 1939: A History*, Collier Books (New York), 1968.

Rees, David, *The Age of Containment: The Cold War 1945–1965*, St. Martin's (New York), 1967.

Statistical Yearbook of the German Democratic Republic, 1971, issued by the Staatlichen Zentralverwaltung fur Statistik, Staatsverlag der Deutschen Demokratischen Republik (Berlin), 1971.

Taylor, A.J.P., *The Course of German History: A Survey of the Development of Germany Since 1815*, Hamish Hamilton, Ltd. (London), 1945.

INDEX

Aachen, 3
Abs, Hermann, 96, 225
Adenauer, Konrad, 93–95, 98–100, 101, 102–103, 111, 149, 151; visits Moscow, 98–100
Air France, 88
Air Ministry building, 32
Alexanderplatz, 197, 199, 201
Allen, Larry, 45
Allgemeine Elektrisitäts Gesellschaft, 96, 113
Allied Control Council, 33, 43, 71, 85
Alsace, rejoined to France, 13
American Committee for Liberation, 108
anti-Communist peasant party, 53
Anti-War Congress (Amsterdam), 19
Apel, Erich, 215
Aquinas, Thomas, 6
Ardennes offensive, 26
Astoria Hotel (Leningrad), 178
Attila the Hun, 3
Attlee, Clement, 32, 59

Bach, Johann Sebastian, 8, 103
Badische Aniline und Soda Fabrik, 95
Bahr, Egon, 148–149, 154, 159, 164, 232
Balkan Wars, 12
Barbarossa, Frederick, 4
Barbusse, Henri, 19
Barzel, Rainer, 221, 230–232
Bauhaus, the, 16
Bayer, 95
Beethoven, Ludwig van, 8
Beitz, Berthold, 123, 124
Beria, Lavrenti, 181–182
Berlin, divided into sectors, 28
Berlin airlift, 50, 60–62
Berlin blockade, 58–60, 75
Berlin Wall, 84–90, 131, 133
Berliner Ring, 156
Berlin-Helmstedt autobahn, 38
Bessemer, Sir Henry, 120, 121
Bierhallputsch, 14, 34
Bismarck, Prince Otto von, 9–10
Böll, Heinrich, 102

271

Bormann, Martin, 38
Borsig Locomotive Works, 148
Brahms, Johannes, 8
Brandt, Willy, 46–47, 93, 147–168, 190–191, 220; elected Chancellor, 159; election, 1972, 233–234; meets with Stoph, 159–163; Nobel Peace Prize, 191, 239–240
Brecht, Bertolt, 64
Brezhnev, Leonid, 165, 174, 188, 189
British zone, 32
Buchenwald, 161
Bulgaria, collapse of, 13; Communist government of, 28
Bundesbahn (Federal Railway), 225
Bundestag (Federal Parliament), 92, 159, 230–233
Byrnes, James, 32

Cabinet of Dr. Caligary, 16
capitalist market factors, 143
Castro, Fidel, 125
Catherine the Great (Russia), 103, 170
Catholic Church, 6, 7
Central Bank, 239
Central Intelligence Agency, 46, 108, 109
Centrist Social-Democratic government, 53
Charlemagne, 3, 242
Children of the Revolution, 40
China, Soviet feeling toward, 173
Christian Democratic Union, 148, 168, 220, 221, 230
Christian Social Union (CSU), 230–231
Churchill, Winston, 29, 31, 32
Clay, Gen. Lucius, 34, 42, 48–50, 59, 111–112
Cologne, University of, 4
colonies, divided among Allies, 13
Comecon, 140, 215, 246
Comintern, *see* Communist International
Common Market, 100, 148, 150, 151, 189, 221, 243, 245, 246, 247

Communist International, 15
Communist Party, organizes in Germany, 15; *see also* German Communist Party
Conference of European Security and Cooperation (CESC), 186–193, 194, 248–249
Conference on Jewish Material Claims Against Germany, 65
Crusades, the, 4
currency, 35–37, 43, 55–58, 112, 178, 200, 256
Cuvillies Theater, 102
Czechoslovakia, occupation of (1968), 140, 145

DDR (German Democratic Republic) *see* East Germany
Daimler-Benz Co., 95–96, 113, 184, 224
Dante, 6
deGaulle, Charles, 28, 100, 150, 243, 245
DeKowa, Michi, 45
DeKowa, Viktor, 45
Demag, 42
de-Nazification, 37–38
Depression (U.S.), 16, 18
Descartes, René, 9
Deutsche Bank, 96, 225
Deutsche Welle, 187
Diary of Anne Frank, 68
Die Aula, 203–204
displaced persons, 106–108
Don Carlos, 221
Dönitz, Admiral, 38
Dürer, Albrecht, 6

East Germany, 70–90, attitude toward reparations to Jews, 67; economy, 131–146; education, 138, 213–214; emigrants to West, 75, 82; future of, 242–259; government established, 59; gross national product, 209; industry, 135–137; insurrection (1953), 79; military, 80, 139–140; police, 75–76; political parties, 73; restrictions on visitors, 158; support of Arab states, 67;

INDEX

East Germany (*continued*)
  tour of (1972), 194–217; trade, 73–74, 138, 180, 209–210; wage figures, 211; workers' strike, 76–77
economy, 15, 36–37; East Germany, 131–146; Soviet Union, 140–146, 175–179; West Germany, 56–57, 111–130, 235–239
Edict of Worms, 6
Eichmann, Adolf, 66
Einstein, Albert, 9, 63–64
Eisenhower, Gen. Dwight, 32
Eisler, Hans, 64
elections (1946), 42
Erfurt, University of, 4
Erfurter Hof, 160
Erhard, Ludwig, 111–112, 220
Esterhazy, Prince, 8
European Advisory Commission, 25, 26, 28, 59
European Advisory Council (London), 132
European Economic Community (EEC) *See* Common Market
European Economic Cooperation, 94
European Free Trade Association, 243
Ewing, Gordon, 78

Fechter, Peter, 86
Federal Republic of Germany, *see* West Germany
Ferdinand, Archduke, 12
Fiat Co., 185
film industry, 16
Finance Division, Office of Military Government, 35
Finland, 81
foreign laborers, imported by Nazis, 106, 115
Foreign Ministers' Conference (Moscow), 33
Four-Power agreement (1971), 227
France, joins occupying powers of Germany, 28–29
Frank, Anne, 68
Frankel, Max, 66
Frederick the Great, 8, 224
Free Democratic Party, 159, 230

Free Europe Committee, 108
French Revolution, 8
Freud, Sigmund, 64
Friedrichstrasse Station, 86, 89

General Agreement on Trade and Tariffs (GATT), 246
General Electric Company, 18
German Communist Party, 15, 19, 35, 40, 51
German language, creation of modern, 7
German Red Cross, 167
Germany (prior to deunification), 1–47; division of (1944–45), 25; early history 3–13, 103–104; formation of government, 40; Protestant reformation, 6–7; reparations, 13, 36–37; Third Reich, 16–17; Treaty of Versailles, 17; *see also* East Germany; West Germany; Two Germanies
Giotto, 6
Goering, Hermann, 38, 39
Goering (Hermann) Steel Mill, 42
Goethe, Johann, 9
Gosplan (Soviet State Planning Commission), 141
Gottwald, Klement, 55
Grand Coalition, 148
Grass, Günther, 102
Great Britain, wants to maintain European balances, 25
Grechko, Marshal, 174
Gromyko, Andrei, 99
Gropius, Walter, 64
gross national product (GNP), 112–113, 135, 209, 233–234, 246
Grotewohl, Otto, 40, 70, 77
Grundig, 123, 124

Hallstein Doctrine, 93, 138
Handel, George Frederick, 8
Hannover Fair, 226
Hanseatic League, 4; map, 5
Hapsburg princes, 6
Haydn, Joseph, 8
"Heartland of the Thousand Year Reich," 45

Hegel, Georg, 9
Heidelberg, University of, 4
Heisenberg, Werner, 9
Helms, Richard, 46
Helmstedt autobahn, 58, 59, 84
Hermes Corp., 184
Heuss, President, 93
Hillenbrand, Martin, 192
Hiroshima bomb, effect on Soviet policy, 34
Hitler, Adolph, 14, 19, 21, 31, 45, 63, 94, 116, 144, 171, 221, 242, 258
Hoechst, 95
Holbein, Hans, 6
Honecker, Erich, 164, 181, 207–208, 214, 215
Hotel Berolina, 198, 202, 205
Hotel Stadt Berlin, 199, 201
Hotel Unter den Linden, 205
Hungary, economy of, 145

I. G. Farben Industries, 65, 95, 113
industries, begin reoperation, 42–43; see also East Germany; West Germany
Interflug (East German airlines), 82, 195
Interhotels, 198
International Air Transport Association, 195–196
International Monetary Fund, 246
interzonal trade, 81–82
Israel, 66; receives reparations, 65; six-day war, 67

Jews (German), 63–69; population statistics, 64–65; post-World War II, 63–64
Johnson, Uwe, 102
journalists (Allied), 38
Junkers (East German landholders), 8

KPD, see German Communist Party
Kadar, Janos, 145
Kaiser Wilhelm Memorial Church, 227–228
Kamm, Henry, 66
Kant, Hermann, 203
Kant, Immanuel, 9

Karlshorst, 35
Kassel art exposition, 126
Kasseler Schloss hotel, 162
Keitel, Feldmarschall, 38
Kennedy, John F., Berlin speech, 82–83
Khrushchev, Nikita, 82, 142, 144
Kiesinger, Kurt, 148, 159, 220
Kissinger, Henry, 148, 190
Koblenz (Germany), 2–3, 16, 20, 218–219
Kohl, Michael, 159, 232
Kokoschka, Oskar, 64
Kollwitz, Kaethe, 45
Kommandatura, the, 33, 71
Kosygin, Alexei, 174
Krupp Co., 42, 65–66, 113, 122, 123, 124

Laenderrat, 43, 52
Lane, Arthur Bliss, 45
Leibnitz, Gottfried Wilhelm, 9
Leipzig Fair, 81
Leonard, Wolfgang, 40
Lieberman, Evsei, 142
Liszt, Franz, 8
Lorraine, rejoined to France, 13
Louis XIV, 242
Lufthansa (West German airline), 88, 113, 225
Luther, Martin, 6–7, 9

Malenkow, Georgi, 181
Maniu, Juliu, 53
Marshall, George, 240
Marshall Plan, 94, 95, 96, 240–241
Marx, Karl, 10, 131
Masaryk, Jan, 55
Maximilian I, 6
Mein Kampf, 14
Military Payment Certificates, 35
Mitbestimmungsgesetz, the (co-determination law), 112
Molotov, Vyacheslav, 97, 99
Mongolian People's Republic, 137
Monnet, Jean, 243
Monteverdi, Claudio, 9
Morgenthau Plan, 25
Moscow Treaty (1970), 165–166, 184, 189

INDEX

Mosely, Philip, 26
Mozart, Wolfgang Amadeus, 8, 9
Muenzenberg, Willy, 19
Murphy, Robert, 34, 46
Mutual and Balanced Reduction of Forces (MBRF), 187–190

NATO, 94, 101, 148, 150, 188–191
Napoleon Bonaparte, 8, 171, 242
National Labor Union, 107
National People's Army, 139
National Socialist German Workers' Party, 20, 37
National Socialists, 18
Nazi Party, block leader system, 41; in Soviet zone, 37; try to use Volksdeutsche, 104; war criminals, 66–67
Neanderthal valley, 3
Neo-Nazi Party, 162
Neue Zeitung, 148
New York Times, 66
Newton, Isaac, 9
Nicholas II, Czar, 12
Niebelungen, the, 3
Nietzsche, Friedrich, 9
Nine-Power Conference (London), 97
Nixon, Richard, 165, 190, 192, 233; Moscow visit, 237
Nordhoff, Heinrich, 118
North Atlantic Treaty Organization, *see* NATO
Norway, 46, 47
Nuremberg trials, 33, 38–40

OEEC, *see* Common Market
occupation currency, 35, 51
occupation forces, 2; effect of new government on, 51–52
Oder-Neisse frontier, 100
O'Donnel, James P., 133
Olympics (Munich), 214, 221, 256
Ostverträge, 191, 230–232, 240
Oxford Movement, 16

Palacek, General, 46
PanAm, 88
Pankow government, *see* East Germany

Parzival, 4
Patton, George, 223
Peace of Augsburg, 6
Peace of Westphalia, 7
Peace Policy for Europe (Brandt), 149
Phoenix Rheinrohr Co., 120
Pieck, Wilhelm, 70
Pius XII, Pope, 34
Planck, Max, 9
Podgorny, Nikolai, 174
Poland, Communist government of, 28; frontier, 44; industry, 122–124; referendum (1947), 53
Polish Corridor, 13
Politbureau, 174
Polyansky, Dmitri, 174
Porsche, Ferry, 117, 118
Potsdam conference, 21, 27, 29–33, 51, 55, 57, 59, 71, 116
Prague, University of, 4
press, Soviet zone, 41; Western zone, 42
Prinzregententheater, 102
prisoners of war (German), in Soviet Union, 99, 105
Prussia, becomes world power, 8–10; invaded by Russia, 12
Puccini, Giacomo, 9

Radio Free Europe, 108–109, 187, 225
Radio Liberation, 108–109
Radio Liberty, 225, 226
Raeder, Admiral 38, 39
Reader's Digest, 133
refugees, 31, 45, 105–106
Reger, Erich, 42
Reichskanzlei (government chancery), 31
Reichstag, 46
Renault Co., 118, 185
reparations, 13, 36–37; paid to Jews, 65–66; Soviet Union demanded from Germany, 99
Requiem Mass (Mozart), 9
reunification, 92–93
revanchists, the, 76
RIAS (U.S. radio station in Berlin), 74–75, 78, 148, 187, 225

Ribbentrop, Nazi Foreign Minister, 38
Riemenschneider, Tilman, 6
Roosevelt, Franklin D., 33
Ruhr region, 26
Rumania, Communist government of, 28
Russia, invades East Prussia, 12; occupation of large area of Germany, 26; soldiers' conduct in Germany, 30-31; sweeps through Poland and Balkans, 26; wants Soviet German Republic, 25; *see also* Soviet Union
Russian Liberation Army, 106, 172

Sachsenhausen concentration camp, 41
St. John's Passion, 103
Sarajevo, assassination at, 12
Sauerbruch, Ernst, 46
Schacht, Hjalmer, 38
Scheel, Walter, 190, 230
Schickelgruber *see* Hitler, Adolph
Schiller, Johann, 9
Schönefeld airport, 195-196
Schopenhauer, Arthur, 9
Schubert, Franz, 8
Schumann, Robert (composer), 8
Schuman, Robert, and Common Market, 243
secession movements, 252-254
Seghers, Anna, 64
Selbmann, Minister, 77
September Plenum, 143, 145
Siemens Co., 42, 96, 113
Skrypcinski, Leo, 41
Social Democratic Party (SPD), 15, 18, 19, 20, 40, 47, 148, 149, 159, 230
"Social Fascists," 19
social security system, 12
Socialist Unity Party (SED), 40, 51, 73, 75, 79, 144-145
Socialist Workers Party, 19
Socialist societies, in Soviet bloc, 131
Sokolovsky, Vassily, 71
Solidarists, 107
Soviet-Czechoslovak Friendship Treaty, 189

Soviet garrison, 42, 71
Soviet Military Administration, 70-71
Soviet Military Police, 44-45
Soviet Union, Berlin Wall constructed, 84; commercial agreement with Germany, 14; Communist governments in Eastern Europe, 28; economy, 140-146, 175-179; import/export with West Germany, 183; industrial products from East Germany, 74; invites Adenauer to Moscow, 98-99; military mission resident at Heidelberg, 71-72; policy on Germany, 169-193; post-World War II conditions, 29-30; repatriation commission, 72; trade with East Germany, 135-136; *see also* Russia
Soviet Zone, 32, 35, 50-52, 70-90; barrier on frontier reinforced, 86
Sozialistische Einheitspartei Deutschlands, *see* Socialist Unity Party
Spaak, Paul Henri, 243
Speer, Albert, 38
Springer, Axel, 42, 113-114
Staatstheater, 203
Stalin, Joseph, 29, 32, 64, 80, 140, 144, 174, 182
Stans, Maurice, 190
Steinhardt, Laurence, 55
Stettin, given to Poles, 44
Stoph, Willi, meeting with Brandt, 159-163
Storm Troopers, 19-20
Strategic Arms Limitations Talks, 187, 188
Strauss, Franz Josef, 231
Strauss, Richard, 8
Stresemann, Gustav, 15-16
Sudeten, Czechs take, 13
Suslov, Mikhail, 174
Sweden, armies during Thirty Year War, 7
Swiss League, 6

Telefunken Co., 42, 96
Third Reich, 16, 17, 258

INDEX

Thirty Years War, 7
Time-Life, 49
Trans-Europe-Express, 222, 223
Trans-Siberian railroad, 164
Treaty of Neutrality and Nonaggression, 14
Treaty of Rapallo, 14
Treaty of Rome, 101
Treaty of Versailles, 13, 14
Tristan, 4
Truman, Harry, 29, 32–33, 59
Tu Quoque, 39
Turkey, collapse of, 13
Two Germanies, outlook for future, 242–259; Potsdam, 27; treaty in 1972, 251; *see also* Germany; East Germany; West Germany

USSR, *see* Soviet Union
Ukraine, invaded by Germans, 13
Ulbricht, Walter, 40, 51, 70, 74, 77, 143, 144, 146, 154, 164, 181, 214, 215
United Nations, 181, 256; Charter of, 57
United Nations Relief & Rehabilitation Administration, 95
United States, depression, 16; financial aid to West Germany, 96–97, military forces (1947), 50; position on CESC, 191–193; resident at Potsdam, 71, World War I, 12–13
U.S. Seventh Army, 49, 101, 169
United States zone, 32; tour of (1947), 48–50
Ussuri River, military conflicts, 163

V-1 & V-2 rockets, 120
VJ Day, 34
van der Rohe, Mies, 64
Verdi, Giuseppe, 9
Vereinigte Österreichische Eisen- und Stahlwerk, 120–121
Vienna, University of, 4
Vietnam War, 165, 193, 220, 258
Vivaldi, Antonio, 9
Vlasov, Gen. Andrei, 106, 172
Volga Germans, 170

Volksdeutsche, 104
Volkswagen Co., 42, 113, 117–119
Volsungs, the, 3
von Eschenbach, Wolfram, 4
von Strassburg, Gottfried, 4
von Trott zu Solz, Adam, 20
Vopos (People's Police), 77, 88, 133, 139, 157, 160, 196
Voprosy Ekonomiki, 141

Wagner, Richard, 8, 102
Walser, Martin, 102
Warsaw Ghetto, 166
Warsaw Pact, 140, 187
Warsaw Treaty, 166–167
Weimar constitution, 92
Weimar Republic, 13–17
Wends, The, 170
Werwolf, 21
West European Communists, 98
West German Communists, 161
West Germany, anti-Semitic incidents, 66; economy, 111–130, 235–239; foreign workers, 110, 115; future of, 242–259; gross national product, 95, 233; industries, 95–96, 113–126; military forces, 101–102; modern cities, 126–128; occupational forces, 101; steel mills, 119–122; tour of (1972), 218–241; transportation, 128–129; unilateral unification of zones, 91
Western Allies, formation of German government, 40, 92; proposed free elections 97–98; zones, 35, 42, 43
Western European Union, 94
Wilhelm II, Kaiser, 10, 13
Winant, Ambassador (U.S.), 26
Wirtschaftswunder, 112–130

Yalta, 28, 55
Yugoslavia, equality deals, 124–125

Zentrumspartei, 93
Zorin, Soviet Ambassador, 55
Zuchmayer, Carl, 102
Zweig, Stephan, 64

ABOUT THE AUTHOR

JOHN SCOTT has been writer, reporter, editor, and executive for TIME from 1941 until the present. His first acquaintance with Germany, however, goes back to 1927 when he spent several months there on holiday, "discovering" it in the company of a German student friend.

In 1932 Mr. Scott went back and again spent some time there, attending several international conferences while waiting for a visa to the Soviet Union, where he was going to work in industry.

In 1945 he returned to set up TIME's Central European Bureau and, during the winter of 1945–46 covered the Nuremberg Trials for his magazine. Mr. Scott lived in Germany, reporting from there, until late 1948. Since then he has made many visits and spent several months there during 1972.

Previous to his assignment to Germany, the author lived and worked in the Soviet Union for ten years, and has also returned to that country a number of times. His thorough knowledge of the two Germanies and of the Soviet Union provides him with the information and insight that make this book both accurate and fascinating.

Mr. Scott, born in Philadelphia, now lives in Ridgefield, Connecticut, when he is not globe-trotting. He has written two other Background Books: *China: The Hungry Dragon* and *Hunger: Man's Struggle to Feed Himself.*